QUIVERS

QUIVERS

ROBIN QUIVERS

ReganBooks

An Imprint of HarperCollinsPublishers

HarperCollins books may be purchased for educational, business, or sales promotional use. For information please write: Special Markets Department, HarperCollins Publishers, Inc., 10 East 53rd Street, New York, NY 10022.

FIRST EDITION

Designed by Caitlin Daniels

Library of Congress Cataloging-in-Publication Data

Quivers, Robin
    Quivers / Robin Quivers.—1st ed.
        p. cm.
    ISBN 0-06-039153-7
    1. Quivers, Robin. 2. Radio broadcasters—United States—Biography.
I. Title.
PN1991.4.Q58A3 1995
791.44'028'092—dc20
[B]   95-2976

95 96 97 98 99 ❖/RRD 10 9 8 7 6 5 4 3 2 1

This Book Is Dedicated To:

My mother and father
for giving me life.

Dr. Sharon London
for teaching me how
to live it.

And
My uncle Leroy
for simply loving me.

CONTENTS

Part III: Breakthrough

Epilogue

Photographs follow page 214.

ACKNOWLEDGMENTS

Special thanks to:

Judith Regan, whose vision and faith in me made my dream of one day telling my story come true.

Carolyn Fireside, who worked tirelessly under great pressure, and whose knowledge of writing and organizational skills allowed me to tell my story better than I could ever have imagined.

All the wonderful people at HarperCollins who worked long hours worrying over every detail, and who in the end performed miracles to get the book finished on time.

Lea, "my Little Sister," for understanding that I had very little time to give during the writing of this book.

Howard Stern for being the best friend I've ever had and the best partner I never wished for.

Fred Norris for being a strong shoulder.

Gary Dell'Abate for caring enough to give the very best.

Jackie Martling for never noticing a thing.

Don Buchwald, who has proved to be my greatest champion.

Mel Karmazin for being a man of conviction and courage.

Angela Russo and Michael O'Brien for making it possible for two computer illiterates to master the PC.

Kathi Diver, my oldest friend, for her understanding and support.

Linda, David, and Becky Zimmerman for always being there even when I'm not.

Charles and Marian Carter for having hearts large enough to allow me back into their son's life.

Tom Chiusano for his guidance, friendship, and support.

All my friends, mentors, teachers, helpers, and kindred spirits, including: Claudia Ascione, Barbara Biziou, Mark Clark, Jody Dunowitz, Michael Gange, Mark Garten, Steve Grillo, Donna Harfenist, John Jeppi, Laura Lackner, Michael Martin, Gloria McKenny, John Melendez, Sherry Morris, Laura Norman, Peggy Panosh, Scott Salem, Jodi Salidor, Cathy Tobin, and Billy West.

PART ONE

BREAKOUT

AUTHOR'S NOTE

The names Lt. Bradley Green, Reggie Small, David Jefferson, and Mary Beth Janus as well as some first names have been changed.

1

A NICE GIRL LIKE ME . . .

I firmly believe, if things are right, you'll click fast and you'll know. . . . I have never said to someone, "Oh, what a hard day on the air with Robin." It never is like that. It's always easy and that's the key to all of this.

—Howard Stern

Girl: I'm nervous! I've never taken my clothes off for anyone except a boyfriend.

Howard: Now what inspired you to do this, I mean, do you listen to the show and . . .

Girl: You're God.

Howard: I am?

Girl: You're God to me.

Howard: I turn you on?

Girl: Ahhhhhhhhh, your height does.

Howard: My height, but my face is the negative.

Girl: You actually look better than your pictures.

It's just seven o'clock on a hot Thursday morning in June. Another typical day on "The Howard Stern Show." This twenty-four-year-old aerobics instructor has come all the way from Dallas to strip before the "King of All Media" in his New York studio. Yes, the girls really do take off their clothes. This is not theater of the mind. This is real.

Howard: So, why are you doing this if you're so nervous?
Robin: Yeah, what possessed you?
Girl: I've got one more year to be irresponsible, and this is one of the things on my list to do.
Howard: So, in your mind you said, "Hey, I don't care. I just want to go down there and be naked and let Howard evaluate my body."

I'm Robin Quivers, Howard's sidekick, partner in crime, first-grade teacher, whatever the occasion demands. We've worked together since 1981, and girls have been coming into the studio to get naked since 1984. It started out as an experiment. Was it possible for a self-proclaimed social geek to now get girls to do anything for him just because he was on the radio? I guess the answer was yes. Since that first girl we've averaged about one girl a week. Sometimes they come alone, and sometimes they come in groups of two or more. They've come with their boyfriends, husbands, managers, and friends. They have been young and old, businesswomen, professors, housewives, strippers, prostitutes, and centerfolds. And they all have their own unique reasons for doing it.

Howard: All right, now I'm going to liberate you. Liberate yourself from your clothes.
Robin: Ha-ha, ha-ha, ha-ha, ha-ha . . . .
Howard: Stand up and let me see.
Robin: Be free.
(Drum roll)
Girl: Don't roll the drum.
(Drum roll stops)
Howard: Are you uptight doing it there? You want to do it over here?
Robin: Now you can't even adjust the lighting.
Howard: I don't need any adjustment. Are you uncomfortable with all these guys in here?
Girl: Yes.

I'm the only woman on the staff of the show. I sit in my own separate booth and look into the studio where Howard sits with the two writers, Fred Norris and Jackie Martling. On this occasion our producer, Gary Dell'Abate, has found a good reason to be in the studio with us. He needs to hold the microphone so we can hear this girl take off her clothes. One thing this job has taught me is that most guys like to look at naked women. Even if they can't see it, most guys will listen to this segment till the very end, though it might make them late for work.

Howard: You're now down to your blue denim shirt and your maroon blousy dress or skirt. What's going to come off next?

Girl: I don't know. What should come off? I've never, I don't know . . .

Howard: I say, take off the . . . take off the skirt. Go wild.

Girl: You want my shoes off?

Howard: No. I want your shoes on the whole time. Let me see what it's like when you're undressed. Want to see if I'd be turned on. So far I'm real turned on. Whoa, you don't even have panties on, do you?

Girl: Yeah.

Howard: Oh, those are panties. Oh, all right, good. Now take off that blue denim top and really let me get a good look at you. She's hot, man. No wonder you're so horny. You got a horny, hot body. You know what it is, you stay in shape. You want guys touching you. I understand that. No one understands that better than me. Let me see. Owwww, wow, oh my God. What a bod on you. Take off your bra. Let me see your chest. That's not small.

Girl: Yeah. It's a push-up bra.

Howard: Oh, it is. Let me see.

Girl: It's not the miracle bra. It's a push-up bra.

Howard: Let me see. You, you got cute ones, though. They're not big. They're absolutely not big. Right? Hey, Jackie, what do you think of those?

Jackie: Perfect!

Howard: Perfectly round (*applause*). Robin, take a look. I see you staring.

Robin: I'm not looking at anything.

Girl: Thank you, Robin.

There will be a bit more *owing* and *ahing*, but it's over for the most part. She has just become another in a string of the most popular girl of the moment.

Women want to know what I'm doing here. Just how is it that I can work on a show like this—and not just because of the nudity. Some women say, "I feel so bad for you." Like I couldn't leave if I wanted to.

NOW members rail, "You should be ashamed of yourself. You're contributing to the degradation of women by just being there!"

And if they can't get to me because of the gender thing, they hit me with "How can you as a black person work with a man who says all those awful, racist things about your people?"

The answer to that one is so simple, it's ridiculous. Why would I care what he thinks of black people? What's important is *my* opinion of black people.

People have even gone so far as to suggest that I'm just a token. That my being there gives Howard the license to say all those things about blacks. I consider that the most racist and sexist thing that anyone can say. It's tantamount to saying that being black and female makes it impossible for me to actually be a creative force on a radio show, and so I sit there taking abuse to get a paycheck. I have nothing more than my presence to contribute. My detractors look at me and merely assume that I have no power.

So when people try to categorize my job as some kind of PC prison sentence with a loudmouthed monster as a jail keeper, I just have to laugh. For the record, Howard is a very sweet man, and there's no way that sweetness doesn't underlie every outrageous joke. He's like a little kid with this beautiful, innocent face. The first time he says a curse word, his face doesn't change. What makes the situation so hysterical and so shocking is that sweet, innocent face saying, "Fuck you." And for fourteen amazing years I have had the pleasure of being the creative partner of that sweet little kid with the dirty mouth in one of the most transforming shows in the history of radio.

I came to "The Howard Stern Show" at a very early stage in its evolution and have contributed to making it what it is. During the fourteen years I've been with Howard, the show's content has always been controversial, and that's why I've liked doing it. As far as I'm concerned, there's never been a subject too hot to discuss. We constantly find ourselves climbing over the boundaries of taste and political correctness as we delve into politics, religion, race relations, the battle of the sexes, and bodily functions. I'm amazed at how upset people get just because of our frank handling of sometimes sticky issues. People often cringe as we dare to talk like real people while sitting in front of microphones. I see what we do five days a week as a work in progress.

That's the great thing about our show and about my relationship with Howard—we're continually growing and changing. It's what drew me to him. He is simply never static. Unlike most people I've met, he continues to grow and learn. That's what fascinates me and keeps me here, because growth and change have always been critical to me. One of the main reasons "The Howard Stern Show" revolutionized the medium of radio, in fact, is because it's never the same show twice.

Until 1981 I thought of radio solely as a stepping-stone to television stardom. Radio was my second career. I had already been a registered nurse for six years. I was twenty-eight years old, which is old to be starting in radio. So I took a shortcut and went to broadcasting school. After only eight months, I was on the air. It was a small station in Harrisburg, Pennsylvania (where they only have small stations), but I was working in broadcasting. In nursing, I did only what was required of me in terms of hours. Radio, though, was a different story. I'd work twelve-hour days without even thinking of asking for overtime. I was having the time of my life.

After six months in Harrisburg, I'd learned everything they had to teach me and was ready to move on. That's when I got a call from the news director at a station in Baltimore, my hometown, so I took the job. I thought I'd found the spot from which I was going to develop myself into a prime TV news prospect—when the calls started coming again. This time, they were from one of my mentors, Denise Oliver, the program director at DC101, a rock-and-roll station in the nation's capital.

I had always wanted to work with Denise, but the timing was wrong and I turned her down. She must have thought I was playing hard to get, because she started really courting me. Still, I just wasn't ready to make the move. Then she played me a tape of this deejay she wanted me to do the news for. What I heard blew my mind. This guy was different. He was interviewing a prostitute, but there wasn't a hint of judgment in his voice. He was so laid-back. I ended up taking the job just to meet him.

My first close encounter with Howard Stern was over the phone—with a third party listening in because Denise had suddenly decided to see if we could really talk to each other. There was no build-up, no momentary awkwardness. He was talking to me like we were old friends, which felt extremely weird. But when he took that direction, I went with him. So we were talking like we'd known each other forever, although it was our first conversation. I hung up the phone and thought, Oh, my God, I just took a job with a crazy man.

The Friday night before we were to begin work together, we met face-to-face over dinner with Denise. I was surprised that Howard didn't look like the tall, thin, long-haired guy I'd seen in the publicity photos. Howard Stern turned out to be tall, short-haired, and not so thin. He had a sore throat and couldn't talk, so I was the one who had to entertain everybody while he kept croaking apologies. I left with few hopes for Monday morning. But Howard came through like the trooper he is.

Howard spun the records and talked between them from six to ten in the morning, five days a week. I was supposed to do the newscasts at the bottom and the top of the hour, starting at 6:30 A.M. I was to have my own studio, but it wasn't ready yet, so that first day I had to sit in the studio with Howard. He was on the air when I walked into the room to prepare for my first newscast, but he immediately included me in the conversation he was having with a guy on the phone.

"It's true, Robin," he said. "If you're going to pick up women, you have to wear tight pants!"

I gave him a look that said he must be out of his mind.

"No," he continued, pointing to some book he was holding, "it says so right here. This guy has slept with sixteen hundred women and he says you've got to wear tight pants."

"He slept with sixteen hundred women?" I asked skeptically.

"Yeah," he replied.

"So when did he have time to put on pants?"

From my statement, Howard went right to the commercial, letting me have the last word. That in itself was unusual. I was used to morning men being selfish, boorish hogs who resented having to give up five minutes of airtime for the news. Yet the idiots never minded the stupid music they had to play. I was still trying to absorb that when Howard reeled back in his chair, grabbed his head, and cried, "Oh, my God, you can talk!" He went on and on, singing my praises, and I'm thinking, What's the big deal? I've been coming back with the smart retort all my life.

From that moment, we were up and running. I would sit in the news office of DC101 typing my next newscast while listening to him on the air. I'd find myself laughing, alone there at my desk. I marveled at how inventive Howard was, how many more ways he knew to use radio to make it more immediate, more compelling. Even when I came in to do the news, the excitement didn't stop. Howard brought me into whatever conversation was going on at the time, and when I did the news he was there, too, asking questions, cracking jokes, or just showing an interest in the day's events.

In fact, I noticed that Howard often referred to current events when I wasn't there. When I was, it became clear very quickly that my newscasts were expected to hold the audience as much as any other part of the show. Howard didn't want five minutes of dry headlines that didn't shake anybody up or keep us out of music too long. Suddenly, five minutes of news had stretched into fifteen minutes of news. We were doing more news than the all-news station. Radio people were shocked that a rock-and-roll audience stayed tuned, even with all this talk, and they were joined by people who would never even listen to rock-and-roll.

I was now talking to more people than I had ever dreamed possible—with more freedom than any other newsperson in the country. In addition, I was attending the greatest radio school ever. And I had finally found another human being who didn't have a limit to what he wanted to do, and with whom I shared an instant and incredible chemistry.

That chemistry has lasted through all fourteen years. Howard and I have discussed the mechanics of what we do on the air on only one occasion. He said that what fascinated him about me from the very beginning was that I noticed when he was changing. He can tell, even if I lay back for a while, that I'm figuring him out. Then, when I have, I start contributing and sometimes make what he's trying even better.

And I said to him that I've always considered our association like a dance. I'm the best dance partner, and the best dance partner isn't good because they know what you're going to do. They're good because if you decide to do something different, they can follow you without missing a beat. It's a hoot working with Howard from day to day because you never know what's going to happen, and it's truly been fun since that first Monday morning in Washington, D.C.

Fun or not, the management of DC101 wouldn't leave us alone. Denise engaged us in constant meetings. She wanted to preplan Howard's unique spontaneity. She recognized Howard's talent but never really understood that he was breaking ground. She spent a lot of time trying to whip us into shape. Since she couldn't get Howard to stop breaking the rules by talking too long about topics deemed unfit for polite company, she tried to get me to rein him in. But it was exactly that outrageousness that I loved most about him. I often thought DC101 was unaware of what they were dealing with. He was a thoroughbred, and they were treating him like a quarter horse. They wanted him to pull a wagon when they should have been giving him his head. It didn't take Denise long to figure out that I was going to be no help at all, so she kicked me out of the meetings.

Denise had already determined her goals before checking out the talent on her team. She had studied all the charts and graphs and, considering the market, thought that if she could just get the station out of the basement and placed third from the bottom, that was as good as a win. Completely unfamiliar with demographics and share points, radio marketing terms, I figured that if there's a top spot, why not go for it? Instinctively, I knew Howard wanted the same thing, but Denise was in the driver's seat and wasn't about to turn over control of a fifty-thousand-watt broadcast signal to two upstarts like us. In any case, she gave up on me and launched a campaign to mold Howard into a big-city, morning-drive, rock-and-roll deejay. She coaxed, cajoled, and, when all else failed, demanded that he conform to the rules—but it didn't work. Five months after beginning this bold experiment, the ratings came out and we were vindicated. Our fast rise caught everyone by surprise and forced them to admit that what we were doing was working. The meetings ended, and Denise managed to parlay the station's success into a network job.

Our problems were over, right? Wrong. Denise's departure left us in the hands of Goff Lebar, station manager from hell. Goff didn't focus so much on what Howard and I did on the air, but he was deeply distressed that he wasn't getting the credit for DC101's skyrocketing popularity. I remember the day I found him poring over a huge article about Howard in the *Washington Post*, probably looking for his own name. Suffice it to say, he was having a lot of trouble finding it.

You couldn't escape Goff. Denise would actually have to come looking for us, but Goff's office faced our all-glass studio. We could see him glaring at us as we did the show. At one point he became seriously ill. I won't say we were praying for the worst, but it certainly would have made our lives a lot easier. Since only the good die young, Goff came bouncing back, hale, hearty, and more horrendous than ever. The situation at the station was becoming claustrophobic, our only fun times the couple of hours really early in the morning before the rest of the staff came to work.

At the studio we were lepers. In the world outside, we were becoming something quite different. One morning we started talking about the Rolling Stones tour. Every tour was rumored to be the last, and we didn't want to take a chance on missing the Stones' farewell performance in case this one was the genuine article. On the air we began clamoring for tickets to the sold-out show at the JFK stadium in Philadelphia. Eventually, somebody came through.

After we were off the air, I decided to go shopping for something fabulous to wear. I wasn't exactly rolling in dough at this point, so I headed for a discount clothing store near where I lived. While I was standing in line at the register, I overheard a couple talking. "Did you hear Howard today?" the guy asked his female companion. When she said yes, he demanded to know if Howard had managed to scare up the Stones tickets. "I think so. I think he did. Yes, he's going," she told him. "Did Robin get some, too?" he asked in the kind of tone people use when talking about personal friends. "Yes, she's going, too," the girl assured him. It was the first time I realized that listeners regarded us as pals. Soon I'd have to confront the fact that our pals wanted to meet us in the flesh.

Since we'd come to the station, Howard had been making personal appearances. At first, nobody knew who he was. Suddenly, it seemed that everybody did, because the crowds were getting larger and larger. Eventually, the demand for Howard became so great that he couldn't be in all the places he was wanted at once, so they asked me to start doing some, too.

My first public appearance was a shock to all concerned. I was sure that the listeners didn't know I was black. DC101 was a rock station whose playlist was almost exclusively white, so it was assumed that the people on the radio were white, too. Plus the fact that whenever people called in and asked Howard what I looked like, and he'd ask them what they thought, they tended to picture me as the tall, blond, Playboy-bunny type. To which Howard would inevitably reply, "You've got it!"

Whenever you make a personal appearance, you're sure nobody's going to show up. So when I peered out of the van window and saw a crowd of about two hundred people waiting for me, I got scared. In this business, there's no middle ground. So I steeled myself to have courage and prepared to meet the public.

The van door slid open, and I appeared. Two hundred people seemed to have been struck dumb. No one said a word or made a move. I stepped down and started taking the promotional bumper stickers out of the hands of the silent crowd, signing them, and giving them back. After about the twelfth person, someone remembered how to smile and speak. Once the ice was broken, everyone warmed up, realizing that I was the same person they listened to every day. They gave up the Playboy-bunny image and replaced it with the one standing in front of them. They'd been shocked by the reality, but they got over it quickly. Once the rumor started that I was black, I'd watch money change hands whenever I walked into a room. People started betting on whether I was black or white.

The people who listened to us wouldn't have believed how

Howard and I were suffering inside the halls of DC101. It was amazing that we could still make people laugh even while under siege by Goff and his minions. But even though things weren't great, Howard talked Goff into bringing in another soldier for our side. Howard first met Fred Norris at a station in Hartford, Connecticut, where they both worked. He had been impressed by Fred's sense of humor and his ability to do voices. When Howard left for Detroit, he promised Fred he'd do his best to find a spot for him at his new station. That hadn't worked out, but Howard never forgot. When the kid who had been acting as our producer at DC101 left, Howard immediately thought of Fred and somehow managed to convince Goff to hire him. Now it was three of us against the rest of them.

Up until now I was having fun, but I was still maintaining a certain separation and distinction as a newsperson. Howard kept asking me to do things that would blur the line between newsperson and entertainer. I felt that that kind of career move was risky without a commitment from him that I was more than just his newsperson on DC101. So I went to him and told him we needed to talk.

Neither one of us is very good at saying what we really mean off the air. So we're just sitting there. I'm not looking at him. He's not looking at me. The conversation actually consisted of sputters and semi-syllables. But somehow, when it ended, we knew what we meant. On the strength of half-words, and without a single signature on a piece of paper or even a handshake, I had thrown in my lot with Howard and had pledged to fight alongside a guy who was about to go to war with an entire industry. It would prove to be the most crucial decision of my life, for the opponents to come were more formidable than I could ever have imagined.

2

DIRTY SECRETS

For a woman to invite and accept the love of a man whom she respects, she must feel herself eminently worthy of his interest and in a deep and abiding sense, a lovable person. Such a conviction carries with it a compelling confidence grown out of the loving engagement of a mother with her precious child, a family with a delightful girl, and a larger community likewise charmed by her.
  —William H. Grier and Price M. Cobbs, Black Rage

Looking back, it seems like I've been a fighter from day one. . . .

What I personally consider as my first heavyweight title bout was in 1964 when I was only eleven years old. Here's the blow by blow:

My opponent outweighed me by about a hundred pounds. He was about seven inches taller than I was and much more experienced. He didn't respect me. He was mauling me, pawing at my breasts with his big, ham hands and forcing his fat tongue down my throat. When I resisted, he laughed and simply picked me up in a bear hug, pinning my arms at my sides. He was wearing one of those Italian T-shirts, so his shoulders were exposed, and when he manhandled me, I wound up with my head over his left shoulder.

Suddenly I saw what might be my only opportunity to win this bout. So, opening my mouth wide, I sank my teeth into his bare skin. When the bastard continued to laugh, I bit harder, my teeth sinking farther into his flesh. Now he tried to push me away, but I wouldn't let go. Break the skin, break the skin, I urged myself, and it worked because he abruptly stopped laughing and with one powerful thrust pushed me off him. My mouth felt funny from trying to bite down so hard. He reached for his shoulder to make sure he wasn't bleeding. He didn't want any telltale evidence, and he was lucky. My teeth marks were clearly visible, but I hadn't broken the skin.

"Why are you trying to hurt me?" my opponent demanded, a puzzled look on his face.

"Because you're hurting me!" I snarled at him.

"Oh, okay," he conceded. "Just don't tell *her*."

"Fine," I hissed as I stalked past. "Fine. I won't tell Mother, Daddy!"

My victory that day was the culmination of months of fear, torture, and guilt. When it started, I was in the sixth grade and I went to P.S. 59, also known as the Louisa May Alcott School, in Baltimore, Maryland. I thought that the worst thing that would ever happen had already happened. That was when President Kennedy was shot. We were in class when the principal made the announcement over the loudspeaker. School was dismissed early, and we all walked home crying. That long, long weekend started on a Thursday, and it seemed that it would never end. I also thought that we'd never be happy again. But we went back to school the following week, and by that afternoon we were laughing and chasing each other around the playground just like we always had. I'd been going to the same school since I was five, and nothing really bad had ever happened to me. Now, in my eleventh year, I thought I might be pregnant. I didn't know exactly how you got pregnant, but I thought I might have been pregnant just the same.

I couldn't talk to my mother about it because I never talked to her about anything, especially not my problems. And this was a big one, because if I was pregnant, then my father was the father of my baby.

It started innocently enough. I had just gotten home from school. Daddy was off from his job at Bethlehem Steel, and my mother was out shopping. I was headed for the front door to go play with the neighborhood kids when Daddy called, "Robin, come here and give me a hug. I haven't seen you all day!"

I thought the sun rose and set on my father, so just like any kid who loves her daddy, I ran to him. He was my favorite parent, my best friend, and my savior. Whenever I couldn't get something from my difficult mother, all I had to do was ask him. Daddy always said yes to me, so how could I deny him a simple hug? And I thought my dad needed lots of hugs because my mother constantly complained about him, argued with him, and spurned his affection. Who wouldn't need a hug under these circumstances?

I clung to my daddy, my eyes closed, my head against his massive chest, my arms barely managing to reach around his back. I tried to give him a really good dose of love. After a reasonable amount of time, I tried to drop my arms—but he was holding me so tightly that I couldn't get free. I pushed against the big muscles in his arms to let him know that I was finished with our hug and wanted to go outside, but he just hugged me tighter.

Suddenly this didn't feel like one of our regular hugs. Daddy had never held me so tightly. He had never pressed his whole body against me. He had never breathed heavily like this, either. Before, whenever I'd indicated that I'd had enough hugging, he had stopped. Not this time. Something was definitely weird.

One of Daddy's arms was on the move now. He put it across his chest, between us. I could move again. That felt better. I thought he was ready to let go, but he didn't. Instead, he used the side of his hand to lift my chin. He kissed me on the cheek. Then he kissed me on the lips.

But the thing was, we didn't kiss on the lips in my family. Kissing on the lips was something only my mother and father did. I just couldn't figure out what he was up to.

After he kissed me, he let me go. I backed away from him in shock. "I love you so much, Robin. I kissed you that way to show you how much I love you, but your mother wouldn't understand. So this just has to be our little secret, okay?" My father had turned back into Ward Cleaver.

He said all this in very reasonable, measured tones. It was probably the same tone he had used when teaching me to tie my shoes or ride a bike. He was so calm, so reassuring. But I suspected that what had just happened was wrong, and I needed to get out of there so that I could think. "Okay," I answered.

"Remember," Daddy said, "it's our secret. You understand?"

"Yes. Can I go out now?"

"Sure, go ahead."

Oh, my God—my father has fallen in love with me, I thought as I bolted from the house. How romantic. But he's married to my mother. He isn't allowed to fall in love with me!

At first I thought it was kind of cute. Later that evening, when my mother returned from shopping, my father seemed to have forgotten the whole incident. He treated me just as he always had. Maybe he wasn't in love with me after all. There was certainly no evidence of it now. And there wouldn't be until we were alone again.

Soon my father managed to work these encounters into our family routine. He was off from work every Thursday, and my mother decided that Thursday would be her shopping day since he could baby-sit for the foster kids we boarded. Shopping day was an all-day affair, so he knew she wouldn't be back for at least two hours after I got home from school. My mother loved her Thursdays. I began to dread mine.

As these clandestine meetings continued, I started to think that they were all my fault. Maybe I had been too nice to my father. I always took his side in his chronic arguments with my mother. Maybe that's how he got the impression that it was all right to kiss me this way. But even if it was my fault, I didn't know how to make him stop touching me.

I thought and thought and at last came up with a plan. Since fathers aren't supposed to allow their children to do bad things, I figured that if I started acting really bad and pretended that I liked his kisses, he'd stop me. That's it, I congratulated myself. The next time, I'll keep my lips open when he tries to jam his tongue in my mouth.

On the next shopping day when Daddy pulled me to him, I put my plan into action. This time, when my father kissed me, my lips weren't tightly pursed. Boy, was he surprised. But instead of stopping, he got even more excited. "That's it," he murmured, "now you're getting it," and he kissed me again, this time holding me closer, grinding his midsection into me. I felt something hard pressing on me from inside his pants. He started to breathe faster and faster, acting as if he'd almost forgotten that I was there.

He stopped just as I was about to panic. My plan had gone terribly wrong. I was obviously in unknown territory. The old rules didn't work, and I didn't comprehend the new ones. All I can say is that my father thought I had given him the green light to go even farther. Every Thursday he took a few more liberties, kissing me on the neck one week, and putting his hands inside my shirt the next. Like a farmer, he plowed a little new ground each time.

It was really scary. I knew how things would start, but I never knew where they'd end. Afterward, I always felt that I must be a really evil person because only a devil could tempt her father into committing such a sin. At least that's what they would have said at the Mount Hope Baptist Church, I thought. Reverend Nance was always preaching about the devil and how sinners would burn in hell. I feared for my mortal soul. I couldn't understand how I had become so awful.

As time went on, though, I started to think that it was my father who was the bad one. I was the one who hated what was happening. I was the one who wanted it to stop. I even tried to avoid him. He was the one who came looking for me. If he had really been in love with me, I reasoned, he wouldn't have been able to hide his feelings so well. If he was so out of control, why was it that he had no trouble controlling himself when other people were around? I was not only beginning to hate it, I was beginning to hate him. He really grossed me out when I realized why he liked doing this in the dining room. He liked being able to take peeks at us in the big mirror over the buffet.

Then suddenly it wasn't just Thursday afternoons. One evening my mother decided on the spur of the moment to go to a lodge meeting. When I discovered that she wouldn't be there, I was devastated. It meant that except for the foster babies, I'd be alone again in the house with my father. Immediately after dinner I ran upstairs and shut myself in my room. I could hear my mother say good-bye and then close the door behind her. Next I heard my father climbing the stairs. He was coming to get me. Terror gripped me and tears filled my eyes. I heard him walking down the hall. I prayed that he would stop at his room, but the footsteps continued on. I watched my doorknob turning. This time, standing in a corner of my little room, my father amused himself at my expense, kissing me until he decided it was time to stop. Couldn't he see that I was upset? Wasn't it obvious that I didn't like what he was doing to me? Why didn't it matter to him?

Almost overnight I'd gone from being a relatively secure kid to one who felt terrified, confused, and totally alone. To make matters worse, I still hadn't unpuzzled the riddle of how to make it all stop. Ultimately, Daddy did it for me by pushing me too far.

One Thursday he pulled me into his lap as he sat on a kitchen chair and stuck a finger in my vagina. That was it. I knew he had done something then, I could feel it. It didn't feel like anything he had ever done before. It was as if he had crossed some invisible barrier. I'm not even sure I knew what the vagina was called, and I wouldn't have known where it was if he hadn't touched it. Fingering me that afternoon was the end of that session for him, but it was the end of the road for me. I thought he'd gone all the way with me. I was petrified that I wasn't a virgin anymore. And if I wasn't a virgin, I might be pregnant.

The next two weeks were hell, although there weren't any more groping sessions. Somehow I managed to avoid him while I waited to see if I'd get my period. I did know that much about reproduction. It was in a book my mother had given me called *Growing Up and Liking It*. If my period came, I wasn't pregnant.

I had a lot of time to think in that two weeks. I thought about the girdle my mother had tried to make me wear a few months before all of this had started. She had said that I was jiggling when I walked and that that was indecent. But the girdle was too tight and cut into the tops of my thighs, so after a couple of days I refused to wear it. "Are you sure?" she asked. "If men see you jiggle like that, they might try to rape you."

At the time, I thought it was just another of my mother's nutty beliefs. I didn't know that the men she was talking about included my father. I don't know if a girdle would have stopped him, but I didn't believe that I should have to live in pain to be safe. I didn't know any other girls who wore girdles, and I wasn't going to either. There had to be another way, because I couldn't live like this anymore.

My period came. Menstruation wasn't one of my favorite things, but boy was I glad to see that blood in my underpants. I'm surprised that I didn't smear it on my face like war paint as a sign that I was back in control and ready to fight. Good and ready.

My poor father had no idea what he was in for. I looked like the same eleven-year-old he'd been molesting, but now I was different. Somehow transformed. Transformed by fear. Transformed by anger. Now I was focused and had only one goal, to make him stop. I was willing to face anything, even death, to make that happen. He was much bigger than I was and incredibly strong. There was no way that I was a match for him physically, but I decided that he'd have to beat me to death before I'd ever let him force himself on me again. That was when I bit him so hard that he threw me across the room.

Once I left the living room arena, victorious, I realized that I could breathe again. It was over. I had expected it to be difficult, but it wasn't. It had only taken a few minutes to end months of abuse, and it had been easy. I was in one piece and unmarked, which only left me questioning why I hadn't done something sooner. Maybe if I'd just said no right away, none of this would have happened.

My father didn't even care what had happened to me. He never said, "I'm sorry." He never said, "I didn't know what I was doing." He never said, "I didn't mean to hurt you." He just said, "Don't tell your mother." Well, at least he was never going to touch me again. As long as he kept his part of the bargain, I'd keep mine, and I was good to my word.

My father might have thought he made a good deal. His life looked the same. He still had his wife, and he still had his reputation. But when he made that deal, he ceased being the undisputed head of the household. Our little secret would change the whole power structure in our family, and nothing would ever be the same. That little secret actually empowered me. The same man who had touched me without permission soon realized that this no-account little girl could destroy him with a word. No one ever talked back to my father with impunity, and when I started doing it and getting away with it, the rest of the family started to fear me as much as they feared him.

Still, this newfound power had cost me a lot. I had lost my innocence, and I'd lost a parent, a friend, and the person I loved the most. With him, I didn't feel that I needed anyone else. I thought he was the strongest and the wisest man in the world, but he'd turned out to be just a paper tiger. I didn't dare trust another person. I couldn't afford to be let down that badly again.

There was going to be no adolescence for me. I went into hiding, and it was a very long time before I came out again. People saw me walking around, eating dinner, going to school, but I wasn't really there. I was hiding in plain sight, trapped in that house where I would never feel safe again with people who would never stop trying to break my spirit, drain my soul, and rob me of all beauty and expectations.

There wasn't much romance in my parents' coming together, and not a lot of beauty or expectations either.

Lula Harvey, who would become my mother, had been raised as one of seven children in a desperately poor family in Tabbs, Virginia. The Harveys never had indoor plumbing, owned only one set of underwear apiece, and during the Depression had to stand in line for food. Lula was forced to leave school in the seventh grade to work in the fields for some white farmers. When she was sixteen, she walked into town, going from door to door looking for domestic work. Though she had no experience, one of the white ladies who answered the door that day decided to give her a chance. This woman hired her and taught her how to clean a house. She didn't only land a job that day, she found a dream.

Seeing how this woman lived, watching her and listening to the way she talked, made an indelible impression on my mother. She worked hard to improve her own command of the language, and would later stand guard over her children's vocabulary, grammar, and pronunciation. There were no lazy tongues in my mother's house. When we went to church, the other children would com-

ment that we sounded white. My mother admired—maybe even
envied—that white woman's life, so much so that when I was born
she named me Robin after that white lady's daughter. Maybe she
thought she could change my fate by giving me that name and, who
knows, maybe she did.

My father, Charles Quivers, had seen front-line duty in World
War II only to return stateside to find that on the home front, he
was still just a "Negro." To add insult to injury, the black men who
had stayed out of the war while he risked his life had made lots of
money and resented the returning GIs as a threat to their newfound
prosperity. Daddy had gotten married a few months before he was
drafted and now had to deal with the fact that his wife had been
sleeping around while he was away making the world safe for
democracy.

Charles Quivers was a bitterly disappointed man, but he managed to find a job, get a car, and take up with a girl. That girl was
my mom. The first time he saw her he said he thought she was the
ugliest girl he had ever seen. But after a few days, she didn't seem so
ugly anymore. All their lives they would be considered a mis-
matched couple. He was a strapping, handsome, light-skinned black
man with green eyes. She was dark brown in complexion, with eyes
so dark they looked black. Even today, a dark-skinned black woman
has trouble getting someone to say she's pretty, and my mother suffered from that stigma. When the two of them walked into a room
together, I could hear women say, loud enough for us all to hear,
"How did she get him?"

When they met, Charles was still married, and Lula was
engaged to marry her childhood sweetheart, who was still away in
the army. They decided to keep each other company until his
return. Before long, my mother discovered that she was "knocked
up." She had no desire to suffer the stigma of an unwed pregnancy.
People had looked down their noses at her all her life because she
was poor. They weren't going to get the chance to pity her, too. She
says she decided to run away to Baltimore, alone, to avoid the scan-
dal, but my father found out and insisted on going with her.

For the life of me, I never understood what these two were
doing together. As long as I've known them, they've done nothing
but fight. If she was looking for stability and security, Charles was

probably the last man she should have chosen. He was a hothead, a quitter. He dropped out of school at twelve, hung out on the streets making mischief and chasing girls. He finally wound up in jail when a scheme to sell stolen cigarettes went bad. He claims it was jail that straightened him out and made him join the service—which he stayed in only because they made him.

The first job he got in Baltimore was with a moving company, but it didn't last long. Someone said the wrong thing to him and he quit. He was always doing that. When he got the job at Bethlehem Steel, Lula, who had started calling herself Louise, dug in her heels, determined that he would stay employed. After all, he now had a woman and a baby boy to support, even if the family wasn't legal yet.

Charles and Louise had trouble saving the money necessary to secure a divorce from his first wife, but they loved to play the numbers. For pennies, you were in the game run by mobsters and based on the daily horse races. If you were in for fifty cents or a dollar, you could win real money. My mother used to say that whenever they really needed cash, they'd hit the number. She thought it was God's way of helping them out financially. So it was illegal numbers' money that eventually paid for my father's divorce, allowing them to get hitched about a year after my brother, Charles Junior, was born.

Louise thought one child was enough. She had no desire to childbear herself into poverty—as her own fourteen-year-old mother had done. Charles wanted as many children as they could have, but he could only talk her into one more pregnancy. That would produce me. I was the one who came after they were married. I was the one they planned. After spending a few years with them, I was fond of saying that they must have taken the wrong baby home from the hospital. The only problem with that theory was that I was born at home.

When I arrived at five-thirty in the morning on August 8, 1952, my mother felt that her family was complete. She had a four-year-old son and a newborn baby girl. Only one piece of the dream was still missing. She wanted to move us out of our tiny little apartment in the ghetto to a home of her own. The first arguments I remember hearing were about the money for the down payment for my mother's dream house. Just before I started kindergarten, they had finally managed to scrape together the two hundred dollars it took to reserve a whopping eight-thousand-dollars' worth of real estate. Yes, the house of her dreams cost just eight thousand dollars. "And it was so pretty," she told me recently. "Well," she added, "it was pretty then."

In reality, my mother's fantasy was a cramped, three-bedroom row house in the middle of the block on a dead end street. We weren't on the wrong side of the tracks, we were practically on the tracks. When we first moved there, the noise of the freight trains would keep us awake at night, but you can get used to anything, and in time we learned to sleep right through it. As if that wasn't enough, our front window faced a metal foundry. At lunchtime, the grimy men from the foundry lined the curbs and harassed all the passing females with catcalls and wolf whistles. Charming. But after a while, that too wove itself into the tapestry of our neighborhood.

I was as happy as Mommy when we got our house because it was supposed to be the end of all our troubles. I assumed that the fights would stop now, and that my parents would start to love each other. The house didn't change anything, though. It just gave them more room for their rows.

It was in this house that I would first see evidence of my father's uncontrolled rage. I was awakened by loud noises coming from my parents' bedroom. When I walked out into the hall, my older brother, Junior, was already there. He opened the door to their room. I saw my mother lying on the floor. My father was crouched over her, pummeling her with his fists and kicking her in the stom-ach. Her dress was torn and she was bleeding. When she saw us standing there, she yelled, "Call the police!"

My brother headed for the phone near the bed in their room. I followed. My father stopped what he was doing long enough to scream at us, "You touch that phone and I'll kill you!"

We believed every word. So even though we wanted to help our mother, we felt that we had no choice but to back out of the room and go back to bed. I laid under my covers, waiting for the noise to stop.

My mother swore she'd never be beaten like that again, but that didn't mean she was leaving. She cut up all of my father's suits a few weeks later to teach him a lesson. She got a recipe for a lye and molasses solution that would severely disfigure a person because he wouldn't be able to get it off his skin. She actually went out and got the ingredients. She said that if it ever happened again, she'd mix it up and throw it on him in his sleep. They even sometimes threatened each other with kitchen knives. At other times she'd boil water and threaten to scald him with it. They never, ever thought of just not fighting.

And the violence wasn't only between them, wasn't only from him. When I was four, my mother beat me so badly that I had to stay in bed for days while she fed me chicken soup. I couldn't figure out why one minute she could hurt me so much and then be so nice the next. Which one was the real person? Early on, I got tired of trying to understand her and wrote her off emotionally. She never beat me that severely again, but I counted on nothing from her but the beatings, slaps, and harangues she tried to discipline me with well into my teens.

I had to face the fact that my mother was a control freak, a petty tyrant who stamped out any display of independence or abandon before it could take root. She was also given to wild mood swings. One minute you could be laughing and joking around. The next, you had unwittingly broken some unfathomable rule and were in big trouble. She even spoiled the good times because you couldn't relax and just enjoy yourself.

Her bad moods could last for hours, even days. It was as if she was probing your psyche, looking for tender spots. Once she found them she'd bore in, picking at the spot until it bled. And sure enough, as soon as you lost your composure, she'd calm right down and even express surprise at the level of your distress. "Well," she'd announce with a smirk, "what I said must be true. Why else would you be so upset?"

You can't imagine what it's like to hear your own mother go on and on about how horrible you are, how worthless and stupid you are, what a burden you are, and how you had ruined her life. If it hadn't been for me, she could have bought herself more things. If it hadn't been for me, she wouldn't have had to stay in that marriage. I was too dumb to appreciate her sacrifices. I was too vain. I was disrespectful. And I was—her favorite slur—a no-good, "imp'kin" (her attempt at "impudent") devil. Making eye contact with her while she assaulted you with her tongue was considered defiance and usually got you slapped in the mouth. So you learned to keep your eyes down. But you'd better be listening, because she didn't like to be ignored either.

She worked really hard at getting a reaction. My brother and my cousin Shirley, who was three years older than I was and had come to live with us when she was five, would start to cry, beg for forgiveness, and thank my mother for putting up with all their shortcomings. I, on the other hand, was just like my father. After hours of abuse, I'd finally explode, she'd hit me, and peace would be restored for the moment.

One evening when I was eight years old I got so sick of her yelling and carrying on that I decided to just leave. "You know what? I'm getting out of here. You hate me so much, I'm such a problem, then I'll just go." I stomped up the stairs and with Shirley running behind, begging me to stay, I began throwing my things into a shopping bag. As I marched downstairs with my bag and opened the front door, I heard my mother call, "Oh, you're leaving now? Well, 'bye!"

I stepped outside. The cool air caressed my burning face. It was quiet. It felt good. I climbed down the steps and started up the street. Halfway up the block, it hit me that I was walking nowhere. There wasn't one person I could call on for help. No one I knew who would give me shelter, not a soul who would understand that I was breaking out of prison.

You see, as far as the world at large was concerned, the Quivers were a model family. We didn't have problems. We were well-spoken and wonderfully behaved. Other kids loved to spend time at our house. Their parents used to urge them to try to be more like us. If I had gone to a neighbor's and confessed that I couldn't live with my mother anymore, they would have told her what I'd said and then sent me straight home. And when I got there, she'd beat the crap out of me for embarrassing her in public. So I turned around and headed right back to "jail." "Oh, you're back," my mother laughed as I resumed my place in this meat locker she called a home. My mother and father were the top of the food chain—cannibals who, with no other food source in sight, began to eat their young.

I guess it was funny that in a way, when all I wanted to do was get away from her, she had made sure there was no place for me to go. Even funnier was that she thought my return meant she had won our test of wills. If I had been anyone else, maybe she would have. But making me angry was the best way to lose a fight with me. My mother had just welcomed home her worst nightmare. She already thought of me as her "imp'kin" devil; soon I'd make those words true by matching her word for word and mood for mood.

So here was our happy family. I was at war with my mother. My mother was at war with my father. My brother and my cousin were so beaten down that they didn't have the will to defend themselves. And soon, in the silent confines of my mother's pretty little dream house, my father and I would be keeping our own dirty little secret.

3

NIGGER TALK

To one who bears the sweetest name,
And adds a luster to the same,
Long life to her for there is no other,
Who can take the place of my dear mother.

—a poem on a plaque in our home

Boom, boom, boom, boom.

"Robin," Junior yelled as his heavy fist pounded on my bedroom door.

Boom, boom, boom, boom.

"Robin, it's time to get up," he yelled again.

"Okay," I managed in a sleepy voice.

Fifteen minutes later he would be at the door again, banging and yelling and warning me that this was the last time he was going to try to wake me up before he had to leave for school. I never wanted to get up anymore. Sleep was so peaceful. The bed was so warm. I felt safe in sleep.

I slept a lot after my father molested me. It seemed that I always needed a nap. Even if I napped, I needed ten to twelve hours of sleep a night, and my brother or my mother would still have trouble rousing me in the morning. That meant that I was always rushing.

Wash my face, brush my teeth, throw on some clothes, and catch a bus to get to school.

I was in junior high now, in a stupid class. It wasn't the stupidest one in the school, but our curriculum didn't include a foreign language. All my really smart friends from elementary school were taking languages, so it didn't take a genius to figure out that my class wasn't considered academically gifted. One last twist of the knife by my sixth-grade teacher, Mrs. Green.

She hated me. Before her, I had never met anyone that I couldn't charm, but she never gave me a chance. Her mind was made up before she ever met me because she had taught my cousin Shirley three years before. I remember my mother complaining constantly about having to go to school for yet another teacher's conference when Shirley was in Mrs. Green's class. The meetings were always followed by threatened beatings if Shirley didn't behave. Whatever it was that was getting her in trouble, I never cared enough to ask. Shirley was never the greatest student, but it seemed that this had to do with her conduct as well as her grades. To me, it was just more of the general chaos that reigned in my house, so I tried to stay out of it.

Shirley's last name was Walker, but even after three years, Mrs. Green instantly remembered having had to meet with a Mrs. Quivers about her. She walked around the classroom on the first day of school going over the seating chart. When she got to my desk, she stopped. "Robin Quivers." After thinking, she said, "That name sounds familiar. Are you related to Shirley Walker?"

"Yes," I replied. "She's my cousin."

She let out an audible sigh. I could tell by her face that she was not pleased. She needed no further introduction. From that moment on it was as if she was looking at my cousin when she looked at me.

Every bad thing that happened in class she blamed on me. If the person sitting next to me wound up with the same answer as mine, I was punished for cheating. If there was talking, I was the instigator. But if there was something fun to do, I was never chosen. Mrs. Green determined my grades and where I'd start next academically. I could have been a budding rocket scientist and she would still have made sure that I got stuck with the slow learners at Pimlico Junior High. Pimlico continued in the tradition of my elementary school—with blacks making up about 15 to 20 percent of the population. The white students were predominantly Jewish. Temple Oheb Shalom was right next door to the school.

I was embarrassed about being in such a low-ranked class and vowed that I wasn't going to stay at that level for more than a year. For the first time in my life, I decided to take school seriously. I lugged five or six big, heavy books home every afternoon. I did all the assigned reading. My homework was always on time.

"Me, me, me," I implored, waving my arm frantically, practically standing at my seat to get a teacher's attention. I was like Horshack, the overanxious sweathog on the TV show "Welcome Back Kotter." I always knew the answers, and the rest of the class was too slow for me. While I was always ready to move on to the next subject, the teachers ignored me, concentrating on those who were falling behind. They finally stopped calling on me. Sometimes I didn't wait to be called on, I just blurted out the answers. At other times I mumbled them under my breath while another student struggled to figure out what to say while staring into thirty pairs of eyes. I pouted when I couldn't participate, arms folded, lower lip poked out.

"Robin, you've got to give other people a chance," I remember my social studies teacher, Mrs. Esposito, saying sweetly.

When pouting didn't work, I decided to try daydreaming. Oh, I was listening alright, but I pretended that my mind was a thousand miles away as I gazed out the window. Mrs. Esposito fell for it. She had just asked a question. "Robin, why don't you tell us the answer?"

"The southerners were called Tories because they wanted to remain loyal to the British." I smiled, turning my head toward her.

"Well, if you know the answer, raise your hand," she said sharply.

By the end of the seventh grade, I had become a really good student. Of course I didn't have the distractions of most girls my age because my interest in boys was on hold. It turned out that this solution for one problem would simply create another. One morning they brought a new black student into our homeroom. Her name was Kim, and there was a certain something about the way she walked into that class full of strangers that made me take notice. I thought she was pretty, but what I most admired was her confidence, something I didn't have. I remember immediately wanting to be her friend and looking for the right moment to approach her.

But the strange thing was that the closer I got, the less I admired her. What I had taken for self-assurance was really a haughty attitude masking a caseload of insecurities. Still, it was quite an act. Kim was the only girl I knew who strolled naked to the girls' shower room after gym class. The rest of us ran, covering our breasts and pubic hair, while Kim's hands swung at her sides as she glided toward the stall. Sometimes she laughed at us for being so modest.

Before school we always met in the courtyard in front of the building. One morning I spotted a bunch of girls I knew all huddled around a bench. I decided to see just what it was that had them so interested. When I reached them, I could see that Kim was holding court. "Girl, then he started kissing me on my neck and unbuttoning my blouse. I put my arms around his neck and then he gave me a French kiss," she announced triumphantly.

When she noticed me, she said, "Look at Robin," directing everyone's attention to me. "Girl, you are so naive. I'll bet you don't even know what a French kiss is."

"No, I don't," I answered matter-of-factly, looking her straight in the eye.

"That's when a boy puts his tongue in your mouth while he's kissing you," she informed me, still smiling a sickeningly false smile.

Maybe I didn't know what it was called, but I had already done it. My father had made sure of that. In any case, I wasn't going to give Kim the satisfaction of knowing she'd gotten to me. The others could think what they wanted. Meanwhile, a voice in my head was saying, You think you're so smart, but you'll probably get pregnant before you graduate from high school and be lucky to get one of these idiots to marry you.

The bell rang. Everyone scurried off to class, and my moment on the hot seat was over. The bottom line was that Kim wasn't someone I needed in my life. The kinds of things she had to teach, I already knew.

I did acknowledge that I wasn't going to figure out this whole sex thing by myself, but who could I turn to? There were no adults that I trusted. I had good reason to believe that they were all evil. Even the best were capable of incredible cruelty, usually directed at those they claimed to love the most. Husbands and wives cheated on each other. Parents humiliated, neglected, and beat their children. Teachers abused their power, making decisions that could affect your whole life based simply on whether or not they liked you. Adults, all adults, were strange, and parents were the worst adults of all. I couldn't afford the luxury of making mistakes that might leave me in their grip forever. That meant that boys and sex were out of the question. I left that to girls like Kim.

Living in the Quivers household all my life hadn't made sex seem all that desirable. Take my mother's attitude about it, for example. As far as she was concerned, men were victims of their hormones, unable to control their sexual impulses. Women had to do the best they could to protect themselves while knowing that they'd eventually have to submit to this animal behavior in order to trap a man into taking care of them. She was definitely from the "grin and bear it" school of sex education.

I knew that my father loved and desired my mother, but it was very difficult to tell if she felt any affection for him. They didn't do a lot of touching. If my father tried to give her a playful tweak, she would angrily bat his hand away. In a reflection from the mirror in their bedroom, I saw her rebuff a lot more than an errant feel. Even when they were supposed to touch, it seemed strained and ritualistic more than affectionate or passionate. Whenever they said good-bye, they gave each other three quick pecks. It was always the same— lips, cheek, lips. If they had been fighting before my father had to leave, he'd still try to kiss her good-bye, but she'd always turn her head away.

Because I couldn't tell if she loved him, I had to ask. I asked a lot because I wanted my mother to love my father, but the answer was always the same. "I guess so," she'd say. "I married him, didn't I?"

She preferred her teenage years. Whenever I wanted to keep her in a good mood, I'd get her to tell me about the dances she'd gone to with her old boyfriend, Clarence. Her face would change. Sometimes she even closed her eyes and paused as she thought about the good-night kiss Clarence had given her at the end of the lane in front of her house. She could go on and on about the good times with Clarence, but if I brought up my father and asked her to tell me about the good times with him, the conversation would come to an abrupt end.

My mother also had a few questions for me. The most offensive of which was had my father or brother ever tried to touch me when we were alone. I was twelve or thirteen at the time and emphatically replied in the negative out of shame and embarrassment even though the answer was yes in my father's case.

I was disgusted by the question. I was disgusted that she would live with people she felt were capable of such action. I was angry that she had included my brother in the question. My brother and I weren't close, but he certanly wasn't a sexual opportunist like my father.

My mother should have known. It wasn't as if she pulled this question out of left field. She had reason. When I was eight years old I walked in on an argument between her and my father. Right away, I knew there was something different about this fight. My mother appeared to be in agony and my father was trying to calm her down. "Lou you're wrong, nothing happened," he pleaded with a worried look on his face.

Daddy tried to touch my mother but she pulled away. She began to pound at her temples with the heels of her hands. Her eyes were red from crying. "This is wrong, Charles" she screamed, closing her eyes. "You're not suppose to touch a child like that."

Again, my father tried to reassure my mother that she hadn't seen what she thought she'd seen but she wasn't buying it. Then my mother noticed that I was watching them, and she yelled at me to go to my room. I knew this was no time to protest and I made a beeline for the stairs. They adjourned this very serious conversation to their bedroom which was right across the hall and I continued to listen to their muffled voices for some time. I decided that this was one of those conversations I'd understand when I got older. I had no idea how right I was.

After my father started molesting me, I remembered that conversation, and believed that my mother caught him doing the same thing he'd done to me to someone else. In a recent conversation, my mother confirmed my suspicions but she swore she never thought he'd do that to his own daughter.

The way I see it, my mother left me in harm's way. Maybe she hoped that she could guess my father's timetable and thwart his attempts. But she did nothing to make sure that I was safe.

After the horses were already out of the barn, my mother did try to teach me the facts of life. She called me into the kitchen one evening after dinner. "Do you have any questions about sex?" she asked out of the blue.

"No," I answered, getting nervous.

"Well, you don't really know how it's done, do you?"

"Leave me alone," I screamed. "You've ruined enough of my life. I don't want you to ruin sex for me too."

She started to laugh at me and kept right on talking. "A man climbs on top of a woman . . . "

I didn't hear the rest of what she was saying. "I'd rather learn about sex on the street," I screamed.

When she kept right on talking, I put my hands over my ears and ran out of the house. She never brought it up again.

My mother did manage to give me other valuable advice. When I asked her if I could use tampons, she said, "No, only married women can use them."

She used to shudder when I bathed during my period. When I started to experience painful menstrual cramps, she claimed, "You see, God is punishing you because you take baths at that time of the month."

When I pointed out that they recommended swimming during your periods in the tampon ads, my mother answered, "Well, maybe they can, but we don't."

It was pretty obvious that my mother didn't think much of women, either. My brother, Charles Junior, was her favorite child. If she'd had her way, he would have had complete control over me. She wanted me to make his bed and cook his meals. Once, when a teacher sent home a note telling my mother that my brother had slapped me across the face, she gave him advice on how to hit me so that it didn't leave marks. And when she applied to become a foster parent, she said that she would prefer boys because they were easier.

I secretly felt that she wanted me to fail. There was never any support for anything I wanted to do. Tap-dancing lessons, which I loved, were deemed unimportant and a waste of money. When I asked for piano lessons, I was told to find my own teacher. When they offered music lessons in school, I asked if I could take violin. No. I loved to sing around the house. "Shut up that noise," my mother would yell.

Sleep-away camp was out of the question. People in my neighborhood didn't send their kids to camp. But more than that, it seemed that my mother wanted me with her all the time. She thought I had been born to be her best friend, and she'd keep me around, sharing all her little secrets. I knew where she hid money in the house. I knew about her secret bank account. She shared with me all her most intimate thoughts and feelings. It never occurred to her that maybe I didn't care about this stuff or that I was too young to be used as a confidante. She seemed to feel that it was my duty.

She never acknowledged my scholastic ability, yet she spent countless hours nagging my brother to work harder in school so that he could make something of himself. I used to wonder why she worked so hard on him when I was sitting right there. "I'm the one," I'd say to myself. "Why are you wasting your time on him and my father? I'm better than they are. If a man is someone who's smart enough to get an education and make his way in the world, then I'm the best man here."

But to her I was just a girl. Once, when I brought home a good report card, she just said, "I don't know why you work so hard. You're just going to get pregnant."

I wondered just how this was supposed to happen. After I got my father off my back, I announced to everyone in the house that I didn't want to be hugged or kissed. "I don't want to be touched anymore," I declared.

I did that to cover my father's tracks and make sure that he never got to touch me again for any reason, public or private. My mother chalked up my strange behavior to "just a phase" I was going through. I had no friends, no social life, and I certainly didn't date or show any interest in boys. Just how was I going to get pregnant, and why shouldn't I work hard? Because I was "just a girl."

The older I got, the more she seemed to resent me. I got the feeling that I had done something wrong by continuing to grow. She didn't seem to like the fact that I was becoming a woman. In a fit of anger, she called me a whore. This was new. She had never used such adult epithets on me before. She glared at my body after saying it and added, "No two women can live under the same roof, and I'm the woman of this house."

The words stung. I had fought off my father to keep him from raping me, and I'd spent the next few years trying to erase this feeling that I had been bad by doing all the right things. How could she call me a whore? I was keeping this terrible secret so that her whole world wouldn't fall apart and she could go on with this delusion that she had a happy family. And this was my thanks.

While I was doing all I could to hide my shame and keep the family together, my father started messing up big time. He started drinking and staying out all night. We used to say that there were only three places my father could be. He was either at work, in bed, or sitting in his favorite chair sleeping or reading a book. He was considered the best husband on the block. You could set your watch by him. Now he was totally unpredictable, out of control, and their fights became louder and more violent. And when my mother had problems with my father, she brought those to me too.

I started to believe that there was no way to escape this craziness. It was in the genes and had something to do with puberty. If that was the case, like some B-grade horror film, I felt that these genes would blow up on me, turning me into my mother and father one day. I wondered if I would know it when it happened. Would I fight every day to keep myself from doing bad things to people only to have it happen anyway? The prospect was too awful to me. That's when I started telling myself that God wouldn't let that happen. He had saved me when I thought I was pregnant. He didn't want these horrible changes to happen to me. I was too good, too special. I figured that the changes became more rapid and irrevocable after eighteen, so that's when I was going to die. God would take me to heaven, thereby saving me from my genetic destiny.

I no longer had to worry about figuring out sex. I wasn't going to be here that long. I could do what I enjoyed and understood, going to school and learning things. School had always been my haven. I went to school even when I was sick. As long as I could walk, I was in my seat when the bell rang. I was the only kid who thought summer was too long and who dreaded weekends. No school meant no respite from that horrible place I called home.

*   *   *

Soon, though, even the tranquillity of school would be shattered, revealing that the world was full of petty, stupid people. Everyone suffered that particular madness of puberty that allows racisim to flourish. I had gone to school with white kids all my life. I was the only black kid in my kindergarten class. It never occurred to me that my color should make a difference, so it didn't. No one told me that I was supposed to be stupid because I was black. No one told me that I couldn't succeed. They always expected the same kind of work from me that they got from the other kids, and I performed well. I was very popular with all of my teachers except that old crone, Mrs. Green, and even that I didn't think was a race thing. The black kids who came to my school long after I'd been there seemed to be the ones with the problem. Every time a new black kid joined the class, I'd have to bring him into the group. The older the black kids were when they joined the class, the less likely they were to ever play with whites.

I continued to play with the kids I had gone to school with all my life, but I also played with the cliques of black kids that sprang up on the playground. Whenever I returned from playing with the white kids, the blacks would ask, "Are they really nice to you?" or "Do they really treat you okay?"

Then one day one of my white friends showed me that I was different. Stephanie and I had been in the same class since we were five. We were never close, but we always spoke, and we shared a common love of the Beatles' music. On a Saturday, I saw Stephanie at the shopping center walking with someone I didn't know. "Hi, Stephanie," I called out when I saw her. No answer. I was getting closer and assumed that she hadn't heard me. "Hi, Stephanie," I said, now almost on top of her. This time there was a very visible response. Stephanie turned up her nose and tossed her hair back. She was very obviously refusing to acknowledge me. She and her friend continued to talk, walking right past me without a backward glance.

I couldn't believe that this had just happened. I had even traded Beatles cards with that bitch. For years I had been urging black kids not to believe what they'd heard about whites. Now this girl who knew me very well had ignored me and I could think of only one reason for the slight: I was black.

Okay, so that's the way it's going to be. You'll stick to your group, and I'll stick to mine. No more living in this fairy-tale world where everyone gets along. It was over. I didn't change that much in class, but during recess I sought out my black friends and stayed with them. We had our own language, our own music, and never ignored each other when we met outside school.

Just as I had no one to teach me how to be a woman, there really wasn't anyone around to teach me how to be black. Was being black really about the slang words we used and listening to the black radio stations? Was it about taking on a tough-as-nails exterior and saying bad things about white people? Was it about calling each other "nigger" and finding other ways to humiliate each other?

"You're so low, you have to look up at your feet."

"Oh, yeah, well, you're so slow you're going to be late for your own funeral."

"Well, you're so ugly that when you were born the doctor slapped your face thinking it was your ass."

"Yeah, well, you were so ugly when you were born the doctor slapped your mother."

"Yeah, well, you're so black that you have to smile at night so people can see you."

"Yeah, well, you don't have that problem, because you smell so bad people always know when you're around without even looking."

Sometimes these verbal battles turned physical. When an insult struck too close to home, fists started flying. But even these fights never ended friendships, maybe because there was nowhere else to go. We clung to each other out of desperation.

At home it was more of the same. "Nigger" was supposed to be a bad word, but people used it all the time and not out of earshot of children. When my mother was angry at my father, sometimes he was a "nigger." When my father was angry at my brother, he was a "nigger." When either of them was pissed off at other black people, they were "niggers." But they didn't have to be angry with someone to call them a "nigger." When men were fooling around, swapping stories, drinking and playing cards, they'd say things like, "You're full of shit, nigger," "Oh, I got you now, nigger," "Nowhere to run, nigger, I gotcha cornered," and the ever-popular, "That nigger's crazy." Even though we heard it all the time, we weren't supposed to say it.

No one talked about the word, they just used it, and no one had to tell us that the time the word was most offensive was when white people used it. White people didn't play with the word "nigger"; when they used it, they meant it. The reaction was always the same. It was devastating, like being hit in the stomach. There was no way to recover. It wasn't fair for white people to use the *N* word. To whites, "niggers" were subhuman. It meant that you were stupid, ugly, shiftless, worthless, and lowdown. A little girl would never want to be a "nigger." But to whites, we were all "niggers."

Once I asked my mother why she and all the other black adults we knew used the word so much if it was so bad. She simply told me that it didn't apply to me. In those days, the theory was that blacks used the term to take some of the sting out of it. My theory is that people who use the word "nigger" mean it whether they are black or white. It was a word coined in slave times to define a new kind of chattel brought to the New World to work the fields, pulling plows and picking cotton. It was not a word that meant a kind of people, it was the word for a new kind of animal. It retains all its meaning today. There is no nice way to use the N word.

It was time for us to start preparing for the inevitable. We were growing up. Black children are cute. Black adults are "niggers." It was only a matter of time before a white person would use the word on us. None of the white kids had done it yet. Even when the little white kid down the street and I had our race wars, which you'll hear about later, that word wasn't used. When the white kids chased us to steal our Halloween candy one year, they didn't use the word. I was the only one who didn't just run away when the white gang descended on us. But even the white kid who threw me across the hood of a car because I talked back didn't use the word. You just couldn't tell when it was going to happen or who was going to do it. You also didn't know how you would react.

One of my friends got her initiation when we were in eighth grade. A bunch of us were all walking home from school together. One of the girls was walking faster and was about half a block ahead of us. When we caught up with her, we found her hovering over a little blond boy. He was sitting on the ground. His face was red, and tears were streaming down his cheeks. "What happened?" someone in the group asked.

"He called me a 'nigger,'" she said through clenched teeth. Her hands were still balled into fists. She looked as though she wanted to hit him again. Somehow we convinced her to leave him alone, walked around him, and continued home. We all patted this girl on the back, proud of her response. She was the first, and instead of shrinking back, she had lashed out and struck this silly little white boy who had dared to call her a name when she was just trying to make her way home. We felt empowered. Striking back had never been an option before. This was the first time we'd ever seen a white person pay for using that word. We knew that our day of reckoning, just like hers, was lurking right around the corner.

The word "nigger" was another fence to box us in. The whites on the outside called us "niggers" to keep us behind the gate. The blacks inside called each other "nigger" to remind you that this was where you belonged, and that no matter what you did or how far you went, you'd still be just a "nigger."

My junior high years were the ones in which I would become aware of how much race would affect my future. Anyone who isn't black can't imagine what it's like to have no one, not even the people who gave you life, expect much of you. No one can imagine having all your childhood friends mock you and then ostracize you because you have ambition. No one can imagine an entire community doubting that you can make it. No one can imagine the distractions and obstacles deliberately put in your path to keep you down. No one wants you to get out.

In Baltimore, in 1965, there were a lot of white people who had talked themselves into believing that blacks wanted life to remain just the way it was, and they were teaching their children the same thing. How else could a classmate tell me during a heated civil rights discussion that black women liked to be maids? Her name was Cynthia, and until that day I thought she was smart.

Cynthia said her mother had told her that black women preferred housekeeping jobs and didn't want to work as cashiers at the five and dime because they didn't want to work the registers. This was her mother's explanation for why no blacks worked at the chain of dime stores in town. It wasn't a racial thing. Whites weren't discriminating. Blacks just didn't want the jobs. I found it hard to stay in my seat at this point. "Only an idiot would make a statement like that," I yelled without waiting to be called on. "Do you really believe that not one single black person in this country wants a job other than cleaning your house? Is that why you think I'm going to school? You think I want to clean house for you when I graduate?"

Cynthia and I stood at our desks yelling at each other until the teacher made us stop. Then Brenda stood up to try to bring some clarity to the situation. "My father is a graphic artist who is in charge of hiring in his office," she said. "He'd like to hire a black person, but the other people in his office said they'd quit if he did."

She was proud of her dad's stand. "Yeah, with support like that we'll get absolutely nowhere," I said, this time from my seat.

"He'd like to do something," she replied.

"Well, that and fifteen cents will get me a cup of coffee," I retorted.

"Well, what's he supposed to do?" she inquired.

"Fire them all and hire all blacks," I yelled. "That's what he'd do if he really wanted to do the right thing."

I was entering my black radical period. I started reading black literature. *Manchild in the Promised Land* by Claude Brown was the first. I identified with this kid of the streets trying to find his way out of the ghetto before it consumed him. I quickly followed that with *Soul on Ice* by Eldridge Cleaver. It became my bible. I had a copy of it with me all the time. I figured that white people would see it and be very afraid that they were dealing with a member of the Black Panther party. I came to believe that there was no way for blacks and whites to live together. My solution to every problem became KILL WHITEY.

I figured that white people had already robbed us of everything. Judging by the level of self-esteem and respect, or the lack thereof, in my neighborhood, blacks had already given up and there was little hope of saving any of us as long as there were so many white thumbs pushing us down. But just when I thought that all was lost, I found a role model. Someone who would show me that I didn't have to wait for anyone's approval to be whoever and whatever I wanted to be.

4

STUNG

We were discussing Israel in class one day when one of the Jewish boys stood up and declared that he was pro-Israel even though he was an atheist. The teacher, who was also Jewish, began to argue with him that he couldn't be an atheist, but the boy insisted. Finally, the teacher ended the argument by saying, "You're too young to be an atheist; at your age you don't know what you believe."

—*1965*

Old habits are hard to break. No matter how vigorously I tried not to let my parents influence my behavior, I would sometimes find myself acting just like they did. I was bound to learn something from them. Why else would you call them parents?

One of the things I'd learned from them was how I was supposed to act around white people. Oh, not with the kids in school. To me, they were equals. It was in the real world that it was hard to know how to carry myself. I had been convinced that white people could and would kill me if I got on their nerves. Baltimore may not be the Deep South, but it was still Southern and we knew that there were sections of the city that we'd better not venture into if we liked living. Even our local version of "American Bandstand," "The

Buddy Dean Show," was segregated. Every couple of months they'd let the black kids on to dance for a day. The show was on five days a week. It went off the air when there was an effort to integrate it.

Every time I went to the store I had a confrontation. White adults thought nothing of taking my turn at checkout counters. Counter people looked past me to wait on all the white faces before serving me. I was actually lucky if I got waited on in turn, but if a white person wanted to take my turn, I'd let him. I was disappointed in myself for not fighting back and demanding to be recognized. Black people in the South were being killed to win me these rights, and I was too scared to speak up on my own behalf.

When I talked to my parents about it, all I got was sympathy. They said that this was the way of the world and that it was the best I could expect. "It's better than getting killed," they'd remind me.

It was just about this time, when I was about thirteen years old, that I really got to know my uncle Leroy. He was my father's oldest brother and the senior living member of the family. My parents acted as though their own parents were coming when Uncle Leroy paid a visit. They were on their best behavior. My mother ran around the house giving it an extra-special cleaning, and all fights were put on hold until Uncle Leroy had gone. I thought it was funny that sometimes, right after he'd left, a big shouting match would break out because of something my father had done while Uncle Leroy had been with us.

Uncle Leroy wasn't light-skinned like my father. He was a big, round, brown man with short-cropped gray hair. He smoked like a fiend and was always coughing and wheezing. But he had a presence. There was no getting around that, and anyone who scared my mother and father certainly scared me. My first memories of him are of his chasing me around the house squealing, "Robin, I love you" in a reedy, high-pitched voice. He would tell me that I used to say "Uncle Leroy, I love you" when I first learned to talk, but I had no memory of this and refused to respond to his squeals. I begged my mother to make him stop, and when she finally told him that it bothered me, he quit and never did it again. But that didn't help me feel any better about him.

He finally got married when he was in his fifties. His wife, Ruth, was only thirty-five. She was a tall woman with dark eyebrows. She was a smoker, too, even though she was asthmatic.

There was something really sweet about her face. I liked her as soon as I met her, and I couldn't imagine why this nice woman would marry cranky, fat, old Leroy.

Ruth showed me that behind that gruff exterior beat the heart of a big, fat teddy bear. It happened on one of their first visits after getting married. Uncle Leroy and my father were playing cards in the dining room while Aunt Ruth sat in the kitchen. She started teasing my uncle about something, and he snapped at her. I was all ready for a brawl to start, but he just continued to play cards and I could see that he was trying to keep a smile from curling the edges of his mouth. He really loves her, I said to myself.

After that, I started hanging out with them whenever our families got together. I liked watching them. They treated each other well. They didn't fight like my parents, and it was obvious that they enjoyed each other's company. It was quite a shock when we got a call from Uncle Leroy saying that Ruth had died. She had a really bad asthma attack and didn't make it. So even though she was much younger than my uncle, and had nursed him through a couple of heart attacks, he wound up burying her.

At first I liked Uncle Leroy because of the way he treated Aunt Ruth. Later I'd love him for the way he treated me. Whenever they visited, they slept in my room. I'd take up residence in the basement, but I still used my room to change. On one particular visit, I was in there riffling through my drawers looking for underwear after having taken a bath when the door popped open. There stood Leroy. Instinctively my hands covered my breasts and I bent forward, trying to hide my body. I thought it was going to happen again, but instead Uncle Leroy calmly and quickly apologized before closing the door behind him. "I'm sorry," he said. "I didn't know you were in here."

Boy, that was easy, I thought. He hadn't tried to sneak a peek. He hadn't planned to invade my privacy or violate my space. He had shown me respect and had restored a measure of my dignity. What's more, he made me wonder. Maybe every man wasn't like my father, maybe some of them were like Uncle Leroy.

While no one else seemed to care that I had no life, Uncle Leroy always asked, "Who's your boyfriend?"

I'd blush and twist. "I don't have one," I'd answer softly.

"Don't lie to me girl," he would said playfully. "A girl as pretty as you. You probably have too many."

Was I pretty? I'd never thought about it, but Uncle Leroy said that I was, and that was enough for me. From then on, when Uncle Leroy came to town, we always spent time together, just the two of us.

Usually we went shopping. Leroy was bigger than your average guy, so he had to shop at Big Man Tall Man stores. There wasn't a store that could fit him in Newport News, Virginia, where he lived. So at least twice a year he came to Baltimore to go on a shopping spree. Shopping with Uncle Leroy was my favorite thing to do.

Armed with a wad of hundred-dollar bills, we'd grab an over-sized cart at the door of Pratt and Pulaski. It wasn't long before the clerks realized that something special was about to happen. In less than ten minutes, the cart was filled with dozens of pairs of under-wear and T-shirts. Then we'd head for the high-ticket items like shirts, pants, suits, and overcoats, collecting merchandise and sales-people as we went. Before I knew it, Uncle Leroy would have two or three of them all jumping around at his command. "Give me ten of these shirts," he'd say with a toss of his hand. "I'll take five pairs of slacks, and I think I'm going to need a suit."

Salespeople darted all over the store. They couldn't do enough for him. As he dispatched another salesman to the stockroom to pick up something else for him, he'd look over his shoulder and give me a wink. I'd beam. I had never seen a black man command such respect or wield such authority over whites. When he worked, Uncle Leroy was just a brakeman on the railroad, but when he shopped, he was a king. He showed me the power of money. The salesmen didn't care what color he was or how much he carried on as long as they got paid at the end. In fact, they often thanked us profusely and were sure to ask us to come back again soon. Money was the great leveler.

Uncle Leroy would let me play, too. Once he was in a suit, he'd come out of the dressing room, with a salesman running behind, and stand in front of a three-way mirror. As soon as the salesman would start to stroke the goods and tell him how nice the suit was, Uncle Leroy would interrupt with, "Robin, what do you think?"

That question made me the most powerful person in the room.

Salesmen would turn to me each time a decision had to be made. Sometimes I said no just to see them run around some more. We had a great time every time we went, and then we'd laugh all the way home.

I never missed an opportunity to be with Leroy. Once a year he and some friends rented a bus and came to Baltimore for the day to see the Colts play football. He always sold his ticket or gave it to my brother and stayed at home with me to listen to the game on the radio. We even bet on the game. But Uncle Leroy spoiled me. Even when I lost, he'd give me the money. I never said, "Uncle Leroy, I love you," but I sure did.

Watching Uncle Leroy made me think that it might be possible to demand respect, even in Baltimore, without your life hanging in the balance. But even when we were running through the aisles of that store, I knew that these white men and I were adversaries. Martin Luther King, Jr., may have been on the television sermonizing about unity and integration, but how were blacks and whites ever going to learn to live together when even kids found it difficult?

Even I participated in regular race wars on my own street. Most of the white kids who lived there were Catholics and went to the Catholic school. Their school was all white. The only time they saw blacks was outside school, and they hated it. There was only one white family with children who stayed on the street. Their son was my age. He never played with us and always made a big deal about the little patch of grass in front of his house. "You'd better stay off my lawn," he'd yell at us as we walked by.

Sometimes I'd step on the edge of the yard just to get him crazy, and whenever his white friends came to visit him, we went to the barricades. Our weapons were words and rocks. We'd yell at each other and throw stones. We were lucky that none of us was much of a shot.

The futility of the situation struck me when I wound up pitching rocks at somebody I really liked in one of these wars. Johnny and I had met when we first moved into our new house. His grandmother still lives next door to my parents. Mrs. Leak watched Johnny once or twice a week.

Johnny would be at his grandmother's door waiting for me when I got home from school. "Robin, Robin, you want to see my new fire truck?"

"Johnny, I have to change my clothes. My mother won't let me play in my school clothes."

"Okay, then hurry up," he'd reply.

Before I could get back to his grandmother's house, he was knocking at the door. We'd sit on my porch or his grandmother's steps for hours. We never had trouble talking or finding things to do. Mrs. Leak and my mother would marvel at how this little white boy and this little black girl could play so well together. For us, the rest of the world disappeared. I'd say that Johnny was my first love.

Johnny showed up one day when my neighbor's son and I were in the middle of a major diplomatic breakdown. When the war broke out, he asked Johnny to choose sides. Reluctantly, Johnny joined the whites. Everybody quickly ran for cover because the battle was about to begin. I hid behind some bushes. It was a great place because it came with a stash of ammunition.

I dug up a handful of rocks and gravel and got ready to throw. When I stuck my head above the bush to take aim, I saw Johnny several feet away, ready to throw a rock at me. After a moment's hesitation, we aimed at each other and let go of the stones we were holding. As usual, before we could hurt each other, somebody's mother or father discovered that we were throwing things at each other again and started to yell. Everyone scattered eventually, seeking the safety of their own houses. Since Johnny was staying right next door, we practically ran home together.

Johnny tried to apologize later. He said he really didn't know what to do, but when he was forced to choose, he felt he had to go with the whites. He had to go with the people who looked most like him, our friendship notwithstanding, and our friendship would never be the same. As Johnny got older, he stopped coming around so often. We still saw each other occasionally, but it was as if we were two strangers.

Once again, I was left with the same nagging question. If this is what the world thinks of me, what am I supposed to think of myself? The white kids I went to school with had fathers who were professionals. My father worked in a dirty steel mill. He did the unskilled labor, handing tools to the white bricklayers. Every few years there was a contract negotiation, and sometimes my father had to go on strike. Once he was out of work for so long, and we

got so behind on the bills, that my mother had to take up house-
cleaning again. This time she wound up working for the parents of
kids who went to my school.

She'd come home tired but full of stories about the little white
girls whose house she cleaned. She thought it was funny when the
youngest one asked her why the soles of her feet were different than
the color of her face. "Bobbi said, 'Louise, why are your heels white
and your face brown?'" my mother said, laughing.

"They call you by your first name!" I erupted.

"That's what children call the maid, Robin," she protested.

All she wanted to do was tell a cute little story, but I was trying
to figure out who I was, and this wasn't helping. It made me angry
that these kids, kids my age, got to call my mother by her first
name. My friends couldn't do that. She would have corrected them.
I pleaded, cajoled, and finally screamed, "You make them call you
Miss Louise."

My mother never understood my distress. She came home one
day and announced that Amy, the older one, was going to look for
me at school. I was mortified that my friends would discover that
my mother was just a maid and that she worked for kids at my
school. For the first time, something about my parents threatened
to spill over into my other life and cause me shame. It was important to me that these kids see me as an equal, someone entitled to
the same things in life that they were. I didn't want to be thought of
as "maid" stock.

My fear of exposure was expressed as anger. "I'm in the same
fucking school as they are and probably getting better grades," I
said to myself. "They're just stupid girls, anyway." I knew something about life they were just about to learn. Women are the "niggers" of the universe, so no matter what color they were or how
many maids they had, they didn't have much to look forward to
either. Their grades were probably already slipping behind those of
the white boys their age. Well, fuck 'em.

I was probably beginning to think that saving what little money
you could make and then going to a store to spread it around was
the only way a poor black person could get any respect at all. And
then I started to hear people talking about this guy named Cassius
Clay. He was a boxer. I wasn't a fight fan. I didn't know anything

about the sport except that the titles were usually held by big black men. The only one I knew by name was Joe Louis, and the only reason for that was because my mother and father would tell me stories about how proud they were of him because he beat up a white guy in front of Hitler.

Mostly it was black men like my father who talked about Cassius Clay. They said he was a "crazy nigger" who was going to get himself in trouble. "He's got a big mouth and somebody ought to shut him up." Whoever he was, he sure made people mad.

He had my father talking to himself. "Who the hell does he think he is, talking like that," he said. "He's going to get himself killed."

What the hell was this guy saying, I wondered. I had to find out about any guy who could cause such a fuss. I discovered that Sonny Liston was the world heavyweight champion and that Cassius Clay wanted to fight him. Clay was telling everyone who would listen that Liston was ducking him because he, Cassius, was the better fighter. It wasn't just what he said though, it was the way he said it. He had confronted Sonny right after a fight, and in his moment of triumph, Clay had stolen Sonny's thunder. He had disrespected the champ, and he bragged too much, always talking about how pretty he was.

I heard that Sonny Liston was going to be on "The Ed Sullivan Show," so I made sure to watch. He was huge. He didn't sing or dance, and he was no talker, so there wasn't much for him to do on the show. Ed decided that they should compare biceps. Both men peeled off their suit jackets and rolled up their shirtsleeves. Then Ed stood in front of Sonny and tried to make a muscle. Sonny followed suit. It was funny. Sonny dwarfed Ed. His huge bicep bulged both above and below Ed's. It was a perfect appearance. Sonny was the kind of black person white people liked. He was the perfect example of a "good nigger," so big, so powerful, and so under control. I have to admit that I liked Sonny too. Sonny was successful.

When I finally saw Cassius Clay, I thought he must have had some kind of death wish. He was young and very good-looking, but he also looked a lot smaller than Sonny. His complexion was also lighter, and just like most people, I bought the myth that a big "field nigger" like Sonny was impossible to beat. The myth says that all blacks are physically stronger than whites, and the darker your skin, the stronger you are. On skin tone alone, Sonny was the clear winner. Liston finally agreed to fight Clay. As soon as the fight was announced, all the black men got excited, and the night of the fight the excitement was palpable. The black men said that this was it. Clay was going to get his big mouth shut. He really didn't even deserve a shot at the title, according to them. He wasn't championship material. Sonny should just beat him up badly and make him go away. A black man who talked like Clay was bad for everybody. He was the kind of nigger who made whites think we didn't know how to behave. Clay reflected badly on the whole Negro race.

Sonny failed the black men that night. He was the one who was beaten badly by Clay, who was too fast and whose punches were too accurate. The radio announcer said that Liston was cut and bleeding. He had hardly laid a glove on his young opponent.

The black men were stunned. Something must have been wrong with Sonny that night. It wasn't possible that Clay could be the heavyweight champ. He was cocky and loud. "I am the greatest," he screamed after the fight.

The black men were afraid. They had grown up knowing that acting like this young boy could get you killed. Somebody had better teach him fast or he wouldn't be champion for long. Joe Louis was a champion, Sugar Ray Robinson was a champion. There hadn't been a champion like Clay since Jack Johnson, and they had destroyed him. Maybe it wasn't hate for Clay that I saw in their eyes. Maybe it was concern for his safety.

I agreed with them. Liston shouldn't have lost that fight. He had underestimated his opponent. He'd get him the next time. This match had been a fluke. The rematch would end all argument as to who was the better champ and who really deserved the title, this uppity, disrespectful loudmouth, or Liston, the champ like the champs of old. You could have a pretty good life in America if you had skills white people could exploit and you stayed in your place. Clay was going to mess up everything and set us back.

If we expected vindication in the second fight, the black men and I were going to be sadly disappointed. Clay was proving to be a worse champion than our worst nightmares could have conjured up. He was threatening to join some wacky religion, the Nation of

Islam. All I knew about Islam was what I heard on the radio. Their leader, the Honorable Elijah Muhammad, was on every Sunday, sandwiched between spirituals and the dime-store preachers who sold "miracle floor wax" to chase the demons out of your home. The Honorable Elijah Muhammad said that the so-called Negro was the original man and that the white man had been created by a mad scientist. Because the white man had not been created by God, he was evil. Junior and I listened to the Honorable Elijah Muhammad and laughed. He was a goof. Now Cassius Clay said that he was joining the Nation of Islam and would follow the teachings of the Honorable Elijah Muhammad.

The championship couldn't have been in worse hands, but Clay would hold onto it by knocking out Sonny Liston in the first round of their rematch. After the fight, Clay announced that he no longer wanted to be called Cassius Clay. He was now Muhammad Ali.

The black men were confused. Some of them refused to call him by his new name, but he was the champion just the same. He had broken all the rules, and he was causing all kinds of trouble. We were on entirely new ground here. Ali was charting a new course, all without the aid of education or philosophy. There were a lot of theories about how to make white people accept us. Promote the talented tenth, work hard at the menial jobs to earn respect, join the army and fight their wars to show that we deserved the same rights.

I don't think Muhammad Ali was familiar with one of these theories. Sure, he represented his country in the Olympics, but if that was all he ever did, I wouldn't know who he was. It was becoming the heavyweight champion of the world and recognizing that he wasn't representing the Negro race by wearing that stupid belt. Boxing was a business, and a dying one at that. Muhammad sold tickets. He put asses in the seats. Some of them were there to love him and some of them were there to hate him, but they all paid the same price and he had a considerable cut of the gate.

This "crazy nigger" had become the first authentic black man produced in America since slavery. We couldn't take our eyes off him. He resisted incredible pressure to conform. He made us accept this strange new name. He was arrogant and boastful, but he was also able to back up every claim. He kept his hair kinky and practiced his wacky religion. He became father to a generation that wondered how it was possible to be black and proud, and he did it without degrees or the approval of the ruling class.

I realized I had the role model I had been looking for all my life. He was the champ. He could make millions, and he didn't have to suck up to anybody to do it. He could have stopped right there, but if he had, he wouldn't have been Ali. Muhammad was a man of principle. In the years ahead, he was to prove that his true measure was not his titles, nor his money, nor his fame, but what he stood for.

5

GOINGS AND COMINGS

I can remember, when Negroes were just going around as Ralph has said, so often, scratching where they didn't itch, and laughing when they were not tickled. But that day is all over. We mean business now, and we are determined to gain our rightful place in God's world.
—Martin Luther King, on the eve of his assassination

In 1967, Martin Luther King, Jr., Malcolm X, and Muhammad Ali were all my heroes. The civil rights movement was in full swing. There was something to feel good about, being black was actually becoming popular. Feeling like we wanted to contribute, a bunch of my black friends and I sat around one day trying to come up with a word for white people that would have the same impact as "nigger." I still don't know where I first heard the word "honkey," but that was the word we chose.

If a white person pissed us off, we'd whisper "honkey" under our breaths. No one had yet tried it out loud on a white person, so we could only fantasize about the effect. I imagined white people cringing in pain, devastated that I'd resorted to the H word.

Then it happened. Lea, this girl who was in my history class, called one of the white girls a honkey right in the middle of the room. The white girl looked at her, confused. "What's that?" she said.

"What's that!" Lea answered. "That's you."

"Oh," the white girl said. She shrugged her shoulders and walked away.

This was not exactly the response I was expecting, and that's when it struck me. White people don't mind being white. So no matter what you call them, if it means they're white, it's okay.

I realized that I had a lot of work to do before I felt that good about being black. I had heard a lot of bad things about my race for a long time, and I had started to believe some of them. Maybe I couldn't march in Selma, Alabama, or integrate a school in Mississippi, but I could make my very own revolution happen right inside my head. The first thing I had to learn to do was to feel as good about being black as white people felt about being white.

To start, I decided that the term "Negro" just had to go. Only radicals called themselves blacks in the 1960s. And I believed I should too. First off, it took care of the old color prejudice I had learned at home. Nobody wanted to literally be black. The more you looked like a white person, the better. The term "black" went right to the heart of that problem. "Black" also felt more powerful than "Negro." "Negro" sounded like an apology. And "black" is the opposite of white. It was perfect.

I started whispering it to myself. "I'm black," "I'm black," "I'm black." I said it to myself every time I thought about it during the day. When I got up in the morning, I smiled at myself in the mirror, and while I washed my face I said out loud, "I like being black. I like being black. I like being black."

I knew I was on my way to improving my self-esteem when I called myself black out loud in front of my school friends. It resulted in audible gasps. "Robin, you called yourself black," Clarice said in shock.

"I know," I said with a smile. Just saying it made them respect me more. Robin is special. She calls herself black. Soon I corrected anyone who referred to me as colored or as a Negro. "I prefer to be called black," I'd say. I even made my parents do it. They hated it. The world was definitely changing. I was changing, and things were changing around me.

*   *   *

On April 28, 1967, in the midst of the Vietnam War, Muhammad
Ali refused to be drafted into the army. The old men who were
beginning to grudgingly accept him as their champion now saw new
hope that he could be unseated. Finally he would meet an opponent
he couldn't "whup," the Federal Government. "Yep, Uncle Sam will
put him in his place," they said.

After all, what was the big deal? They simply wanted to put
him in a uniform and take his picture. They did the same thing to
Elvis. But Ali said that his religion was opposed to the war. A lot of
people would have said, "So what, Muhammad! The country's done
a lot for you. They're not asking for much in return."

Ali saw it differently. Why were young black men going overseas to die in a war that they didn't understand, against a people
they didn't know, for a country in which they were not free?

The black men who hated him failed to recognize what he was
doing. They had served in wars, and even though things weren't
great, each time they got a little better. They only saw the money.
He was crazy to give up the title and all the wealth it could bring.
Now he would probably go to jail and never be able to fight again.
That was an awful lot to do just for a bunch of "niggers." They
would have taken the money. They would have gone into the army
and they would have led every "nigger" who would have followed
them right to the draft board. At least Ali was getting paid. That
was more than most "niggers" could expect. They cursed him once
again, this time for being stupid as well as crazy.

I was in awe of him. I had never known a fully empowered black
man. I'd never even known anyone with principles. My parents
spouted rules all the time, but they were the same rules I saw them
constantly breaking. A promise was kept only if it was convenient
and didn't cost anything. I had read about people like this, but here
was a man I could watch, and I began to watch everything he did.

I'd argue with anyone who bad-mouthed him. I even bet my
uncle Leroy that he would never go to jail even though I secretly
believed that he might have to. I fantasized about knowing him, but
because he was a Muslim, I stopped short of wanting to marry him.
I wasn't going to walk two paces behind anyone, not even Muhammad Ali.

Ali went to court and fought the draft. The case slowly made its way through the system. The debate about whether he was right or wrong continued. With each passing year, fight fans lamented the wasting of the greatest boxing skills ever displayed in the ring. It would take four years for the case to make it to the Supreme Court, where eight white justices, with Thurgood Marshall abstaining, would side with Ali. The government and the boxing commission had been wrong. But when Ali decided not to be inducted, and lost his championship belts, he couldn't have known all the consequences of that action. Yet when he discovered how great an impact that decision would have, he still refused to back down. He threw his whole life into the breach. Four years is longer than most people can wait to see the outcome of anything. If this was the only lesson that Ali would have taught me, it would have been enough. But he had tons of lessons to teach and quite a few tricks up his sleeve. He would surprise us all, just as I was about to be mighty surprised by what was going to happen to me. Like Ali, my luck was about to change.

Change was a Quivers' house rule. People seemed to always be coming and going at my house. There was the core group—me, my mother and father, and my brother, Charles, Jr. Then there was everybody else. My uncle George, who was my father's youngest brother, lived with us for a while, but then he moved out so that his daughter Shirley could move in.

I was two, she was five, and Junior was six when she came. Since we were both girls, she and I shared a room. I assumed that Shirley would be with us until she grew up, so I treated her like a sister. I didn't know if I liked her. You don't think about whether you like the people you have to live with, they're just there. I didn't know if she was pretty. I didn't think about that, either. I was the baby of the family. That meant that I was automatically the cutest one.

Shirley was bigger and lighter than I was. When her girlfriends started worrying about boys, I remember them all congratulating Shirley because she could pass the "brown bag test." The darker girls were worried that boys wouldn't like them. Shirley said she wasn't sure if she was lighter than a brown bag, so someone pulled one out, and sure enough, she was.

If the talk was about boys, when my mother came into the room Shirley would clam up. God, she was passive. She used to drive me crazy. I think that's why I fought with her so much. That plus the fact that it seemed to me she was competing for my father's affection. She had a father of her own. What did she need with mine? I would gladly have given her my mother instead, but they never seemed to get along.

My mother would hit the ceiling if she saw Shirley with boys. According to her, Shirley was the kind of girl who was surely going to get "into trouble." That meant only one thing when applied to girls: getting pregnant before getting married.

Shirley's abrupt departure from our house when she was eleven or twelve has always been mysterious to me. The way I remembered it, my mother decided that she wanted her gone, and within a week she was living with her father and his new wife, Miss Annie. We weren't even consulted. I was used to seeing my cousin every day for most of my life, and suddenly she wasn't there. I figured that if she was going to be living with her father, I'd get to see her sometime, but Shirley didn't get along with her new stepmother either, and before long was on her way back to Virginia. I knew I'd never see her again once she got there.

We wrote to each other for a while, but it was clear that she was going to grow up very different from me, and I was only eight when she left. It was hard to keep up the correspondence.

Even before Shirley left, my mother started taking in other children. She decided to become a foster parent after a steelworkers' strike forced her back into a maid's uniform for what she declared would be the last time. The state paid money to board and feed these kids, and my mother looked at that money as steady income. Her work would now be foster mothering.

Getting into the system involved an extensive application process that included family interviews. When they interviewed Junior, Shirley, and me, the authorities had no idea that my mother had coached us. First she told us what to say. Then she had us role-play with her as the social worker. We were to answer that we wanted these children to come to our house, that our parents never fought, that we were very happy, very religious, and that we'd love to open our homes and our hearts to needy children.

I could tell that the social worker was quite impressed with our performance. She went so far as to say, "What mature and well-behaved children. I'm sure we'll have no problem approving your application." If she'd only known!

In a very short time we were accepted as a pre-adoptive foster home, which meant that only infants and toddlers who were considered adoptable would be placed with us. My mother didn't want older children. Since they had already been around for a while and been raised by others, they were probably damaged. She didn't want to inherit someone else's problems. She definitely preferred to create her own.

Pretty soon after that, the front door become a revolving door. Our little boarders were from six months to a year old and stayed a year or two before being placed in permanent homes. Since I wasn't doing anything else, I helped out with the kids. I actually didn't mind it. I knew they were too young to hurt me. I trusted them. It was all right to share affection with them, but I knew not to get too attached because they could leave at any moment.

We were only supposed to have two foster children living with us at a time, so our house was already full on February 27, 1967, when a frantic social worker called to tell us that they had a four-day-old baby and no available homes. So my mother consented to boarding a third child.

His name was James, but we started calling him Jimmy right away. He came to us straight from the hospital. He was still wrapped in those thin, pastel receiving blankets. My mother had to borrow some things from the neighbors to get through his first few days because he had been delivered on such short notice. Most of the other kids who came to live with us were coming from other homes. They usually had clothes, bottles, and diapers, but Jimmy had only the things he was wearing. He needed everything, including a crib.

I remember rushing home from school the day he arrived. There was a newborn baby in my house. I had never seen a baby that young. When I opened the front door, there he was, lying on the living room sofa guarded by two pillows. He looked like a pale blue bundle. I dropped my books into the chair by the door and walked softly over to the couch. Inside all the wrappings was the face of a little old man with his eyes closed and his bony fingers grabbing the air.

My mother had been on the phone since she'd found out that she was getting a brand-new baby, so the neighbors were already there. "You want to hold him?" my mother asked.

"Uh-huh," I said, staring at him.

My mother told me to sit down on the couch, then she gently picked Jimmy up and placed him in my arms. "Make sure you support his head," she instructed me.

He was warm, and after I took him he started to squirm around. It felt good. I wanted to just sit there with him resting on my lap, but after a few minutes my mother said I had to put him down. "It's not good to hold babies too much, you'll spoil him," she said, ever the killjoy.

I did my homework sitting on the steps of the living room that afternoon so that I could watch him and check out the neighbor women streaming in and out of the house to look at the baby. I got to observe an interesting ritual that afternoon. They all looked into the blankets and then began to comment and compare notes. "He's got a nice color," someone said. "Yes, and by the look of his ears, I think he's going to stay light," someone else volunteered. "And it looks like his hair is going to be straight," another said, stroking the top of his head.

Listen to them, I thought. I wondered what must have been said about me at birth. Jimmy had just been declared okay because he was going to be light with straight hair. This carrying on continued for days, every time a group of people gathered around him. Didn't they know that what they were saying was wrong? Weren't they listening to what was going on in the world? Hadn't they heard anything that Martin or Malcolm was saying? Didn't they care about their own children and what this kind of ridiculous talk did to their spirits? This was the kind of crap that seeped in and strangled the very souls of black folk, and here they were, all too eager to reinforce it one more time.

Jimmy's layette was a large box on the dining room table. My mother thought it was the perfect size. It was large enough for him to lie in comfortably, yet small enough to still give us room to eat. We'd have to get a crib soon, though, because in a few weeks he'd be able to move around and then he wouldn't be safe in the box. "Mommy, why does he sleep so much?" I asked.

My mother told me babies slept a lot because they had a lot of growing to do. I had changed diapers before, but he was so little that at first I had trouble figuring out how to make them fit. This was before the days of disposables, and we were using cloth and pins. I had to make sure I didn't stick him. As I got more comfortable with Jimmy's size and age, I started spending every moment that I wasn't in school with him. I stopped doing my homework in the basement and started lugging my books up to my parents' bedroom, where Jimmy slept.

I'd throw my books on the bed, turn on the TV, and then take Jimmy out of his crib. There was this black dance show on one of the DC stations, but it came in very fuzzy. I didn't care. I'd watch it anyway. Jimmy watched the show upside down as he lay across my lap. I wondered what he thought of those grainy, upside-down people swaying to the music. When I was actually doing homework, I'd lay him beside me. I'd feed him and then have my own dinner.

We stayed together until it was time for me to go to bed. By then, Jimmy was already asleep in my arms. The only time he cried was when he woke up in the middle of the night and found himself actually lying in his bed and not with me. Then he'd scream. My mother started waking me up to put him back to sleep even though I had to get up to go to school in the morning. She finally just moved his crib into my room as a solution to this nighttime problem. That was just fine with me.

Shortly after Jimmy arrived, as if by some miracle, the two children who were already living with us were each sent back to their real parents. Jimmy was the only baby in the house for a long time, and he got my undivided attention. I found out, too, that his real mother was only fourteen, the same age I was. These few coincidences convinced me that Jimmy was my personal gift from God. He had sent me someone to love again, someone who would love me without hurting me.

For the first time in years, I completely forgot about not getting too close. Jimmy needed me, and I needed him. I wanted to make sure Jimmy was safe and wouldn't be affected by the crazy things that went on in my house. I vowed to myself that I would protect him. I cared more about him than I thought possible. I cared about him enough to start wanting to live again. I even started thinking about a future with him. I decided I'd adopt him after I graduated from college. We'd move out of the house and get an apartment of our own. My life was set. I knew just how it was going to be: Jimmy and me against the world.

Jimmy's arrival coincided with high school selection time. I had been going to school with the same people for nine years. Most of the kids who would graduate with me would go on to Northwestern High. It would be Pimlico all over again, but on a larger scale. I decided that it was time for something new, something both more challenging and less so all at the same time, so I took the entrance exam for Western.

Western was a public high school, too, but it had a great academic reputation and required a test, a transcript of your grades, and a teacher's recommendation to enter. There were also no boys at Western. I could get a great education and completely avoid the boy problem. Western would get me prepared for college and give me time to grow up before I had to deal with men.

Western was really scary at first. Everyone there was really serious about this academic stuff. Before, when I made good grades, it was an added benefit. At Western it was mandatory. But it was also fun. When these girls weren't surrounded by boys, they began to shine intellectually. Even in the cafeteria, we sat around discussing weighty topics and comparing notes. At Western nobody took us for granted, nobody thought of us as just girls.

I was looking forward to the Jewish holidays coming up a few weeks after school started. I was going to take this much-needed break to regroup and get over the shock of my new high school workload. Thank goodness I didn't go with my first thought that morning and leave my books at home, because when I got to class, to my surprise everyone was there. All through school, Jewish holidays had meant a class comprised of me and the substitute teacher. Even though I had to go to school, since no one else was there, I still got a day of rest. All morning I wondered what the hell everyone was doing in class today.

By lunchtime I could no longer stand the suspense. "What the hell are you people doing here?" I asked a group of white girls at the table. They looked confused. "It's a Jewish holiday," I continued. "You're supposed to be in temple!"

"You think we're Jewish?" one of them asked in a tone that indicated that this was not a compliment.

It was my turn to be confused. I didn't even understand the question. "Do we look Jewish?" someone else chimed in, perturbed.

"I don't know," I said. "What does Jewish look like?"

At this point they proceeded to educate me. Jews were supposed to have kinky hair and big, hooked noses. They also had obnoxious personalities, according to these girls. They were loud and pushy and liked to show off how much money they had.

I was beside myself. I had obviously been surrounded by Jews all my life and I hadn't noticed how different they were from other white people. I thought that being Jewish was belonging to a religion like a Baptist or a Catholic did. I didn't realize that it made your nose grow and gave you a bad personality. I thought better of telling these girls that I didn't see much difference. But I did begin to lose hope that whites would ever accept blacks. They didn't even like one another.

The life lessons were coming fast and furious now, and even little Jimmy would end up teaching me as much as I would teach him. By caring for him, I learned what it really meant to love someone. He helped me to forget all the cruelty in my own life—and to see beyond the "spare the rod, spoil the child" philosophy of child rearing my parents practiced. My mother used to tell me that she beat us because she loved us, and although I don't think I ever believed that, when I was in charge of the foster kids, I beat them too.

I might have gone on thinking this was okay if Jimmy hadn't come. He embraced the terrible two's with a vengeance. When he threw his first tantrum, I just didn't know what to do. The more I yelled for him to stop, the louder he screamed. With no other options, I resorted to that old standby, spanking. I took off my sandal and started whacking him on the butt. With each smack, he cried even louder. In the midst of all the action, I suddenly saw what I was doing, which was being just like my mother. I was beating a little boy I claimed to love. I wasn't fixing the problem, I was physically abusing a child. Thank goodness I was hitting mostly diaper.

I fell to my knees, crying, and took him in my arms. I promised him and myself that I would never hit him again. I promised to be patient with him and not to try to work out our problems with belts, switches, and paddles. For the first time, I realized that I had hit those other children because of my problems, not theirs. As time went on, I was amazed at how easy and loving even discipline could be.

I was also determined that Jimmy wasn't going to be hit by anybody else, either, and I made my mother's life hell as only I could if anything "happened" to him while I was away. I assumed total parental control, and my parents let me. If Jimmy misbehaved while I was in school, my mother got him in line by threatening to tell me that he had been bad. That's the way I wanted it.

I think I was a good parent. I treated Jimmy like a little person. I never talked baby talk to him, so by the time he was three and a half, he had an amazing vocabulary for his age. People always thought he was older because he was so mature. We used to have incredible conversations.

Some people thought that he was stuck-up. Jimmy knew that he didn't have to submit to being touched by anyone just because they thought he was cute. I've always found it odd that total strangers walk up to children who don't know them and start touching them. Jimmy would pull away if he didn't want to be touched. He was oblivious to the ribbing some other kids tried to heap on him. For him, they didn't even exist. He knew unconditional love and found nothing wrong with himself.

Even the rough stuff, such as toilet training, was easy with him because I was fascinated by everything he said and did. I wanted to be there for every moment of his life, and I knew that meant forging a life for myself. By the time I was seventeen, I knew I had to reenter the world.

I had never really been very far from home. My parents had a rule: Unless there was a very good reason, a girl didn't go out alone. I was seventeen and had never taken a bus downtown until I got accepted into a pre-nursing program at Maryland General Hospital. It was for girls in high school who were thinking about becoming nurses after they graduated.

I didn't want to be a nurse, but when I was a little girl I had fallen in love with the TV show "Ben Casey." I identified with the smart woman doctor who was married to Dr. Zorba but who I knew secretly loved Ben. Even in the summer, on Monday nights I'd come in early, leaving my cousin and my brother outside. I'd sit through "Stony Burke" just to make sure I didn't miss "Ben Casey." I still thought I wanted to be just like them, and I figured that a nursing degree would allow me to work my way through medical school.

Ethel, who was one of my best friends in high school, found out about the course and we both called for applications. But she lost interest, and I wound up taking the course by myself. This was the first thing I had ever done outside the school system, and I was scared to death, scared that I would find out that the world would reject me. I was a black girl, and I had been told that this would hold me back, that no one would give me a chance, and that I wasn't expected to have ambition.

To my surprise, I was accepted into the pre-nursing program. On the first day of class, I was one of the two blacks among the forty or so other students. The other black girl was also from my high school. In fact, at first it seemed just like high school except that we had to wear uniforms. They issued us these starched white blouses and pink pinafores. That's why we were called "pinkies."

Being a pinkie in training got very interesting after a couple of weeks. We had been sitting around in classrooms learning how to take temperatures and count pulses. We also learned to make beds when they were both empty and full. We learned about urinals and bedpans and giving baths to bedridden patients. Now it was time to practice on real people. They took us into the hospital, assigned us to floors, and gave us real, live patients of our own.

My anxiety level rose to an all-time high. All the girls were nervous about working with real sick people, but I think I was even more nervous because I was black and I was afraid it would become a factor. The nursing instructors had treated me okay, but they were professionals. Maybe the patients wouldn't be so enlightened.

When I heard my first patient's thick Southern drawl, I knew I was a dead woman. He sounded like those sheriffs from down South whom I saw on the news at night using dogs and hoses to break up protest marches. They wanted me to touch this man and make his bed. I was sure he wouldn't let me. The white nurses from the night shift reported that he had been a horribly difficult patient. What was he going to think when he saw me?

Now, while all these thoughts were going through my head, I was the picture of calm. I didn't share my concerns with anyone. I didn't want people to know how really scared I was. I didn't dare tell my parents for fear they would discourage me. As always, even surrounded, I was alone, alone with my thoughts, but I was too much of a fighter not to confront my fear head-on.

I walked into the room and over to his bed. No matter what the outcome, I had to try. I had to see for myself what the world was really like. If it was going to reject me, it would have to do it to my face.

The Southern man's back was toward me as I approached. I reached out and touched his shoulder. "Mr. Johnson, it's time to wake up," I said, trying to keep the trembling out of my voice.

He rolled over, looked up into my face, and said, "Good mornin', darlin'. What can I do for you?"

He turned out to be one of the sweetest old men I've ever met. From then on, I knew I had to test everything I'd ever been told. I finished the course and was one of the four students from the class to be offered a job by the hospital. I worked one day a week, on the weekends, my entire senior year. We made a couple of dollars more than the minimum wage, and I couldn't wait to get my first paycheck. The one thing I wasn't prepared for was income tax. I almost cried when I saw what the government had done to my sixteen-hour check.

Even so, I loved having a marketable skill. I loved the responsibility and the acknowledgment of people whose opinions I respected. Within a few months I had impressed the staff so much that they started giving me the plum assignments, like the intensive care unit and the emergency room. Jimmy would get up with me, see me off to work, and be waiting for me when I came home.

A hospital is a great place to learn about people. Patients come from every segment of society. I took care of both the rich and the poor, the educated and the illiterate, the young and the old. I found out that I could talk to all of them. No one recoiled from my touch, no one disliked me, and no one assumed that I wasn't capable of doing my job. I seemed to be the only one thinking about my race. It was a good thing that I had gotten this preview of life in the real world before graduation. It made the prospect of leaving the safety of public school that much easier. I could actually look forward to moving on.

Graduation from high school was a trip. We wore long white gowns onstage in the school auditorium. I was so convinced that I'd never get married when I bought my white dress that I just knew it was the only time I'd wear one. Seating was determined by class rank, the valedictorian being number one. I was number forty-two out of the five hundred seniors. I had graduated with honors and been accepted at the University of Maryland.

I had applied to only one college. My parents wanted me to go to Morgan State because it was practically right down the street from my high school. I was determined that I was going to go away to college. I told my mother that the university was right downtown even though I knew that it was near Washington, D.C. It was a risk, but one that I thought I had to take.

So here I was, seventeen and a high school graduate. Yet, aside from work, I wasn't allowed to go anywhere. I always had to try to talk my friends into doing things with me to get out of the house. By this time they were all interested in boys, and most of them had boyfriends. I was going to get stuck sitting at home. I knew I needed to find out what else went on outside my house and my little community, and that meant that I had to find a boy to take me.

6

TWO JAMESES

Despite everything that had happened to me, I still expected that one day I'd fall in love even though I had no idea what that was. I watched everyone to see if I could see it. But I don't think that love lived in my neighborhood, or if it did, there was nothing pretty about it. Made me wonder why everyone wanted to fall.

The summer before I went off to college could be called "The Summer of My Two Jameses." My little Jimmy had brought me so far back from the edge of collapse that I was actually giving this dating thing real thought. And the other James, James Benjamin Talley, was just what the doctor ordered for a seventeen-year-old black girl just out of high school who had almost never had a date.

I say "almost" because in a totally uncharacteristic moment of weakness during my last year of high school, I'd agreed to let my father fix me up with a date for the senior dance. He was some guy who worked with my father at the steel mill. I should have known better, but my objective was to go to the dance, not find true love. It's a good thing, too, because the boy turned out to be a complete cretin. I can honestly say that there wasn't one thing I liked about him. He was an ugly, semiliterate hulk totally devoid of charm, grace, or tact. He arrived in his Sunday best, and it didn't do a thing for him. I, on the other hand, looked wonderful in a form-fitting black velvet number, which was my first really sophisticated dress. The cretin's eyes almost popped out when he saw me.

As soon as we got to the dance, I scoped out my friends, planning to ditch the troglodyte, but he had already learned to heel off his lead and wouldn't be shaken. Even after I'd beaten a cold and hasty retreat when he dropped me off at the end of the evening, he called me the next day, asking me what he could do to make me like him. I came right out and told him that it was not in the cards no matter how he acted and slammed down the phone. When my father heard about this, he crowed, "Gee, he must really like you!" To which I replied, "Of course he liked me, so what?" and promptly left the room. I guess that any boy around the house would have been a relief to my parents, but I knew that I could do better than him.

What I didn't know was that I'd find my Prince Charming as close to home as my friend Marlene's kitchen. Marlene was one of my last classmates who didn't have a guy. We became partners on the prowl. On our first outing, we met at her house. I was early, so she was still dressing. I had on my "man-trapping" outfit—we're talking a lime green tennis skirt and a navy blue shell, the colors of the day, and all you could see were legs for days. I forgot all about fashion, though, when I walked into Marlene's kitchen and saw *him*.

James Talley, an engineering major at the University of Delaware and an old friend of Marlene's older brother, was sitting at the table, leaning back on the two rear legs of a kitchen chair, rocking. His skin was almost black, his hair was in an Afro, and he was wearing dark glasses inside the house. I thought he was the coolest male I'd ever seen who wasn't on the tube. Marlene introduced us, I sat down, and James continued to talk to her as if I wasn't there. He seemed so worldly, so confident, so intelligent, so beautiful that I couldn't help lamenting the fact that this was the man of my dreams, the one I was looking for, and he didn't even know that I existed.

When Marlene went upstairs to dress, James's interest in me perked up, but I assumed that he was just being polite. I had never been so nervous. I didn't say much. I wasn't sure my mouth would work, and I could feel myself sweating. I was actually relieved when

Marlene reappeared and it turned out that James wasn't going out with us. I really didn't care about going out anymore because I was sure that no other boy I would meet that night would measure up to James.

You can imagine my surprise when he called a few days later. This time I didn't feel awkward at all. We talked for hours, and at the end of the conversation, he asked me to go bowling with him and a bunch of his friends. I thought this was perfect. I really didn't know what to do with a boy, and since we'd be in a crowd, I figured nothing much could happen. But once we got there, James kept asking me to go to the parking lot. I was so naive that for the life of me I couldn't figure out why.

Once we got to the car, it became clear that he wanted to kiss me. Kissing was a problem I hadn't considered. I needed a boyfriend to get out of the house. I hadn't given much thought to what they'd want from me. I simply wasn't used to being touched like that. I touched Jimmy and I touched my patients at the hospital to take their pulse or give them a bath, but what James was proposing was more intimacy than I could handle. I never even lowered my guard enough to hug someone. That first kiss was a complete fiasco. Later James would describe it as like kissing someone through a screen.

Luckily, at the time James must have thought that I was just an old-fashioned girl or was playing hard to get, because he called the very next day to ask me out again. Before long, to Jimmy's chagrin, James became a permanent fixture on my front porch. Jimmy wasn't used to having to share me with anyone. He didn't like James and refused to speak to him. He often asked my mother to send him away. I thought it was cute that Jimmy was jealous and that he must know that there wasn't a human on earth that I preferred to him.

In time I learned to tolerate James's kisses, then to get used to them, then to really start enjoying them. We became great kissers and used to go at it for hours at a session.

Best of all, we enjoyed each other's company. We were both trying to save money for college, so we couldn't spend a lot on elaborate dates, though James did take me to some of the best restaurants in Baltimore. I once got sick in the middle of a great Crab Imperial because I was wearing too much perfume. Remember, this dating stuff was all new to me.

Most of the time, though, we just took a bus downtown and roamed the city, visiting historical sites and museums and sitting in the lobbies of expensive hotels fantasizing about what it might be like to be staying there. I felt incredibly fortunate that I could feel this way after what had happened with my father, and I knew it was because of who James was as a person. He was everything that I had first thought and more. He was also sensitive and considerate. Not a brute or an animal as I'd been led to expect. Then, after James and I had been dating for about a month, Marlene announced that since she'd sort of been responsible for getting us together, it was her duty to tell me that James had a girlfriend at college.

Oh, so it was only going to be a summer romance. That was okay; after all, my objectives had been met. I was really only looking for a summer escort anyway. In the fall we were going to go our separate ways. I was grateful to Marlene for being a good friend. She was surprised at how well I took it. She thought I'd throw a fit and make a scene. No, I said, we'll go on just as we have until the summer's over and that will be it. I was used to people coming and going, and I liked knowing something that James didn't know I knew. I felt that it gave me the upper hand. I thought I had everything under control and that nothing could shake me. I was on top of the world; I had everything I wanted.

Then, just a month before I was to begin my new life, the rug was ripped from under my feet. My mother met me at the door one day when I came home from work and announced: "Jimmy's going to be adopted."

"No, no, no. You can't let them do it. You've got to adopt him for me. Please." My brain was on fire. What was she talking about? Jimmy belonged to me. How could someone just come in and take him away? I immediately thought that I was being punished for leaving him to spend time with James. If I'd been here, it wouldn't have happened. That stupid boy meant nothing to me.

Jimmy was my life. How was I supposed to live without him? Didn't anyone understand?

While I'd been off working hard to get my life back together, the social services agency had put Jimmy on a local TV show that offered kids for adoption—an early version of QVC. Need a kid? How about this model right here? We honor all major credit cards. Jimmy was gorgeous as well as brilliant, so of course he was "sold." I hadn't even known they'd put him on television. When I found out about the adoption, it was already too late.

I considered running away with him, but quickly wrote that off as a really bad idea. A year or two before, I'd begged my parents to adopt him, but they had refused. Now, seeing my horror at the thought of losing him, they honestly tried to make it happen, but the agency was set on placing him with a family outside the social services system. There was nothing to be done. I was devastated.

Jimmy was three and a half by now and had lived with us for so long that the agency decided that the move had to be made gradually. I didn't want to know much about the process. I simply assumed that they were taking him to meet with his new family. Every day the social worker would pick him up and take him on an outing for a few hours. When he'd return, he'd run to the basement to find me and tell me all about the fun time he'd had. I didn't want to hear it. One day I just plain lost it, saying, "One day Mrs. Fine is going to take you away and never bring you back!" The next time he returned from one of these trips, he ran to find me and proudly told me, "See, Robin, I came back!" I fought the tears welling up in my eyes and gave him a big hug.

My job was to be strong for him and to help him get through this move. He never again saw me cry. I knew at the time that letting him go would be the hardest thing I'd ever do, but I also knew it was for the best. After all, I was just a kid myself. I was going to college in a few weeks, and he'd be left in the care of my crazy parents. At this point, my father was a full-fledged alcoholic, and he and my mother still fought like animals. Maybe Jimmy had a chance of finding a couple of parents who could provide him with some normalcy, stability, and support. The day he left was just like any other day. He thought it was just another day trip. His clothes were taken from the house later. So there was no tearful farewell. I said good-bye that day just as if he'd be back in a few hours.

The worst thing for me was realizing that I would no longer be a part of his life. I wouldn't get to see him start school. I'd never get to help him with homework, never check a report card or attend a

PTA meeting. There would be no graduations, no first love, no first broken heart to help him through. I'd never get to tuck him in bed again, and I'd never know what kind of man he'd turn out to be. I retired to the basement after he left for the last time and stayed down there, crying, for days. Every time my parents passed me on the way to the laundry room, I was huddled in the same spot, weeping my heart out.

I'd never fallen apart like this, so I guess I kind of scared my mother. She'd been trying to bring me to this state for years and now, when she saw me this way, she didn't know what to do. She eventually resorted to her usual tactics and yelled at me, "Why don't you get up and do something!"

"Like what?" I asked.

"Go upstairs and sort the laundry and put in a load of clothes."

I didn't even bother to argue. I brought the laundry downstairs and turned on the machine. I was just standing there watching the water fill the tub. I'd never noticed how pretty it looked as it swirled around the agitator. I could feel the warm mist from it on my face. It was as if a trillion tiny beads of moisture were hitting my face at once and then exploding. It felt good. It felt so peaceful that I was startled when I hear my mother scream, "What are you doing?"

That's when I realized that my head was all the way in the machine. That's why I could feel the mist on my face. When I told her that I didn't know what I was doing, I meant it. I wonder to this day what might have happened if she hadn't walked in when she did. I was in terrible shape. All the progress I had made while Jimmy was with me had been erased when he left.

Marlene called while I was in the midst of my grief. My mother handed me the phone, but I couldn't speak. She thought that James was the cause of this malaise and she called him to berate him for hurting me. He immediately phoned to see what he'd unknowingly done, but I couldn't talk to him either. I had never told anyone what Jimmy meant to me, and I certainly couldn't explain it now. I was utterly miserable.

I honestly can't remember how I snapped out of it. Maybe I just managed to repress my grief the way I repressed all of my other feelings and once again donned the mask, the mask that I wore for my family, the mask that I wore for friends, and the mask that I wore for the world. The mask that said, "I'm just fine."

I picked up my life just where it left off. James and I continued dating, and we never spoke about that night on the phone. As summer came to a close, he asked me what I wanted to do about our relationship. I told him that since we were both going to different places, it was probably best that we stop seeing each other when school started. He agreed, and I thought that that was the end of that. But after James got home that night, he called and told me to sit down, that he had something to say that would be difficult for me to hear. Choking back tears, he told me about the girl he had left behind. He had dated her all year, and they had agreed to be true to each other over the summer, but he said that he hadn't expected that he would fall in love with me. I let him stammer out this whole story, and then I said, "I know."

He was furious that I had allowed him to go through such torture when I already knew. But I figured he deserved it for not telling me right away. After that, he said that he didn't want to break up. He didn't like the idea of my going off to college and dating someone else. So another chapter of my life was about to start. I was going to college, but it wasn't exactly the way I had planned it. I no longer had Jimmy to anchor me, but I did still have James and that would make going off to these strange new surroundings a little bit easier.

7

B.S.

I attended a number of lectures sponsored by the Black Student Union while I was at the University of Maryland. Most were the usual brand of revolutionaries screaming about the system. But one very unpopular speaker actually had the nerve to encourage us, while we were there, to dedicate ourselves to our studies and to make the most of our educations as a service to our community. He was never asked back, and I never got his name, but I thought what he said made sense.

I began college in the fall of 1970, the same time that Muhammad Ali returned to boxing. He climbed into the ring with Jerry Quarry, a white man, on October 26 in what everyone called the "Battle of the Draft Dodger versus the Great White Hope."

It had been three and a half years since Ali had last been allowed to ply his trade, and it showed. In the old days, I used to be afraid for his opponents. Now I was afraid for him. No one had ever come back from such a long layoff. No one knew what effect those three and a half years would have on the champ until they saw him, flat-footed, standing in the center of the ring being hit by another fighter for the first time in his career.

Muhammad showed great courage. No longer capable of dancing away from every blow, he took them. Then, out of nowhere, Ali delivered a shot that opened a wide gash above Quarry's eye. The fight was stopped and he was declared the winner. Ali had returned. Ali had once again done the impossible.

With each successive bout, Ali would have to confront three opponents—the ghost of the fighter he had been before his forced retirement, the other guy in the ring, and the multitude who wanted him to fail. But he kept on fighting because he had a goal. He wanted to be the only man in history to regain the heavyweight title.

I was so into Ali's comeback that I began collecting pictures from every bout. Eventually, I created an Ali collage on my dorm-room wall. The first picture to go up was the *Time* magazine cover with Ali's face bathed in sweat, staring straight into the camera. His eyes followed you around the room. When my white roommate, Jeanne, discovered what I was up to, she protested, "I'm not living in any room with that guy!"

"Well, then when are you moving?" I asked, continuing to hang the photographs.

Once she realized that there was no room for negotiation, she learned to live with this black man watching her study, sleep, and undress. I think that she eventually came to like him. In any case, the collection grew with every fight. It became quite the conversation piece.

I identified with Ali in a lot of ways. Here was a black man who tested the boundaries of convention and was willing to put his life on the line. But in one crucial way, we were polar opposites. Ali had a dream. I, on the other hand, felt as if I was afloat, with no real goals that first year of college. I had been waiting to be free for as long as I could remember, and now that I was, I didn't know what to do. There was no one to yell at me, no one to say no to me, and no one to avoid. I suddenly realized that everything I had ever done was in defiance of my family or my background. There was a certain security in having them to fight. With them to measure myself against, I knew who I was. Without them, I was no longer sure.

And I had been alone too long. Now I compensated by throwing myself into the social whirl with a vengeance. I usually made it to my first class of the day, but I'd invariably wind up spending the rest of the day talking and playing cards in the Student Union. Instead of studying at night, I socialized with my dorm friends. I learned to smoke, drink, and stay out late, things I had never done at home.

James and I kept in touch by phone and by mail and we saw each other whenever we could. My Christmas present from him that year came in a small black velvet box. I opened it and found myself staring at a ring with a six-prong setting around some sort of stone. In the dim lights of the Christmas tree I couldn't tell whether or not it was a diamond. I stared at it silently for a long time before James announced that it was my birthstone, a pale green peridot, and that it was meant to be a pre-engagement ring.

I heaved a huge sigh of relief at the "pre" part as he slipped the ring on my finger, because getting married wasn't at the top of my agenda. Still, I spent the rest of the school year explaining that I wasn't engaged. As long as the wedding was a long way off, though, I felt comfortable with the situation. To me, it was like being on lay-away. I was still a virgin, and James wanted me to stay that way until we were married. So I partied on and ended up out of the honors program with a dismal first-semester grade average of .09. Somehow, I miraculously managed to convince my mother that academic probation was a good thing. Don't ask how!

So, by my standards, I was being absolutely wild, but my friends saw me as a prude and a perfectionist. You can imagine, then, how out of control they must have been. They took great delight in flaunting their sexual exploits in great detail in front of me. They couldn't believe that James and I hadn't done it. Little did they know how hard I had been trying to get James to relieve me of this burden of virginity—to no avail.

The summer after my freshman year of college proved to be my last with James. I grew up a lot in that one year, and yet when we got back together that summer, James seemed not to have grown at all. What I had once taken to be worldly sophistication on his part now seemed square and immature. I was tired of make-out sessions that ended only in frustration. I had no desire any longer to observe some old convention that said "good girls" are virgins when they marry. I wanted to do what I felt like doing, and his constant denials were only proof of his desire to control—not respect—me.

The relationship just didn't feel good to me anymore, but I kept fantasizing with him about the M word—the life he wanted us to have together, how many children, what their names would be, what kind of house we'd live in.

Still, I didn't realize how seriously James took all of this until the day we wound up at a jewelry store looking at diamond rings. The night after the ring shopping, I actually woke up in a cold sweat, realizing that I didn't want to get married! Just the thought of it made me feel that walls were closing in on me. It was then that I knew beyond a doubt that we had come to the end of the fairy tale.

What began so beautifully ended badly. When I told James it was over, he just didn't get it. He sobbed. He begged. It was terribly sad because I still liked him, deeply appreciated the tenderness he had shown me at a time when I really needed it, and genuinely wanted to be his friend. But I couldn't spend the rest of my life with him just because he'd been a nice guy. I didn't really want the kind of life that he had been offering.

James thought I wasn't hurting, but I was. Like my uncle Leroy, he'd offered me proof that sex didn't turn men into gross animals, and I valued him in my life. But he was beginning to make me think that love was even more intimidating than sex, because in its name, he was trying to make me into something I wasn't.

The breakup was incredibly painful, and the worst of it was that it took months to play itself out. I felt like I was being stalked. He would show up at the hospital when I arrived at work. He was at the door, waiting, when I left. As soon as I entered the house, the phone would ring. It would always be him, tearfully imploring me to take him back. He acted as if losing me was killing him. Finally, I had to tell James that I would no longer take his calls, answer his letters, or see him again. But to this day, I'm grateful that he was my first love, and I'm sorry that he wasn't my first lover.

I was aware of the fact that people were curious about my sexuality, and now that I had discarded a perfectly acceptable boyfriend they were mystified and started wondering if I was gay. That lesbian question has dogged me ever since. Granted, I've never been like other girls. I'm not afraid to compete with men, and I have never been given any good reason to defer to them just by virtue of their gender. I'm definitely not the cheerleader type. Quite frankly, my attitude was that if a man could do something better than I could, he'd have to prove it. I wasn't in awe; I had no respect for them, and I couldn't be talked into anything.

Still, for all that, the guys liked me. My girlfriends couldn't understand it. They did everything they could to please these guys, but I was the one men came to visit. None of them ever got any sexual favors from me, but they came back again and again. I guess I represented quite a challenge. I never paid much attention to all this scrutiny until Morris, one of the cutest black guys on campus, called me a dyke to my face.

I had just walked into a conference room in the boys' dorm only to find one particularly wacky classmate dancing drunkenly on a table to chants of "Take it off." Just as she started to pull her dress above her waist, I grabbed her arm and pulled her down. A struggle ensued between Morris and me, with my friend in the middle, being jerked back and forth like a rag doll.

"She's coming with me," I yelled at him.

"No, leave her here, she's having fun," he yelled back.

We continued to struggle as our shouts of "She's staying" and "We're going" continued to overlap.

Suddenly Morris dropped her arm and announced, "Okay, then, you take her, you dyke. You want her more than I do."

It was probably that kind of peer pressure that convinced me that now was the time to shed my virginity. It had never occurred to me that I could be a lesbian, and I figured that if I wasn't a virgin anymore, it would end the speculation of others. With James out of the picture, I was free to find out. The lucky man turned out to be a friend of a roommate's ex-con boyfriend. His name was Billy. He was like all the boys back in my old neighborhood, a decent sort but not much ambition. He'd finished high school and had gotten himself a job. The next thing on the agenda was to find himself a woman. He flipped for me the night we met, so I thought, Why not?

I don't think either of us knew what we were doing. For all I know, Billy might have been a virgin too. The big event took place in his mother's converted basement, which served as his Washington, D.C., bachelor pad. I had no idea what I was in for.

The pain was excruciating; I would have preferred to have been stabbed repeatedly, but here I was instead with my head repeatedly banging into the headboard of his bed. But I was determined to rid myself of this dreaded virginity, so I gritted my teeth and stuck it out. Just as the pain was beginning to subside, he stopped thrusting, shuddered, and collapsed on me like a dead man. My first thought was, Was that what all the fuss was about? But my second was that I was now a proud member in good standing of the sisterhood of the sexually active.

I awoke that spring morning with a new sense of confidence. I would return to school with my own story to tell. I must admit that when I recounted the story to my girlfriends, I did gild the lily just a bit. I admitted that there was a bit of discomfort at first but insisted that the pain soon gave way to a kind of intense pleasure that I couldn't wait to experience again. Unfortunately, when poor Billy discovered that I'd been a virgin, he thought it put our relationship on a whole new level. He thought I was in love with him. We continued our affair, and soon the whole school seemed to know about it.

Some of the same guys who had been trying to sleep with me for over a year were shocked when they found out that I was fooling around with a guy who didn't go to the school. "Why not me, Robin?" they all asked. They were even more shocked when they discovered that the door was still closed to them even after I had crossed over the sexual threshold. The campus grapevine started to sizzle with my name. My reputation went from virginal to sexually active to kinky. No one quite knew what to make of me, but at least they weren't calling me a dyke. This was when I first became Robin Quivers, mystery woman. I still didn't fall neatly into any conventional category.

Muhammad Ali's life and mine were still weirdly paralleling. The winter of 1971 was giving way to the spring. I had just lost my virginity, and Muhammad was also experiencing a loss, his first inside a boxing ring. I hated Joe Frazier even before he fought Ali. After all, he held Muhammad's title. He didn't deserve it. No one had beaten Ali in the ring. Frazier had just been in the right place at the right time. Ali had to fight several opponents before he could even get a shot at reclaiming what was rightfully his.

I think I hated Joe Frazier most because he was a good fighter, much better than the other guys who had plundered the spoils after Muhammad's belts were stripped from him. I had seen a lot of Joe's fights. Joe was scary. Joe had never seen a punch he couldn't take. He'd just stand there and let you punch him until you got tired, and then he'd knock you out. I didn't want Muhammad to fight Joe Frazier. Wasn't it enough that he had been able to fight again? Wasn't it enough that he'd managed to just come back after a three-and-a-half-year layoff? Couldn't he just concede that he wasn't the fighter he'd been before all that happened and just go home and be safe?

I knew the outcome of the fight before I saw the pictures. It had been a terrible bout. Terrible in its ferocity. Ali had been soundly beaten, but he wouldn't give up. It went the whole fifteen terrible rounds. From the photographs, you couldn't pick the winner. They were both beaten up. Ali was always slightly banged up after his fights now, but he had never looked like this and neither had Joe. At least Joe Frazier hadn't won easily. At least he knew he had been in a fight. Those were the arguments I'd use when my father came in to look at my wall and guffaw, "Where are those pictures of your man on his ass?" He hated it that I loved Muhammad so much. Even this defeat didn't stop Ali. He would fight again in July.

And I continued my relationship with Billy through the summer and into the fall. I was a junior now, and I'd had to declare a major. Since I had no idea what I wanted to do, I decided that at least as a nurse, I knew I could get a job. Nursing school meant moving back to Baltimore. I still intended to live on campus, but my mother offered me an enticement to move back home—a little mustard-colored Ford Maverick.

I had just two years left to get a degree, but because of that wasted first semester I needed to make up some credits so that I could graduate on time. I was carrying a full class load and also working three to four days a week at University Hospital. Except for the five-hundred-dollar honors scholarship and a small loan my second semester, I worked to pay for my education. I was getting tired. I knew I had to do this in four years. I couldn't keep up this pace forever.

Being at home again also reminded me of what I was trying to escape. My father was having blackouts and disappearing for days at a time. He'd gotten really sloppy about his extramarital affairs, so that everyone now knew about his young women. Billy became jealous of all the time I spent on my schoolwork and forced me to make a choice between him and my future. It wasn't even a contest—Billy went.

My mother was quite shocked at how easy it was for me to get rid of him. She thought I really cared about him and she couldn't understand how I could discard him with so little emotion, really without a backward glance, but she didn't dare question me. Two years away from her had only made me more of a tyrant upon my return. She now believed that I was everything I said I was. I was scary. Nothing stopped me. What I said I'd do, I did. What I said I wanted, I got. The rules that seemed to apply to everyone else didn't seem to apply to me. The whole family tiptoed around me. Even my father wasn't allowed to speak to me when he was drunk. He'd discover that I was in the house and retire to his room to sleep it off. Sometimes I thought that I might be even worse than my mother had ever been, but I didn't have time to change. Outside the house I managed to appear as a sweet, jovial, and reasonable person.

My tenacity paid off. Nursing school was going quite well. I had a couple of brushes with authority figures, which I then took to be racial but now feel were more about my rigidity, perfectionism, and defiance. I also made some significant friendships in nursing; the one with Kathi Stout continues to this day. Kathi and her family lived on that other side of the city where blacks were personae non grata, but her parents never seemed concerned about my race and I loved being in their home. Kathi's mother seemed like Betty Crocker to me and her father seemed like John Wayne. They had a cute relationship. I'd go to Kathi's house just to watch her parents.

Ali hadn't given up his goal of regaining the title either. He had four to five fights a year. There were ten more after the loss to Frazier before he lost again to Ken Norton in 1973. I was working part-time as a student nurse in the Shock Trauma Unit that night. As we ran back and forth taking care of patients, one of the technicians sat by a radio calling out the score at the end of each round. They said Ali's jaw was swelling and was probably broken. Norton kept aiming for it. The fight went the distance, and the judges awarded it to Norton. Tears filled my eyes as again I thought it was time for Ali to quit. I don't know about him, but for me each fight was hell.

Six months later, Muhammad was back in the ring with Ken Norton. This time he won. That meant another fight and another fight. He was determined to fight his way back into the ring with Joe Frazier and another crack at the title. And then something terrible happened. Frazier fought a young guy named George Foreman who had turned pro after the 1972 Olympics. The way I saw it, George Foreman had one punch, but he was as strong as an ox, and that one punch was a knockout. It was all he needed. Joe Frazier walked into that punch and his lights went out. He lost the heavyweight crown. I felt worse for Muhammad than for Joe. It would have been tough enough to take the belt from Frazier, but how was he going to get it from Foreman, who looked like a big tree?

The rematch with Frazier was scheduled for January of my senior year. I was just praying that Muhammad didn't get killed this time. He had wound up in the hospital after their last fight, and since then Ken Norton had broken his jaw. It was stupid to go through all this, Frazier didn't even own the title anymore, but being a man, Ali had a score to settle. This time Ali controlled the fight. Frazier wasn't even able to do that much damage. It went twelve, but Ali won.

That summer, after a lot of hard work and very little play, I earned my Bachelor of Science degree in nursing. We actually wore mortarboards for this one. My mother said that my father cried when my name was called. I was the first person in my family to graduate from college. Even I had to admit that I'd done the impossible. I'd overcome plenty of obstacles, but had made major sacrifices to do it. No boyfriends, few parties, lots of work, and no distractions to speak of. Still, it was all worthwhile. I took a job as a nurse in the same Trauma Unit I had worked in my senior year, and within a month I was living in my own apartment.

The place was only fifteen minutes from my parents' house, but I was the only one with keys to the locks on the door. Never again would anybody barge into my space uninvited. I could choose who I spent my time with. The whole apartment was mine. Of course, it was practically empty except for the bedroom furniture my parents let me take. I vividly remember sitting on the floor, soaking in the quiet, the peace, the tranquillity, and basking in the fact that I'd done it. I had realized my lifelong dream—escape. I never experienced a second of loneliness or any fear of being alone. After putting down the first month's rent and the security deposit, I was almost literally penniless, but I vowed to make do. The peace and quiet were priceless.

My mother must have really missed me, and within a week of moving out, I got a phone call from her. She was in rare form, screaming away about what an awful daughter I was. "Mom," I told her calmly, "I moved away from home because I didn't want to do this anymore."

When she continued shrieking, I replied, "Scream all you want, but I don't have to listen."

"What are you going to do, hang up on me?" she demanded.

"No," I countered, "but I'm going to put the phone down. Talk as long as you want."

I placed the receiver on the nightstand, walked out of the bedroom, and closed the door. When I returned, the phone was making that noise which indicates that it's been left off the hook. As soon as I replaced it on the cradle, it rang again. I picked it up only to hear my mother screaming. "Mom," I announced, "I'm putting the phone down again." This time I left it off the hook for a full eight hours. When I eventually hung it up, my mother didn't call back. And she never tried to berate me over the phone ever again.

I passed my boards the first time out and was declared a full-fledged registered nurse. I had my own place, my own profession, and it was now time to start living again. The year my dream came true was the same year that Muhammad Ali would achieve the goal he had set for himself several years and too many fights before. He met George Foreman, a man just in his twenties who'd gone into boxing to be like Ali, in an African country called Zaire. It was a tough night for me. I knew Foreman wasn't a great boxer, but he was a dangerous puncher. If he hit Muhammad, I thought it would be all over. It was hard to listen to commentators keep saying, "Ali's against the ropes, he's just staying there, his corner is urging him to fight his way out of it, but he's doing nothing," round after round. Finally, in the sixth, some good news—the man on the radio said Foreman looked tired. In the eighth round, Ali knocked him out and regained the heavyweight crown. Seven long years after he'd been stripped of the title, he had it back. He never gave up.

I was ecstatic, jumping up and down, beside myself. I had never really believed that he could do it. Yet even as it got tougher and it looked as though his goal was slipping away, he simply fought harder, never lowering his sights. How did he know all the things that he knew? How did he know how to do it, and where did he get the courage? I couldn't imagine. I've never been so happy about something that wasn't even happening to me. God bless you, Muhammad, I thought.

Maybe some people are just born with a special task they and they alone can achieve. I certainly didn't think I was going to do anything to shake the world. With no more challenges on my horizon, I thought I might as well have some fun. It was time to reenter the dating game. I found my next conquest right in the radio room of Shock Trauma. We used radio communication to track incoming patients, and the two guys who manned the room were old elementary school chums of mine. One, Gary, had been a major crush of mine in fifth grade, but the other, the head guy, whose name was Dwayne, I had loved from afar since the age of seven. The first time I saw him, I thought he was the most perfect-looking boy I'd ever seen. The trouble was, Dwayne hadn't grown much since then. He was now a perfect-looking little man. I dwarfed him in every way but one, as I would soon discover.

We struck up a casual friendship at work, and pretty soon he was confiding in me that he had a huge decision to make. His longtime girlfriend wanted to get married, and he wasn't sure if he was ready or if she was the one. My advice was to date a little before deciding and I proposed myself as the candidate. Dwayne quickly overcame his shock at my boldness and asked me out. The good-night kiss he gave me at the door after our first date was perfect. It was inevitable that we would wind up together in my narrow little twin bed.

I loved the way Dwayne kissed, but problems arose when we started making love. For one thing, Dwayne was hung like a mule. I used to joke that God used so much of him to make his dick, there wasn't much left for the rest of him. I was a novice, and he was simply too much for me to handle. He obviously wasn't too much for his girlfriend, though. One night when we were caressing each other, I noticed scratches all over his back. Clearly, I was no match for her in the passion department. I knew that Dwayne and I weren't going to last very long, but when he told me it was over, I went ballistic.

The breakup was both ugly and revealing to me. I, who was always rejecting, felt rejected. If he'd only waited a short while, I would have left him, but he had decided to take away all the things I liked about him before I was ready to give them up. I missed the attention, the time we spent together, the endless phone calls. I wanted to make his life hell for taking all that from me. Work became a battleground because we still had to deal with each other there in a professional capacity. The tension was unbearable.

I began at last to feel like all the other women I knew, since I could now share my heartache about a brute who had used me and discarded me. The upside of this terrible period was that I proved myself to be not only human, but also one of the girls. Sharing the story with my friend Marlene was a definite eye-opener. I was sputtering, weeping, actually wailing in pain when she told me, "I know how you feel, Robin. I've had my heart broken too. The sad part is that it takes years to get over something like this."

I stopped crying and stared at her, incredulous. "Feel this bad for years?" I repeated. "Are you crazy? If it lasts six months I'd be surprised," and that was the end of that.

It's hard for me to judge from this vantage point exactly what the condition of my heart was then, but at the time all I thought I felt was a thirst for revenge—a burning desire to beat the piss out of Dwayne for subjecting me to such public humiliation. I actually convinced him that I would do it, too. When he ran into my brother, Junior, at an Orioles game, he begged him to get me off his case. After Junior dutifully reported this to me, he sighed into the phone and told me, "Robin, I don't know what you do to people, but you scare them." I wonder if I still do.

In that simple phrase, my brother had become the only person ever to try to give me some insight into how the world perceived me, but it didn't matter to me then. I was thrilled that I'd gotten to Dwayne. I found it a real hoot that he was afraid I was plotting against him when it was really all talk.

Shortly after the Dwayne fiasco, I found myself dissatisfied with everything. I was beginning to think that maybe I'd be happier somewhere else. I left Shock Trauma for the Intensive Care Unit at Maryland General, where I'd spent all those years as a pinkie, and I moved to an apartment all the way out in Owings Mills. I was searching for something, but I didn't know what. That's when I noticed those prepaid postcards for the army, the navy, and the air force in one of my nursing magazines. On a whim, I filled them out and dropped them in the mail.

The next thing I knew, I was being plied with information and repeated calls from recruiters. After awhile, I began to pay attention. Even the changes I'd made hadn't taken care of the restlessness I was feeling. I wasn't happy, although I couldn't quite pinpoint the cause—Baltimore, the job, or Dwayne. One thing was for sure, though. I was ripe pickings for a fast talker with a good story.

PART TWO
BREAKDOWN

8

CLIPPED WINGS

One night when I was walking from the garage to the hospital, I remember looking up at the window of one of the rooms. The light was on, and I could see a nurse of about forty handing a bedpan to a male patient. The very sight caused a spontaneous prayer to spring to my lips: "Lord, please don't let that be me."

—*1975*

It's funny how you often can't remember the names of the people who've had the biggest impact on your life. But, believe me, I'll never forget the face of the enlisted woman who sold me that bill of goods on the air force. The military was her career, and recruiting was just a way to put another stripe on her sleeve. She had a monthly quota to fill. When we met for lunch, I had no idea how crucial I was to her moving up in the ranks.

I should have noticed good old Sergeant-what's-her-name's air of desperation, but I didn't. Maybe I wanted to believe that there was such a place, a place where neither gender nor race mattered. She raved about the fact that advancement was based on performance and that authority was based on rank. Bars and stripes meant the same thing whether worn by a man or a woman.

She hit all the right chords. We were both single women on our own. Who knew if Mr. Right would ever come along? And even if he did, shouldn't we be having fun and fulfilling some of our own dreams while we were waiting? If traveling was my thing, I could see the world and still be building seniority and have job security in the air force. The only thing women couldn't do was fight on the front lines. Even so, all the advantages offered to fighting soldiers would be open to me. I could go back to school with the air force footing the bill, hop on military planes to practically anywhere in the world for free, even ask to be stationed in exotic locales. If I decided to do just one tour of duty, I'd have great experience—military service looks good on a résumé—and I'd have all the benefits of the GI Bill.

But who would want to leave? The air force was full of great people. Since there was no longer a draft, the military had added incentives to attract a better brand of recruit. People like me who were looking for more than average lives. And to cater to our needs, the bases offered gyms, tennis courts, riding stables, and golf courses. On-base housing was luxurious, but it wasn't mandatory. I could get a housing allowance if I wanted to tough it out in the real world.

I was aching to get out of Baltimore, and here was this woman promising me that I'd have friends waiting for me wherever I wanted to go. I could choose to live in any state in the country where there was an air force base with a medical facility. If I wanted to stick to my expertise, which was Intensive Care, I'd have to stick to the bases with the larger full-service institutions instead of the ones with the small infirmaries. But I was assured that both assignments came with advantages and that I could try either. The air force would do everything in its power to give me my first choice.

I was woozy after that first lunch, but the afterglow soon faded. I would probably have forgotten all about it if the good sergeant hadn't continued to call, even setting up another lunch with a genuine air force nurse. She too was career military and had even more glowing things to say about life as an officer. She'd been stationed all over the world and wouldn't trade her military experience for anything. She was just six years shy of completing twenty years of service. She was going to retire at a very young age with a full military pension and veterans' benefits to see her well into old age. This was not to be taken lightly by a woman alone.

As it turns out, there's a limit to how much time a recruiter can spend wooing a prospect, and they were running out of time with me. The phone calls were coming more frequently, and I was told that I had to make up my mind within forty-eight hours. The night before that final call, I'd gotten together with some of my old friends from Shock Trauma. I was whining about life at Maryland General. It had turned out that the grass wasn't greener on the other side. I found the job less challenging and less rewarding. I missed the kind of camaraderie and excitement I had found behind the metal doors of my old stomping ground. And I had trouble kowtowing to the black head nurse on my shift, who treated her fellow nurses as her courtiers.

You might say that I was crying in my beer because I had quite a bit to drink that night and got in late. The phone woke me at eight in the morning.

"Hi, Robin." It was the recruiter, sounding irritatingly cheerful. "Today's the day!"

"The day for what?" I mumbled groggily, putting a hand to my pounding head and realizing that I had a wicked hangover.

"Today's the day you have to make your decision," she chirped on. "Is it yes or is it no?"

When I asked if I could get back to her, she insisted that she had to know right then. When I pleaded for a couple of hours more, she launched into another sales pitch. I just wanted her off the phone so that I could go back to sleep. The more I tried to say no, the more she talked. The only way to get her off the phone was to say yes. So that's how I wound up becoming a second lieutenant in the United States Air Force. The one concession I managed to win was a delayed entry of January 1976. I didn't have to report for six months, and I vowed to make them as pleasant as possible.

The tension between me and the "diva," who was my head nurse at Maryland General, was intensifying to the point where it threatened my ability to give safe and effective patient care. When I complained to my old nursing buddies from Trauma, they surprised me by asking me to come back, and I leaped at the chance. Those last months in Shock Trauma were the happiest I ever spent as a nurse. I loved my job and didn't even mind having to deal with Dwayne. By the time December rolled around, I didn't want to go anywhere, but I had signed an official piece of paper. Like it or not, I was air force bound.

As the days passed, I became more and more convinced that I was making a big mistake. I was scared, although I would never have admitted it. Having selected California, Hawaii, and Las Vegas as my assignment choices, I was regretfully informed by the air force that there were no openings at those bases. Of course there weren't. They were the ones everybody selected. Notification came that I would be relocating to Ohio. Yes, Ohio! In its infinite wisdom, the air force had decided that since my first choices were unavailable, I'd be happiest at Wright Paterson. That's what I always say—if you want to see the world, see Ohio.

The notion that I was really leaving Baltimore made me kind of sentimental, and I asked my mother if she thought it was a good idea for me to spend my last month of freedom under her roof. She seemed thrilled by the idea, so I quit work, terminated the lease on my apartment, and shipped my furniture to Ohio. Maybe it was just my proximity, or the fear of losing me, but I wasn't at home an hour before my mother launched into one of her rants about what a horrible person I was. Graphically reminded of why I'd escaped in the first place, I picked up my keys, jumped in my car, and drove back to my empty apartment. I spent the night sleeping in my clothes on the bare floor. Anything was better than dealing with my crazy mother.

The next day, after I'd arranged to stay with friends, I went home to pick up my things. I refused to even look at my mother, so while I packed she pleaded with my back not to leave, promising never to behave that way again. And she didn't. There were no fights and no arguments for the rest of the month. When it was time for me to leave, the whole family caravaned with me to Fairborn, Ohio, just to make sure I got there okay.

My friends and acquaintances were five hundred miles away. The Quivers family soon would be. Now I was completely on my own. But I put on a brave face and told myself that I'd be fine. Oh, if I'd only known.

*   *   *

Just before I left Shock Trauma in Baltimore, a former navy nurse joined the staff. When I asked her what basic training had been like, she told me about the time she'd been made to scrub the steps in front of her quarters with a toothbrush because she hadn't folded the clothes in her drawer properly. I couldn't believe she'd tolerated such treatment for six years and told myself that things must have changed. Surely that wasn't the same armed forces I'd be joining.

By the time I headed off to the air force, Muhammad Ali had already spent more than a year as the world heavyweight champ. He remained an incredibly active one, fighting three or four times a year. His fights were longer now and lent themselves to debate. Even though it often seemed that younger opponents deserved more points at the end of the fight, announcers got used to saying that you have to take the title from the champ. No one was ever just going to give away Ali's title again. The "Thriller in Manila" took place in September 1975. It was the third time Muhammad would meet Joe Frazier in the ring. Both men rose to the occasion, probably fighting better than either of them had a right to expect at this point in their careers, making it another memorable contest. Ali won again, retaining his crown. And although I didn't know it, I was headed for some heavyweight confrontations of my own.

In January 1976, I reported as ordered to Shepherd Air Force Base in Wichita Falls, Texas, where all medical corps inductees were assigned for two weeks of basic training. Our quarters were small flats complete with maid service. We didn't even have to make our own beds, much less stand by while someone pawed through our drawers.

Nurses, doctors, dentists, and pharmacists all sat in the same auditorium learning what it meant to be an officer. About the most difficult thing we did was get sized for uniforms. They had long ago eliminated the bivouac, an overnight camping trip complete with C rations, from the medical corps basic training curriculum. We were taught to salute and were supposed to learn to march, but it was always too windy. We wound up spending all of our time chasing our caps. So they simply settled for a dress inspection with us standing at attention. The rest of the time they plied us with booze and food at nightly banquets.

At one of our more serious orientation lectures, the speaker had informed us that the only facility competing with the hospital for hours open on any military base was the liquor store. Booze was a big problem, yet the air force was offering us alcohol everywhere we turned. As the days trickled by, I watched each morning as more and more new officers looked like victims of the night before.

The good news was that the military seemed a lot less draconian than I'd feared. The bad news was that I quickly got a glimpse of what would become a source of unimaginable hell for me.

One lunchtime I was at the condiment bar of a crowded fast food joint on base when a guy diving for catsup almost tipped my tray. I yelled at him to watch it, and he started to reply in kind until the sun bouncing off my bright gold bars caught his eye. "Oh, I'm sorry, Lieutenant," he said, instantly changing his tune. "I'm really sorry. You want some catsup? Can I carry your tray?" I knew right away that he was an enlisted man, a grunt who had been convinced that his very life depended on not pissing me off. He acted like a battered puppy afraid of getting whacked across the nose one more time.

I was experiencing for the first time the almighty power of rank, and it made me incredibly uncomfortable. Having been born black in the South, I had no desire to see another person grovel and consoled myself with the thought that once I got to my duty station, things would be more normal.

People did act more like people at Wright Paterson, but bars were still a lot better than stripes. They had simply tried to replace the race thing with a rank thing, and the results were still the same—demeaning and belittling, and awarding to people with little minds the right to control others. Commissioned officers weren't even supposed to socialize with noncommissioned officers. To marry a noncom could disastrously affect your career. I watched officers flaunt and abuse their power, and I saw higher-ranking enlisted men do the same to their underlings. It was clear that I was going to have a problem. I couldn't tolerate the injustice, and there was no way I was going to enforce it.

On the positive side, I found a homey little town house with a full-sized washer and dryer about twenty minutes from base, but it turned out that my apartment was about the only thing I'd enjoy about the whole air force situation. Within six months, I realized why I'd been so restless. It wasn't where I was, it was what I was doing. I didn't want to nurse in Baltimore, and I didn't want to nurse in the air force, but I was sentenced to it for the next eighteen months—and military medicine left a lot to be desired.

The Intensive Care Unit was a fifteen-bed combination Coronary Care and Surgical Intensive Care Unit staffed by nurses with little if any Intensive Care experience. A few weeks after I got there, I was giving my head nurse, a major with absolutely no experience in the field, a quick course in ICU care. I'd always worked in teaching hospitals, in state-of-the-art units on the cutting edge of new treatment protocols and with experts in the field. This unit was furnished with old equipment. The staff hadn't even heard of many of the procedures that were routine in the real world. It was obvious to me that no one, from the major down, knew anything about medicine. I felt nervous leaving the unit after my shift because I was afraid for the patients.

Then I made an amazing discovery in "the squeaky wheel gets the grease" mode. A superior officer's top priority is that everything run smoothly. Professional advancement depends on it. If officers can't handle the personnel assigned to them, they can very well be looking at the end of their careers. As the number one complainer in the unit, I was a potential stumbling block on the major's road to glory.

Instead of getting me into trouble, my grousing and thoroughly unmilitary-like behavior were earning me preferential treatment. My uniform was never quite right, I wouldn't salute and showed no respect whatsoever to my superior officers, but I always had the best hours in the unit and rarely worked weekends. They even sent me along with the major on an all-expenses-paid trip to Columbus to attend a workshop on ICU management techniques—partly to pacify me and partly, I think, to explain to her what the speakers were talking about. Granted, I was a very responsible staff member, with more valuable experience than the rest of them put together. But, oh, was I one colossal pain in the ass!

No matter how much disinterest or lack of military discipline I displayed, I kept failing upward in the air force. Even with the ruckus I was causing, they kept promoting me right on time. After six months I became a first lieutenant. By the time I was discharged, I was a captain.

Now that I knew I wasn't going to be a nurse for the rest of my life, I was sort of treading water on the job, and in no time, I was bored. So what do you do when you're feeling bored, unfulfilled, and you're me? You have an affair with a married man. His name was First Lieutenant Bradley Green, and he was only in the air force to fulfill an ROTC commitment he'd made to pay for college. He couldn't wait to get out of the military and start his life. Bradley was smitten with me right away and made no secret of his intentions when we met at the Officers' Club. I had a moral streak a mile wide and was sure I'd never have an affair with a married man. What I didn't know was that I was courting danger by merely becoming his friend.

Our association was never innocent. He was at my place every night after work, and the conversation on the couch always wound up as a make-out session with me calling a halt at the eleventh hour. The boundary between cheating and not cheating kept shifting, but I eased my conscience by convincing myself that it wasn't adultery unless we went all the way.

One day after a particularly hot session, Bradley declared that he couldn't take the frustration anymore and was going to stop asking me to go to bed with him. If I ever wanted to, he added, I was going to have to be the one to say the words. Since I was sure I'd never do that, I felt that my virtue was safe. From then on, whenever he got to the boiling point, he'd just get up and go home.

Before long, it was me who didn't want to stop. No matter what I did, though, Bradley refused to stay. He turned it into a real contest, always declaring, "I told you you'd have to ask!" Just before he'd leave, he'd gaze at me and say, "What do you want?" Even though I was going crazy with desire, I couldn't find the words—until one night when, overcome by passion, I threw myself against the door. "Bradley, don't go," I pleaded, my arms barring his way.

"Why?" he whispered.

I closed my eyes and summoned all my strength. "I want to make love to you," I said softly.

"Are you sure?" He smiled.

"Yes . . . yes . . . yes, yes, yes, yes!" I gasped as we ran up the stairs toward my bedroom and fell rapturously into each other's arms.

That evening I at last discovered exactly what all the fuss was about. My body seemed to have a mind of its own. I was astonished that it knew all the things it was doing, but they sure felt good. So began my first four-alarm physical affair. Sometimes we barely made it indoors before the fireworks started, the passion was that tremendous.

Since Bradley was married, we tried to be discreet. We rarely went out, but when we did, we picked places where none of our friends were likely to see us because it was so obvious that we were more than pals. As time went on, the rigors of cheating began to take their toll on me. It was really difficult to be denied his company most weekends and every holiday. We started to fight, then break up. The breakups led to incredible reunions, but the strain was showing on both of us. When our affair forced him into therapy, Bradley pulled the plug.

I was truly devastated and in real physical pain. I thought my heart was literally broken and bleeding. I started drinking wine in the morning to dull the pain, and would end up drinking all day. After two days of that, I realized that I was flirting with an even greater danger. My father, after all, was an alcoholic. I had no desire to wind up like him, so out went the wine.

The hurt was still so intense that it forced me to seek another painkiller. I thought I could find absolution in church and ended up sitting in a pew crying profusely. When the minister made a call for sinners, I staggered, blurry-eyed, to the altar, begging for forgiveness. I'd never do another bad thing. I promised God that I'd become a good, Bible-reading churchgoer if He would just make the hurt go away.

I came to my senses later that Sunday afternoon in the bathroom of the library where I'd gone for my first Bible reading. Sitting on the toilet, I realized that this whole remorse thing just wasn't me. I wasn't going to change my whole life because of one stupid mistake. I knew the difference between right and wrong, and I didn't need anyone else telling me what to think or how to feel. That was the end of my brush with salvation.

Still, it wasn't easy to get over ol' Bradley Green. Just when I thought I had finally done it, I saw him from a window, parking in the hospital lot, and was thrown into a tailspin. I knew I had a vacation coming up, so as part of the healing process, I decided it was time to pay a visit to an old friend in Newport News, Virginia. Someone my tour of duty in the air force was keeping me from. Someone whose love I didn't question.

I hadn't seen Uncle Leroy in more than a year. He was in his mid-sixties now, a decade that few of us had thought he'd make, given the steadily deteriorating condition of his heart. He was surviving, but my parents, who were planning to visit him the same time I was, warned me that the years and coronary disease had taken their toll. Still, I wasn't prepared for what I soon saw.

Uncle Leroy had shriveled into a skinny old man, with a tuft of inch-long white hair circling his shiny bald pate, who needed a walker to get around. He could have shopped anywhere for clothes now, if he could manage to get to the store. But his mind was still sharp. He knew everything, including what bad shape he was in.

On my last night there, I sat alone with him by his bed.

"This is the last time we're going to get to talk," he told me.

"No it's not," I insisted, fighting back tears.

"Yes it is, but it's okay," he replied, patting my hand. "I just want you to know that I love you and want you to always be happy."

I continued to protest that he had years ahead of him, but I could tell that my uncle Leroy hated living the way he had to now. He still defied his failing body by attempting to do things of which he was no longer capable. He was constantly trying to travel around the neighborhood by manipulating the walker as he once had his two good legs, but he almost always had to be rescued after falling down in the street. He had lost the thing he valued most—his independence—and he was well aware that it was gone for good. It struck me that he was saying good-bye to me while he still could.

I went on smiling at him until I said good night, but once outside the door of his room, I broke down. The one person in the world who truly loved me was dying. In that light, Bradley suddenly didn't seem all that important. I went back to Dayton ready to relegate that part of my life to the back burner and get on to a more important chapter. Uncle Leroy wanted me to be happy, and his wish would never be fulfilled as long as I was working in ICU.

*   *   *

I had to get out of ICU. I considered the level of medicine practiced there so low as to be dangerous. When I demanded a change
of department, the chief nurse was accommodating. "We have a
number of floors that might interest you," she said and smiled.
"There's medicine, surgery, where would you like to go?"

"I want to go someplace in this hospital where you don't have to
practice medicine," I replied grimly.

"And just where would that be?" she asked, growing a little
vexed.

"Pediatrics," I announced, although I didn't know if they had
openings and wasn't experienced in the field.

I'd done my research and knew that the Pediatrics department
was an eighteen-bed unit. The hospital had no pediatric residency.
Most of the patients were simply there to have their tonsils yanked
or tubes put in their ears. Really sick children were sent to civilian
hospitals. If I had to work in this stupid institution, it seemed like
the best place. How badly could they screw up a tonsillectomy, after
all? The chief nurse gave me the job right off the bat because the
powers that were still wanted to keep me happy.

A few days before my transfer, I was tending to a baby who had
developed heatstroke after being left unattended in a parked car on
a hot summer day. She had stabilized and was now awaiting a technician to transfer her to Pediatrics. I was just finishing her chart
when I heard a male voice, obviously the technician, say, "Oh, so
you're Lieutenant Quivers," but I didn't bother to look up.

I had the world's largest chip on my shoulder, and the guy's
words hit me the wrong way. I preferred that people keep their distance, and here was this tech openly approaching me. Contemptu-
ous of his familiarity, I finished my notes, hung the chart on the
crib, and told him, "You can take her now," without giving him so
much as a glance.

My first day on the new floor, I was individually introduced to
everyone at a staff meeting. "David Jefferson, Lieutenant Quivers,"
the captain of the unit announced as she presented me to the most
gorgeous young man I'd seen in a long time. I couldn't understand
why at the time, but this caramel-colored Adonis gave me the cold-
est handshake and barely looked at me. During the meeting I

learned that David Jefferson would soon be leaving the unit to work in the Emergency Room. My heart sank. It sank even lower when I put two and two together and realized that he was the technician I'd blown off in ICU. Now I wasn't ever going to get the chance to show him how friendly I could be.

I'd chosen Pediatrics without much thought as to what the job would entail. My first full day turned out to be quite a challenge. The captain put me on medications. Getting children to drink out of medication cups and take pills was no easy task. My first patient was a long-termer who was suffering from juvenile arthritis, and he really knew the ropes. He must have spotted me as a novice the moment I walked in the room. I offered him several baby aspirin in a cup. He folded his arms across his chest and clamped his mouth shut. No amount of coaxing was going to work. I walked out of the room destroyed, afraid that I'd bitten off more than I could chew.

Just as I was about to head back to the nurse's station and throw in the towel, another technician, Reggie Small, showed up. He noticed my distress, and when I told him my problem, took the cup, went back into the room, and demanded in a stern voice that the little boy take his pills. Without a word of protest, the kid grabbed the cup and gulped down the pills with a grin. I promised myself never again to let my compassion for sick children get in the way of doing my job.

I subsequently found out that this same little boy had every nurse in Pediatrics jumping through hoops. He demanded bribes of candy or toys for his cooperation in medical procedures administered for his benefit. If he didn't get them, he threw a tantrum. He would have pulled me into this same routine had I not been wised up by Reggie. In the end, that little boy and I learned to respect each other. I discovered that I could use some of the same techniques on him that I'd learned with my little Jimmy. He came back to the floor for a visit a few months after his discharge. I was the only nurse he remembered by name.

Reggie proved to be more annoying than instructive once we got to know each other. He was an outrageous flirt, and he hit on me at every available opportunity. I hated getting the same treatment from him as did every other female around but became more tolerant when I found out that David, the gorgeous guy who wouldn't even give me the time of day, was his roommate.

Eventually, I convinced Reggie to become my partner in crime as I set out to snare The Unobtainable One. He would invite me over to their house when he knew David was just sitting around watching TV, then conveniently disappear. Nothing ever came of these forced meetings, and I was about to give up when Reggie proposed one last scheme. His family was coming up for the weekend and he needed David's room, so I was to offer David my spare bedroom along with one of my famous lasagna dinners. My heartthrob swallowed the bait and the lasagna. And he never made it to the spare bed.

I was amazed at my own boldness. Just as he was about to say good night at the door of my second bedroom, I found myself suggesting, "You don't have to sleep there if you don't want to."

This too became a very hot, physical affair. David had just had a circumcision a week before our first night together. He was under doctor's orders not to even get aroused, but we wound up busting a stitch or two that night. David was a very good lover, and I developed quite an appetite for this young man.

In the course of pursuing him, I'd developed an appetite for something else, too. Weed. I'd never been much of a pot smoker—I'd tried it a couple of times in college but had never even experienced a buzz. Reggie and David smoked incessantly, and on one of my first visits to their place, they offered me a hit from the water pipe they called a bong that was ever present on the coffee table in their living room.

A person never forgets her first bong hit. I didn't want to appear square. After all, I was a worldly twenty-five, and David and Reggie were only about twenty-two, so I took the contraption when they passed it. I put my mouth over the large hole as I had watched them do, but even after inhaling with all my might, I couldn't keep the damn thing lit. After a good laugh, David showed me the secret, the little hole in the back that you have to cover in order to close the system. With David's finger on that little hole, I inhaled again, and a powerful blast of smoke filled my mouth and my throat, causing me to cough uncontrollably. I was sure that I hadn't gotten any of the smoke into my system, but soon the music from the stereo started to sound better and I started to feel mellower and mellower.

This was 1977, remember, when it was all right to get high and engage in conversations that didn't make sense with people you otherwise wouldn't give the time of day to. I was high for the first time and liking it fine.

In no time at all, I discovered that marijuana mixed well with music, sex, and sugar. It was the era of Led Zeppelin, Fleetwood Mac, and Steely Dan. The drink of choice was sangria, but when we couldn't get that, Kool-Aid would do. The TV set was always on, but the sound was always muted so that we could hear the stereo. Sometimes we provided our own dialogue to whatever was on the tube. The only show we both watched and listened to was "Saturday Night Live."

What amazes me to this day is how David and Reggie managed to pass their mandatory drug tests. They were noncoms. I was an officer, which meant that I was on the honor system. Unless I did something really stupid, I didn't have to worry. My superiors never seemed to notice that I was wearing dark glasses to work. I didn't generally come to work high, but I wanted to hide my pupils just the same. I sort of liked being a druggie and getting away with using illegal substances when the air force was so dead set against it. It's certainly possible that I unconsciously wanted them to catch me.

David and I didn't have a lot in common intellect-wise, and marijuana gave us something to talk about. All our conversations revolved around drugs—the best high, the lack of good product, who had the best stuff. We even entertained the idea of going into the drug business for a while, but only to cover the cost of our habit. When I actually came face-to-face with real drug dealers, I decided that it was no business for me. The two black people who sold us the pound of pot were hardened criminals, and I could tell that if we'd gotten them on the wrong day the deal didn't have to go down just this way. They could have taken our money, or killed us, or sold us the pot. It really was their choice and my last drug deal.

I actually had more in common with Reggie than David, and our friendship survived my relationship with David, which self-destructed relatively quickly. Since women were always throwing themselves at him, according to the law of averages it followed that some of them would get caught.

One morning after I got off work, I just couldn't sleep. Every instinct in my body told me that there was something I needed to check out at David's. When I got there, I spotted a red car I'd never seen before parked in front of the house. I rang and rang the bell, but no one answered. Finally, I found a phone booth and called. David answered. While I was on the phone with him, the red car zoomed past, with a young Asian woman behind the wheel.

That phone call was a study in pretense. I pretended that I just happened to be in the neighborhood, and he feigned sleepiness. When he asked me over, I consented as pleasantly as you please, but inwardly I was fuming. When I told him I'd seen "Suzy Wong" drive away, he was honestly puzzled by how I knew that her name was Suzy. David had lots of swell attributes, but he was never going to be a rocket scientist. I decided that we were through and prepared to exit in grand style.

To me, the worst part of the whole sleazy episode was that he was screwing her on the lion-print sheets I'd gotten him for his birthday. I proceeded to rip them off the bed, roll them up into a ball, grasp them in my arms, announce, "Sleep with anyone you want, but not on my sheets!" and stalk out, slamming the door behind me. On my way back home it occurred to me that the last souvenir of David that I wanted was those sheets, so I stopped at a dumpster by the road and hurled them in.

A couple of weeks without David's amorous charms and I was missing the steady diet of sex I had become used to with him, so I took him back. He was very repentant and I'm sure tried to be good, but a few months later I got that certain feeling again. This time my instincts told me that he'd started sleeping with one of his friend's wives. Before I could spring another trap, he sat me down and told me that he thought it would be good for our relationship if we opened it up and started seeing other people.

Pissed off that he would dare to dictate to me how my life should be led, I replied angrily, "I'll tell you how it's going to be. You'll see other people, and I'll see other people, and we won't see each other!" I guess that he wasn't ready to break up because he started to cry, but I hardened my heart and ended it for good right then and there. My pride left no room for sharing or constantly uncovering his indiscretions.

It wasn't long after this that I remember sitting on my living room floor alone, smoking a joint. I had the TV on with the sound down and the stereo blasting. I felt that I'd been sitting in that position for a year. Was I better off now, I asked myself, than I had been a year before? The answer was a resounding no. I hadn't done anything new or learned anything new. An entire year of my life had literally gone up in smoke.

So I stamped out the joint and got up off the floor. It was time to start moving again.

You never know when people are watching you. I had been working in Pediatrics for about eight months when Dr. Herrera, the head of the department, came to me and asked me if I wanted to run the Pediatrics clinic. He said that he'd been very impressed with my work, and even though I had less than a year left in the service, he urged me to take the job. For once the chief nurse was opposed to my getting such a perc, but Dr. Herrera prevailed, and I became head nurse of the Pediatrics clinic.

The work intrigued me because it was different. It was more administrative than anything I'd ever done before. I arranged schedules, made assignments, and ensured that the five doctors who worked in the clinic used their time efficiently. But my favorite part of the job was the detective work. Every morning we started the day with about twenty open appointments for emergency Pediatric patients. Parents called in and described their children's symptoms over the phone. I had to determine from their descriptions which children got these slots. I became quite an expert at it, once even diagnosing a case of pneumonia over the phone.

Working with all of these children made me think of Jimmy a lot. I'd see a child of three and think of Jimmy the way he'd been the last time I'd seen him. Then I'd see a kid of about ten who was going through some childhood trauma and wonder if that had ever happened to Jimmy. I carried two pictures of him in my wallet. I thought I'd need them to remember what he looked like, but I never did. In fact, it was painful to look at them. Sometimes at night, though, when I was alone, I'd take them out for a second and wonder where he was and what he might be doing. I always stopped myself after a couple of questions because I'd never know the answers.

At last, in the summer of 1977, it was time to start thinking about getting out of the air force because I was due to be discharged in January. At the start of my enlistment, I'd made the decision not to continue in nursing, so I went back to school to find out what I'd really like to do with my life. I signed up for two courses at Dayton Community College, one in criminology because I was interested in the law, and an introductory acting course because I'd always loved movies and wanted to know more about actors and their craft. I could actually feel my future about to begin when the air force threw me a hard, fast curve.

One payday, when my affair with David was winding down, I'd noticed that my check was short and had gone to the finance office to get the discrepancy resolved. Maybe if I'd never questioned that check, everything would have been okay. As it was, I discovered that the air force had been overpaying me the entire time I'd been in. I could have kicked myself for not noticing that something was wrong a long time back. Every other officer, even those who out-ranked me, was always complaining about money. I had chalked it up to my being a better money manager. The overpayments now amounted to a staggering $10,000.

This time I was dealing with the real air force. Its heavy guns rolled into position, preparing to mow me down. I actually became the subject of a criminal investigation. It was ludicrous. I was the one who'd brought the matter to their attention, and these assholes had the nerve to accuse me of intentionally ripping them off. When I asked why they weren't investigating the people who filled out my forms in the first place, I was told that those soldiers weren't liable for their mistakes. I was.

Ultimately, the investigation proved that the whole thing was the result of a clerical error, but that didn't stop the air force from wanting me to return the cash.

"Where's the money?" this full bird colonel yelled at me.

"I didn't know it was yours, so I spent it!" I screamed back.

"If you don't lower your voice, young lady, you're going to find yourself in even more trouble," he said with a sneer.

He wasn't used to anyone like me. "Well, you'll just have to forgive me," I continued to yell at him, "but I'm a little bit upset."

The injustice of the whole thing made me nuts. I had done

nothing to cause the problem, but suddenly it was mine to fix. I was the one who needed a lawyer to work out a repayment arrangement. Ten grand! There was no way I had that kind of money. My only bargaining chip was my time, so I extended my tour of duty for six months, taking a huge salary cut to expedite the payback. They didn't even consider the additional time as part of the deal, behaving as if I should feel privileged to be granted the six extra months. It was a bitter pill to swallow, but I had no other options.

After the settlement agreement was firmed up, I went right out and ran up all my credit cards. If I was going to have to spend six more months in the service, I reasoned, I deserved a few creature comforts to make it more bearable. I was in such a shopping frenzy that the only thing I actually remember buying was a nineteen-inch color TV. Until then, I had been watching TV on the same nine-inch black and white set that my parents had bought for me when I went to college.

My saving grace was school. I loved being in a civilian environment again. On campus it was as if that huge military base right outside town didn't even exist. I guess this exposure to the outside world made me resent the pomp and circumstance of the military more than ever, because on base, I wouldn't let anyone salute me, and I greeted my superior officers with a casual wave. They were so shocked, I was usually gone before they had a chance to react. After a while, I stopped wearing my air force–issue coat and hat and came to work in a bright green ski jacket.

At school, I joined the theater group and helped build the stage for the fall production of *A Midsummer Night's Dream*. I worked props during the show and got to go to all the rehearsals and see the play take shape. I was fascinated by the magic of theater and liked hanging around these artistic types. The last show was sad because we knew that months of work had now come to an end and that this troop might never act together again. The company chose the musical *Applause* for their winter production. I had been bitten by the bug, so I auditioned for a part although I didn't expect to get cast because they already had a lot of good actors. Imagine my delight when I saw my name posted on the board a few days later. The director had actually changed the sex of one of the characters, a lawyer, for me. It was a small part, but it meant that I was in the play.

* * *

I never got to find out what it was like to be on stage, though, because rehearsals started after January 11, 1978—the day my life began to unravel completely. It was my original discharge date, and from that day on, I stopped seeing people and stopped paying bills. My phone was eventually shut off. For the first time in my life, I couldn't manage to do anything.

The first outward sign that something was wrong was the sudden onset of chronic lateness. I actually caught myself waking up early one morning to turn off my alarm clock before it rang so that I would oversleep. I had to move it across the room so that I'd be fully awake when I turned it off. Even when I did get to work, I couldn't finish my shift. I'd burst into tears at the drop of a hat. Soon I was crying at the beginning of my shift, too. My supervisor really wanted to help, but she couldn't just let me out of the air force, and I didn't know of anything else that would work.

It was the fifteenth round, and I was down for the count, the first time I'd ever been knocked down by an opponent. The referee had started the count, and I didn't know if I'd make it to my feet in time.

Meanwhile, Muhammad Ali, continuing to ignore the call of father time, climbed into the ring with another young former Olympian named Leon Spinks. The fight was supposed to be a cakewalk, but at the end of fifteen, Ali lost it on the judges' cards. He had gone in undertrained and overweight. He had underestimated his foe and was now suffering the consequences. The belt and his reputation were gone. That fight, his fifty-eighth professional bout, marked his worst performance in what was now a string of poor showings in which the judges simply refused to take away his title. It had been getting harder and harder to defend Ali when his detractors said he couldn't fight anymore. This loss appeared to be a confirmation of that sentiment. Ali had stayed too long at the dance—just like me.

Even in my weakened state, I wouldn't let anyone demean the champ in my presence. When a sergeant from another clinic came into my office crowing that the slimy draft dodger had finally gotten what he deserved, I roared, "Got what he deserved? That draft dodger could buy and sell you with what he's got in his pocket."

The sergeant couldn't understand how another member of the service could defend Ali, but when he checked out my collar, he knew that there was no room for argument. Any other time I would have been glad to wave the privilege of rank to take him on, but I was about as tired as my hero, and I let my silver captain's bars do most of the talking.

Eventually, I gave up my head nurse position because I couldn't function anymore and returned to Pediatrics, where they put me on the night shift, the least demanding shift of the day. Even when I didn't have to be at work until eleven o'clock at night, I managed to oversleep. Working all night and sleeping all day, I lost track of time. I stopped watching TV and listening to music. When I was awake, I cried. I had become consumed with the thought that I was going to die in the air force, that it was killing me. I prayed in the dark, lying on the living room floor, "Please, Lord, just one day of freedom."

My diet went to hell too. I no longer cooked. If it hadn't been for McDonald's, Burger King, and Wendy's, I would have starved. I developed this strange notion that I had to hide being single, so when I went to a fast food place, I ordered enough for two. The only thing that really made me feel better was ice cream. Soon it became my entire diet. I was putting away up to a gallon a day, and I didn't feel secure unless there was at least a half gallon in the freezer. I stocked up every day, I was eating so much, and took to rotating stores so that the clerks wouldn't see me every day. My favorite was Friendly's Vanilla Chocolate Chip. There was a whole circuit of Friendly's stores that I visited. At holiday time, I liked the yule log and eggnog flavors too.

As my new discharge date neared, I could see light at the end of the tunnel and began to pull myself together. I had already decided I was going to head out to California—one of the places I'd wanted to go when I'd joined the air force. Since I was driving, I had to get my car serviced for the trip. With no friends and no phone, I drove to the dealership one morning after work. Since it was a short drive, I figured it would make a nice walk home. That pleasant stroll turned out to be an eight-mile trek along a deserted road. Once I got home, I collapsed on my bed, my legs aching, but that afternoon, I started back to the dealership.

It didn't take long to know that I wasn't going to make it, and when a car appeared and stopped for me, I climbed right in. My guardian angel must have been looking out for me because the driver turned out to be a really sweet, elderly gentleman who took me all the way to the car place.

When I came out of my emotional coma, I had about two weeks of vacation left, and I used them to terminate my bondage early. My furniture was already on its way to San Francisco. I'd managed to save a thousand dollars, and my credit card balances were within reason. I'd visit my family in Baltimore for four days and then spend the rest of the time in Pittsburgh with Linda and David Zimmerman, two former air force buddies whose friendship I value to this day.

I told my parents that I could only get a long weekend because I didn't want to spend my final days on the East Coast with them. I was tired, I needed rest, and I was too weak to deal with them. Even though my father had gone through rehab and taken the cure while I was in the service, and they had assured me that things had changed, I was afraid to go home. I had to go somewhere I'd feel safe and that was with Linda and Z, as we called him. Donning my mask with the happy face, I reentered the world.

I arrived back on the base the day of my discharge, picked up my papers, signed out, and pointed my car west. I was free again, and I was off to California to seek my fortune. I had managed to survive the terrible darkness that had surrounded me and now embarked on a quest to find myself in a place where nobody knew me.

With my final paycheck, I now had two thousand dollars in cash and no deadlines, and I was headed for California, where for me there was no past—only the infinite possibilities of a brighter future.

9

PLAYGROUND

*I'm standing center stage behind lush velvet curtains, eyes closed
and head bowed in a moment of silent meditation. Mike in one
hand, I use the other to stroke the beautiful fabric of my gown.
Out front, the house is packed and the crowd is abuzz with antici-
pation. The house lights go down, the orchestra strikes up the
introduction to one of my biggest songs, and the curtain rises.
Searching spotlights find me on stage, the crowd erupts in thun-
derous applause, and I drink in the love pouring forth from this
adoring throng.*

—a favorite dream

Discharge papers in hand, I jumped in my car and headed for I-70,
the road out of town. I was free. I still owed the air force a few
grand, but my military lawyer assured me that they'd never come
after me for such a paltry sum. Even though I'd promised to set up a
new payment schedule as soon as I found a job, I was leaving the air
force without looking back.

It was June, and the sun beating down on the flat Ohio land-
scape felt good. I heaved a huge sigh of relief as I passed through
the gates of Wright Paterson for the last time, thanking my lucky

stars that I hadn't done something stupid out of boredom while waiting for this ordeal to end. I could have gotten married or, God forbid, I could have gotten pregnant. If I had, I would have been running away now instead of going to a new place to find myself.

I really needed to be out and on my own. Some people handle things better surrounded by friends and family, but I've always found that I do my best work solo. It might have scared another person to have no one to call and no one to leave behind, but for me, having no strings felt just right. My first stop was Indianapolis. I'd lived in Dayton for two and a half years but had never gotten any farther west. So even though Indianapolis was about a hundred miles away, I decided I'd better see it now. I wasn't planning on ever coming back this way again.

I started the trip staying at Ramada Inns, although as my funds dwindled, I would have to cut back and end it at Motel 6's. I had gotten Reggie to score me an ounce of pot before I left Ohio, and after stopping at a convenience store and picking up some beer my first night on the road, I settled into a nice little Ramada room and rolled a joint. Smoking and drinking alone wasn't my cup of tea, so I stamped out the joint, rolled up the baggie of pot, tucked it into the side of my overnight case, and forgot about it for the rest of the trip.

I broke up the driving into two-hundred-mile chunks following a route mapped out for me by Triple A. When I reached someplace interesting, I stopped for two or three days to take in the sights. I managed to do all of the major cities across the southwest—Houston, Albuquerque, Las Vegas. While in a town, I'd go to museums, state houses, zoos, and Indian reservations. The angry eyes of the young Indian guides were familiar. It was the same look I'd seen in the glare of angry young blacks hanging on ghetto corners. Seeing that hate directed at me made me feel ashamed. They were right, I belonged to the system that had stolen their land and forced them onto reservations, killing the spirit of their people.

Vegas was so tempting, it was scary. Especially frightening were the signs heading in and out of town that proclaimed, "We pay cash for your car." By now, my travel bank was getting low and I could just imagine going into one of those casinos and losing all the rest of my money. I decided to enjoy the lights from the highway and kept going, stopping only to see the Hoover Dam.

I had planned to use this time on the road to recharge my battery. Taking in the vastness and the beauty of America did have a restorative effect, but I'd been on the road for almost two months now and felt that it was time to get where I was going. I still had about five hundred dollars, but car trouble cut that amount in half just after I crossed the Arizona state line. I was desperate to get to San Francisco as soon as I could.

Crossing the mountains into California was some of the hardest driving I encountered on the entire trip. I had to do it in one long, exhausting session, which took a lot out of me. But late one afternoon as dusk was falling I saw houses nestled in hills and knew I was close to the city that would be my new home. I was surprised at the lack of uniformity of San Francisco architecture. An orange house stood side by side with a green house, then a pink one. I thought the people who lived here must be crazy.

California was supposed to be warm, or so I'd always heard, but the closer I got to San Francisco, the colder it got. It was a startling contrast to the drought-scorched desert I'd just crossed in record heat. Finally surrendering to the temperature, I rummaged through the trunk of my car for a jacket. California was not like I'd pictured it, but I'd come all this way and there was no turning back.

I found my first nest, the Nob Hill Women's Residence Hotel, while driving around looking for a temporary place to stay. It turned out to be the perfect spot for a girl from the other side of the country who didn't know a soul in the city. The room I took was small, with a twin bed right in the center of it. There was a sink, but the toilet and the shower were down the hall. You could pay by the day, week, or month, and the price included the room and two meals a day. It was like dorm living again.

The hotel was right on the edge of the ritzy Nob Hill section of San Francisco, which was famous for its Victorian residences. But if you walked the wrong way, which I did that first day, you landed right in the heart of the strip of gay, male pickup joints on Polk Street. It was Sunday afternoon and I had slept through breakfast at the hotel, so I went looking for a quiet place to eat and stopped at the first coffee shop I saw. I took a stool at the counter, began to read the want ads in the paper I'd brought with me, and ignored the very obvious and rude stares I'd noticed the moment I walked in. A whiskey-voiced waitress took my order, but she too seemed surprised by my presence. When my omelet arrived, I took a second look at my waitress. That's when I discovered that she was no waitress, she was a man. I definitely wasn't in Kansas anymore.

At least I had a lot in common with my fellow hotel residents, who were all in the midst of major transitions. They either had just arrived in California, were starting out, or were starting over after a divorce. There was a wealth of worldly knowledge behind the doors of these small rooms, and in time many of the other residents would prove to be invaluable resources for me.

In plotting out my job-hunting strategy, I decided to pick a field in which my nursing degree would be an asset. After some thought, I recalled a pharmaceuticals lecture I'd heard during my stint in Shock Trauma. The speaker, who had once been a nurse, was a sales representative for a drug company. It just so happened that a number of drug companies called California home, and there were tons of listings for pharmaceutical sales reps in the Sunday paper.

Bright and early that first Monday morning in the city, I picked up the phone and made a few appointments. I showed up for my first interview wearing a flower-print cotton wrap skirt, a white shell, and a brown leather jacket. Needless to say, the interview was a short one, and I never heard from that company again. When they heard my account of this episode, my newfound career counselors at the women's residence lost no time in whipping me into shape. Nothing in nursing had ever prepared me for the world of business. In my experience, interviews were just a formality. If you had the license, the experience, and the references, the job was yours. Since I'd only worked in hospitals, I was a babe in the woods as far as office protocol was concerned. Thanks to the women at the hotel, I quickly acquired a professional-looking résumé and cover sheet, business cards, and a spectacular interview suit. It was my first real makeover, and when I wore my interview outfit, I looked like a million bucks.

Before I could concentrate fully on my job search, I was going to need some money. I knew I'd be tapped in a couple of weeks and I also knew that I wasn't going to score the kind of job I wanted that fast. That meant that I was going to have to do some nursing, at least temporarily, and I wound up driving all the way to Sacramento to get a temporary license. My Intensive Care experience put me in demand at the temporary agencies, and almost immediately, I was working two or three days a week, which put money in my pocket and gave me time to look for a non-nursing job.

I could have gotten lazy about finding a new career, since the temporary nursing jobs were so plentiful and the money was so good, but something happened that would make finding a different way to make a living a top priority. I was sitting in report on a medical floor in a hospital I'd never worked in before when I started seeing spots in front of my eyes and realized that I was about to faint. The other nurses never noticed my condition, but just handed me an assignment card. If a student hadn't offered to help me find my way around, I might have hit the deck. She got me to a rest room, where I sat with my head between my knees to get some blood to my brain. It was then that I realized how sick I was of the people in my profession. They were so burned out after a couple of years that they couldn't even see what was happening right in front of them. It was then that I promised myself that I was getting out of nursing. It was the last time I worked in a hospital in California.

Meanwhile, word had hit the street that a great black sales rep candidate was looking for placement with a pharmaceutical company. Employment agencies actually started recruiting me, and I got to interview with all the best firms. But because I stopped taking nursing gigs, another money crunch forced me to jump at my first real offer of employment.

I had seen an ad in the paper for an R.N. to help start up a new temporary nursing agency, followed it up, and got the position. My duties consisted of interviewing and checking the references of applicants and filling orders from understaffed hospitals with the best candidate for the assignment. I still hadn't severed all my ties with nursing, but it was the first job I'd ever held where I didn't have to wear a uniform.

Now that I knew where my next meal was coming from, I settled in for a long stay at the residence hotel, even installing a phone line in my room so that I could field weekend calls from my new job. I was feeling so up, I even checked in with my parents. I had given up making the mandatory weekly call during those dark days in the air force. They hadn't heard from me in a while and were worried because I was so far from home. I actually hated talking to them.

Never one to look on the bright side, my mother's conversations were filled to overflowing with tragic tales of misfortune. This one was pregnant and not married, that one had lost a job, someone's son had flunked out of school, and someone else's was going to jail. Once I'd been away for a while, I'd noticed that she was telling me exclusively sad stories about people I didn't even know. Once I asked if anything good ever happened to the people she knew. When she answered yes, I asked why she never bothered to tell me those stories. After that, she never had much to say when I called.

It was the fall of 1978, and I could lie in bed with my hands behind my head and my ankles crossed while I watched my little nine-inch black and white TV. It had traveled across the country with me in the backseat of my car. I never wanted to be without the television, it kept me in touch. It was television that showed me all those great Ali fights, alerted me to his losses, and informed me that he had regained his title in the rematch with Leon Spinks.

Muhammad was probably reclining in a similar fashion, savoring the sweetness of this particular victory. It made him the only man in history who had won the title three times. I secretly thought Ali had chosen Leon Spinks, an inferior fighter in my opinion, to lose just so he could achieve this record. Whatever the case, I was happy for him.

San Francisco turned out to be a friendly place where total strangers struck up conversations on the bus or walking down the street, but I still hadn't made any connections outside the little group I socialized with at the hotel. One day a makeup artist came to give us a demonstration. After dinner, though we hadn't a dime to spare among us, we decided to check it out. I wound up being the model for the demonstration. Usually, I shied away from such obvious attention, but I was in a new place and in a mood to try new things. Jill, the makeup artist, was a pretty blond woman who seemed to be about my age. She spoke with incredible ease and confidence, and even though she didn't make one sale, she remained pleasant to the end. As she was packing up to leave, she called me over and told me, "You seem like a really nice person, someone who might be open to new things." I was flattered, and when she asked me to attend a meeting with her the following night, I accepted without bothering to ask what it was.

That's how I found myself in an industrial park in South San Francisco the very next evening. After we'd pulled into the parking lot of a warehouse, I began to have doubts. My fellow passengers had difficulty explaining just what kind of lecture I'd be attending. I didn't have the faintest idea whether it was a reality-based group or some wacky California cult. Just what had I gotten myself into, I wondered.

Inside, I was relieved to find, it was warm and brightly lit, with a lot of attractive, well-dressed people standing around sipping coffee. When the lecture was about to begin, first-timers like me were ushered down a long hallway into a large room with brown, egg carton-covered walls. Folding chairs were arranged in rows, and we were encouraged to take seats at the front near a small riser. One by one we were asked to stand and share our names and who had invited us, after which the speaker for the evening was introduced.

She was a tall, slender, short-haired woman who called herself Kathryn Starfire, and she radiated even more self-confidence than Jill as she prowled the stage telling her story. For forty-five minutes Kathryn Starfire held us rapt as she recounted how lost and confused she had been before the day a few short months ago when she'd found herself sitting just where we were now. She claimed that after taking a workshop called Playground, her whole life had changed. Now she was a happening human being with a great job and a wonderful relationship with a man. She'd been taking workshops ever since and conducted guest lectures for free because she believed in them so much. Ever the skeptic, I tried to rattle her with some biting questions. Never losing her cool, she fielded each one with aplomb.

For the first time, I felt I'd found a group of people I might consider joining. Even though I'd had friends, and even a few lovers, I'd always remained separate and apart. Suddenly I craved that same sense of belonging that Kathryn Starfire had described. I wanted to believe that anything was possible and that I too could have whatever I wanted. I was tired of being afraid, and I was tired of running away, and I was tired of being alone. The next Playground seminar was that very weekend, and I signed up that night to take it.

Come Friday evening, I was back in that same room with about a hundred other people, all dying to know what was going to happen. Soon, two group leaders, a man and woman called "trainers," entered and took seats on stools in the front. Randy, the male trainer, explained that we'd spend the next couple of days doing processes, some of them written, others involving an activity, and still others consisting of guided meditation. Inside these doors, we were assured, there were no right or wrong answers and no failing grades. Playground was a return to childhood, meant to be fun. The rest of the evening was spent on the first process. Each of us got to watch ourselves on a monitor as a camera made a complete circle around us. The purpose, Randy explained, was to give us an idea of how we appeared to others.

In the next two days, I would confront my fear of being on stage, discover that I too held prejudices against other people, and realize that in every human being there's a wonderful person just dying to get out. One hundred total strangers had walked into the workshop on Friday night, but by Sunday evening we were best friends sorry to be parting. Ninety-nine strangers had supported and loved me while I confronted my own fears, and I had gotten to do the same for them.

Playground was just one of the many workshops and seminars conducted by this organization known as Summit, and I wanted to be around the wonderful energy I found that weekend all the time. I offered my services as a volunteer and signed up for the next available workshop, the women's workshop, assuming that it would be as warm and embracing as Playground. Was I in for a surprise! The big smile I was wearing when I entered the workshop room soon faded, for the women's workshop was no laughing matter.

Beth, the trainer for this workshop, led us through grueling confrontational processes designed to unearth the secret traumas of growing up female. When I discovered what we'd be doing, I wanted to run but instead hung back and barely participated as others told tale after tale of abuse at the hands of fathers, brothers, friends, even strangers. Old and young, all had secret histories of dashed hopes and shattered dreams.

One particularly poignant sharing came from a middle-aged woman who had introduced herself at the beginning of the workshop as the happily married mother of two grown boys. She had probably never before confided this story to another living soul. Standing in the middle of a circle of women, she told us that when she was eight, her adored older brother had allowed his friends to see and touch her naked body. He did it so that they would like him, and she did it to win her brother's love. Listening to her struggle through tears to reveal her long-hidden shame, I thought my heart would burst. Still, I refused to join in this collective bloodletting and kept my mouth shut, desperate to maintain the illusion that my childhood had been fine.

How I managed to get through the entire weekend, I'll never know, but by Monday I realized that I was losing my voice and assumed that I was coming down with a cold. No other symptoms ever appeared, but for the next several weeks, I couldn't speak above a whisper. I was reduced to writing notes to communicate. I did manage to croak out my problem to one of my fellow Playground alumni, Danielle, who suggested that I consult with someone at the Center. When I wrote out my problem for a staff member, she suggested another workshop. The next one available was a parents workshop at the Summit center in San Jose. As anxious as I was to get my voice back, I was sure the parents workshop wasn't for me because I didn't have kids. "Do you have parents?" the staffer asked. I was on my way to San Jose. The parents workshop was just as difficult to sit through as the women's workshop. I had never known such anger, and I wasn't even doing the exercises. Merely hearing others share their stories churned up all my rage. After another excruciating weekend, I was livid and still couldn't talk.

Since I was planning to attend a follow-up meeting on the Wednesday evening after the workshop, I spent Tuesday night at my friend Danielle's. To my surprise, she came right out and asked me what it was that I didn't want to say. What I did in response astonished me. For the first time since my father had molested me, I confessed to another person what had happened. "You'd better talk to Beth about this," Danielle urged me.

I sat through the Wednesday meeting without hearing a word that was said. After everyone filed out, I approached Beth, who was still standing on stage. As I walked toward her, it became clear to me that I had been holding on to my secret for so long that I didn't want to let it go. I had convinced myself that if I told, people wouldn't like me. That's why I'd been so terrified to speak. Somehow I knew that it was time for me to stop guessing about what happens when you tell and really find out.

Tears were spilling down my cheeks and my lips trembled as I struggled to make myself heard, but the more of my story I shared with Beth, the louder my voice became. By the time I got to the end, an hour had passed, Beth was holding me in her arms, and I had my voice back. "You're one hell of a strong bitch," Beth blurted out with what can only be discribed as moxie. "You sat through that whole women's workshop without saying a word. You're lucky your voice was the only thing you lost!"

I was amazed at how much better I felt, and it wasn't just getting my voice back. It was finally having someone listen to me and tell me it was okay. I still feared that eventually my confession would come back to haunt me, but that night I allowed myself to be taken care of. Danielle even sat outside for an hour and a half, waiting patiently for me to collect myself so that we could drive back to San Francisco. For a brief moment, that scared, battered little girl inside me had shown her face, and she didn't get slapped. It was a beginning, but she was still very scared and incredibly vulnerable. Even the air hurt, but she knew she was alive.

I was incredibly grateful to the staff of Summit for having created a safe haven where such a breakthrough could be made. As a result, I became what is known in the field as a workshop junkie. Summit was created by a guy named Paul Larson. Legend has it that Paul had studied Eastern philosophy for many years and had once worked with Werner Erhardt, the founder of Est. The workshops were designed to produce the enlightenment of the East by using Western techniques. Every moment at the Center was a training session, whether you were attending a workshop, scrubbing toilets, or answering the phones, all of which I did just to be there. Soon my friends from the residence hotel saw less and less of me as all my spare time was spent inside the warehouse structure in South

San Francisco. My new friends at Summit wanted to walk the path and live with Paul. For a while, I did too.

I knew who Paul Larson was the first time I saw him—although he'd only been described to me as not looking like anybody else. I guess his disciples found it difficult to deal with the questions a description would create because Paul didn't look like a guy who had it all together. He was about six five, with receding gray hair, and he weighed about three hundred pounds. The people at the center were fond of saying that Paul had a Buddha complex, and the resemblance was uncanny. There was a light and a joy about his face that was unmistakable. After I started working reception, Paul and I developed quite a phone relationship. We rarely saw each other, but you didn't have to see him every day to fall in love with him. I had a whole Oedipal thing going with him. One weekend when I was assisting at a workshop, he flirted outrageously with me, but I knew he did that with all the girls. Paul lived with Beth, and after a while, I decided that if I couldn't have Paul, I was glad she did.

Although I don't see him or talk to him now, Paul remains the father I never had. That relationship was cemented the day he walked through one of the Center's side doors, saw me, rushed forward, swept me up in his arms, twirled me around as he said hello, then disappeared. I'd been suffering with a stiff neck that afternoon, but the moment my feet returned to the floor, I felt completely loose, and the pain was gone. But that hug had more than just a curative effect on my spine. It reminded me of the ones I'd shared with my own father before he betrayed me. For the first time in years, it felt safe to have someone bigger and stronger touch me. Whenever Paul was around, I would just go up to him, say, "I need a hug," and get one.

People loved being around Paul because he brought out the best in them without even seeming to try. I wanted everyone I knew to experience the joy I'd found at Summit; I even thought that if my parents took a workshop, we might learn to love each other. I actually tried to sign them up long distance and almost had my mother convinced, but she eventually declined, citing money and distance as the reasons. Of course, I took my inability to get them to do a workshop as a personal failure. Since no one who hadn't experienced a workshop could understand my enthusiasm, a lot of people thought I had joined some kind of cult, especially after the whole Jim Jones thing broke.

Summit was home to me. For the first time in my life, I had a circle of friends so large I was never without support or companionship. I always knew what I would be doing on weekends because there was always something going on at the Center. My whole social calendar was filled with great friends who truly wanted me to be the best I could be. Whenever I was wallowing in self-pity or being negative, someone called me on it and refused to play along.

We had wonderful times, too. Everyone was so talented. Danielle had been a child prodigy on the piano, and our blond buddy, Ted, played the guitar. It wasn't unusual for a bunch of us to show up at a piano bar and just take over the place. Surrounded by this group of bohemians, I reconnected with the desire to perform, which had surfaced during my last days in the air force. But, even though many of my friends made their livings in the arts and recognized my talents, that self-defeating part of me refused to believe that I could ever make my living on the stage. That's why I tried as best as I could to replace my dreams of being an actress with fantasies of being on staff. I was considered one of the Center's best volunteers and kept taking on greater responsibility, eventually handling all the travel arrangements for Paul and the trainers at the five Summit centers throughout California. It was ironic how well everything was going inside the egg carton-covered walls, because outside, things weren't so great.

I ended up quitting the job that paid my rent at the temporary nursing agency, even after getting a raise, because the work bored me, and I never seriously looked for another. I began doing bizarre things to make money. I tried selling encyclopedias, life insurance, and Kirby vacuums door to door, but was a dismal failure. Next I tried phone sales, hawking gold, magazines, and subsequently sales training tapes for radio stations. That job provided me with my first introduction to radio. I worked early hours and talked to radio stations all over the East Coast. I got the distinct impression that radio people liked their jobs. Radio, I thought, must be a fine profession.

With all the time I was devoting to the Center, I was really too busy to think about having a relationship. Besides, I had learned a few things about myself and men at Summit. In one of the evening seminars, I discovered that I had developed a distinct pattern as a result of my childhood trauma. There were always two men in my relationships, a friend and a lover, and my lover was usually unavailable. David and Reggie were a perfect illustration of that pattern, which was actually the same triangle created when my father molested me. My father had been my best friend, and when he betrayed my trust, I learned that friends and lovers don't come in the same package and that the most exciting lovers were already attached. Just knowing something doesn't mean you can change it, and since I didn't think I could, I decided not to bother.

That's why I was shocked when this atypical little affair sort of fell into my lap. I was in my own little world, singing as I walked home down Polk Street, where I'd just grabbed a late night snack, when a very handsome young man interrupted my reverie by saying hello. He wound up walking me home and, after the world's fastest courtship, I sneaked him past hotel reception and into a first floor bathroom so that we could be alone for a few minutes, if you catch my drift. At that moment I didn't even know his name and never really expected to see him again.

A few nights later, I was in my room getting undressed when I heard something hit my window. At first I thought it was the wind, but when it happened again, I decided to take a look. There, standing in a halo of lamplight, was the beautiful young man from that incredible night encounter. When I raised the window, he yelled up, "I thought I dreamed you." He'd waited outside that night after he'd left me, and had guessed which window was mine because he'd seen the light come on shortly after I'd left him. I felt like the heroine in a fairy tale.

His name was Audry, and he claimed he was going to play football that fall at Stanford. The only reason I believed him was because his legs were as hard as rocks. He was the most incredible lover, and after having sex with him in a parked car at the beach, I discovered something a little disturbing about myself. My car was parked right next to a truck, and the whole time we were making love, I knew we were being watched. I think that's what made it so exciting. When we finished, the guys in the truck applauded and I didn't feel the least embarrassed.

I lost Audry when I tried to introduce him to my other passion, Summit workshops. I took him to an introductory lecture one night, and to put it mildly, he was not impressed. We never really saw each other again after that night, but the exhibitionism that surfaced while I was with him would later lead me down strange and desperate paths.

Shortly after the Audry thing ended, I moved out of the residence, got my furniture from storage, and took a three-bedroom ranch-style house in San Mateo with three other people from Summit. It was a great place, and whenever we were all home together, we'd have a party—which turned out to be a rare occurrence because we all kept different hours. We used to call the place International House since we were all from different ethnic backgrounds. Phil was Korean, I was black, of course, Gayle was a white Southerner, and Alan was Jewish.

It was a good thing I got my furniture back, because when I lost the telephone sales job, I had to start selling my possessions to live and to pay for workshops. I abandoned the job search entirely because I'd decided to go on staff. All I had to do was convince Paul that I was ready, but I didn't seem to be having much luck. I wanted him to ask me and, although I was already treated like staff, he still hadn't. Then Paul announced his latest brainchild, "The Nine-Day Training." He called it the first intensive workshop ever, and made it a mandatory requirement for going on staff. The debut sessions were going to be held in Los Angeles, and tuition was a thousand dollars. But it seemed worth it because Paul assured us that it would finally blow out any fragments of old patterns that were still keeping us from fulfillment. I simply had to take it.

Assessing my own situation, I had to admit that I was still recovering from that nervous breakdown I'd experienced in the air force. I was also, to my surprise, still suffering several aftereffects of childhood abuse—anger and an inability to trust chief among them. I was painfully aware that I was still afraid to show what I considered my real face to the world, always hiding behind a smile and a giggle. And it was getting harder and harder to maintain the disguise. I needed to control every variable in every moment of every day to avoid cracking up. The nine-day session was just what I thought I needed to steer me in the right direction for the future. I had to sell my car to afford it, but I was absolutely certain that the wisdom I'd gain would be well worth it.

Even before the new workshop got underway, I had a feeling that things weren't going to turn out exactly as I had expected. I had already begun to see traits in my friends that disturbed me. All of a sudden, I got the feeling that they wanted to be on staff because they needed to be with Paul. They didn't really believe that they could ever translate what they had learned inside Summit to the outside world, so they were choosing to cut themselves off from it. I, on the other hand, had this nagging feeling that I belonged in the world and not some workshop monastery. I headed for L.A., hoping that things would look different when the workshop was over. They most certainly did. It was during the nine-day training workshop that I cut off all my hair for the first time. And not only was I looking different when I got back to San Francisco, I felt like my whole insides had been churned into butter. Believe it or not, I was in worse shape than when I had left.

The training had been the death knell of my participation at Summit. All my friends went on staff after we got back and wondered why I wasn't. They called and called after I stopped showing up at the Center. Somehow, I just felt that it was time for me to go. The magic safety net wasn't working for me anymore.

At first I thought the key to my post-Summit life was getting a different kind of job, and I found myself scouring the papers again, this time for work in the skin trade. The exhibitionism that had surfaced with Audry began to move to the front of the line in my thoughts about what to do with myself. Maybe, coupled with my desire to entertain, it would calm my restless spirit. I found myself auditioning for a porn film director, allowing him to take a Polaroid of me naked, then I made an appointment at a strip joint downtown.

Since I was a novice, the woman on the phone said that I had to come in and dance once for free just to prove that I was going to take the job. She claimed to have been burned too many times by girls who chickened out at the last minute. The first thing I noticed when I walked into her office was a life-sized poster of Blaze Starr. Blaze was a world-famous stripper and Baltimore celebrity. She owned a club in the red-light district of the city, and I'd seen her on

talk shows dozens of times. The boss lady warmed up to me immediately when she discovered that I knew of and admired her idol.

The club itself left a lot to be desired. Strippers danced on a
stage under a proscenium arch, and the audience consisted mainly
of derelicts who slept through the show. This wasn't exactly as I'd
imagined it. In my fantasies, I performed to a well-dressed and
appreciative audience like the ones in the movie *Gypsy*. When I
went inside to watch the girl on stage, I was shocked by her beauty.
I surveyed the comatose audience, unable to believe that they were
ignoring her.

After the strip was over, the boss lady led me backstage. I didn't
even recognize the girl I'd just seen dancing. In real life, she was
incredibly homely. She had rushed backstage and thrown on her
cat's-eye, Coke bottle–thick glasses to work on her latest costume
because she was being groomed for Vegas and needed at least seven
different outfits to break into the big time. What an illusion she had
created on stage. She was good. The boss was very proud of her.
Much like me, she had just walked in off the street one day.

The other girls at the club paled by comparison. They possessed neither the homely girl's skill nor her ambition. When they
danced, they got out of their clothes as fast as possible, then, lying
on the lip of the stage, simply spread their legs. They were a sad lot,
showing the mileage of the rough road they had traveled. My education in stripping continued way into the night. I had made an
impression on the boss, and deciding that she didn't need to audition me, she put me on the schedule for the next day and assigned
me to the other black stripper in her stable for my orientation.

The black stripper she assigned me to gave me a glimpse of
what a stripper's life would be. "Give up your day friends," she
warned. "You're a night person now and your day friends won't
understand." She gave me a wig, because men who watch strippers
prefer their girls with hair. Dancing naked is different than dancing
with clothes on, so don't jump around, she told me. Be nice to the
cops, they get to come back to the dressing room whenever they
want, and you can develop a nice little side business turning tricks
for your regular customers.

After that night, I knew I wouldn't find whatever it was I was
looking for on that stage. I left that night and never even called to

say I wasn't coming in. For the moment, I was back in control of my faculties and I chided myself when I got home, wondering what I had been thinking of to even consider stripping.

The calls from my friends at Summit were still coming. I decided I needed to get out of town to figure out on my own how to live in the world the way we lived at the Center with Paul. Besides, it was time for the rent, and I had only a couple of hundred dollars to my name, so I skipped out on my roommates in the middle of the afternoon without even saying good-bye. Since I wanted to be in show business, I might as well go all the way to Hollywood.

This bird had to fly. I had learned a lot at Summit. It was like a crash course in life. All the things my parents couldn't teach me, Paul had put into those workshops. I had all the information I would need to take me where I wanted to go, but that still didn't prevent this little chick from falling flat on her face the first time out of the nest.

When I touched down at LAX, there was no one there to greet me, and it suddenly occurred to me that I really didn't know much about Los Angeles. When I'd been there before, I was never in L.A. proper, I was always in the valley, West Hollywood, or Tarzana. I didn't know if these places were sections of the city or the suburbs outside. I didn't even know if Los Angeles had a downtown, but I was about to find out.

I hopped on a bus, and once we reached downtown L.A., I understood why I'd never heard of it. It was dirty and seedy, full of flophouse hotels. I can't imagine what the state of my mind was, but I walked into one of these fleabags and registered. The room was just six dollars a night. A neon sign blinked right outside the window in my dirty room. Again, the bathroom was down the hall, but even after I showered, I couldn't feel clean in this place. That evening after dinner, I went to the TV room and watched the fuzzy picture with a bunch of sleeping drunks, sitting in the very rear of the room, afraid to let anyone sit behind me. That night I was awakened by what I thought was the sound of gunshots.

The next morning at breakfast, I shared the want ads with the few men in the place interested in looking for work, then headed for the state employment office. I wanted a job, and fast, and was even willing to be a nurse, but there was no way for me to get a license so far from the capital. I spotted a counter at the employment office just for vets, took my place in line, and waited my turn. It was the only time I had ever tried to apply for any kind of public assistance in my life.

The pleasant-looking black man behind the desk was very solicitous as I poured out my heart, recounting my sordid job history since getting out of the service. He took my hand and told me that I needed time to relax and get my head together before I'd even know what I wanted to do. Finally, he referred me to what he said was a nonprofit agency that dealt with GIs having trouble readjusting to civilian life. He even called the guy there to tell him I was coming over. "Remember, ask for Mel Jackson," he reminded me as I started off. "Don't speak to anyone else, only Mel. We got to take care of a fine sister like you." I thanked him profusely and sincerely as I left.

The office I was sent to was a mass of partitions. I rounded a corner and encountered a young man who asked if he could help me. A look of disappointment crossed his face when I asked for Mel, but he promptly got up and led me to the back of the office. Mel, a leathery-skinned black man with a bad complexion, was in his own messy little cubicle. I was struck by how much he looked like the photographer Gordon Parks.

I introduced myself and extended my hand. He took it but remained seated. He recognized my name right away and asked me to tell my story again. He, too, expressed great compassion, offering to help me get out of the dump where I was living. He wouldn't even let me go back there alone. I spent the rest of the afternoon sitting in the front of the office waiting for him to get off work. At the end of the day, Mel rolled himself into the lobby and for the first time I realized he was a cripple. That wheelchair was a souvenir of Vietnam, I thought to myself, trying not to stare. Outside awaiting us was his customized Lincoln Continental. The disability checks must be awesome, I imagined.

I checked out of the rattrap downtown and threw my bag into the backseat of Mel's car. Then we headed off to Fat Burgers Restaurant, where he told me he'd once seen Diana Ross sitting on a stool at this very counter. Aware of my aspiration to stardom, Mel added, "One day someone will be saying they saw you sitting on that stool." I blushed.

Then Mel got serious. He figured that I needed a stake to give me some time to consider my options. In order to get a stake, though, you needed money to invest. I wasn't sure I was following the conversation, and he must have noticed my puzzled look. He asked how much cash I actually had on me, and when I told him about a hundred and fifty dollars, he sighed heavily. To get into the game he was talking about would take about five hundred. With five hundred, I could buy some cocaine, split it, dilute it, and turn my five hundred into about two grand. Two thousand dollars would give me room to breathe. Today I'm shocked that I didn't just get up and leave. I actually considered buying and selling cocaine.

Later, after we left the restaurant, Mel offered me a hit of cocaine, which I declined. Next, he decided to prove to me what a social elixir this white powder could be. Pulling the car to the curb at a bus stop, he asked a pretty blond girl if she wanted to party. She hopped into the car and snorted a line of the stuff after pouring it from a little vial as Mel circled the block. When we got back to the bus stop, she thanked him and resumed her spot under the canopy. "See how easy it is," Mel said and smiled. Although I continued to refuse his drugs, he took me to a much more expensive hotel that night.

I thought he had taken care of the bill and settled into my new, clean bed worry-free. The next morning I awoke well rested and feeling good until I passed the front desk on the way to breakfast only to be asked to pay the bill. I parted with twenty-two dollars of what little money I had and spent the rest of the day watching game shows and soaps on the TV in my room. Mel showed up as promised, this time revealing another part of the plan. I needed more ready cash. He knew men, white men, who would pay for certain services. It wasn't any big deal, according to him. Sometimes they'd pay big money just to look at you.

"Stand up and take off your clothes," he ordered. "I have to inspect the merchandise." I stood and removed what I was wearing. He beckoned for me to come closer, and when I did he leaned forward, wrapping his lips around one of my nipples.

"And just what do you think you're doing?" I demanded sternly.

"I told you, I have to check out the goods!"

"I don't recall giving you permission to do that," I said, stepping back and putting on my clothes. He spun the wheels of his chair around and headed for the door, nonchalantly saying that he'd be in touch. Even after that episode I waited for him to return, but when I didn't hear from him for two days, I finally put it all together. Mel was a pimp, and the guy at the employment office was a spotter. They were trying to get me strung out and then turn me out. That nice guy at the employment agency must have been an expert at picking out women at the ends of their ropes. Mel was simply waiting for me to run out of money. Well, I wasn't waiting around for that.

I found the number for the YWCA in the Yellow Pages and got a room for fifteen dollars a day, including meals, and found a job selling ad space in a free newspaper. The boss really liked me, but I never found out if I would have been any good at the job because it was straight commission and I had run out of money. I was about to panic when who should call one day at the Y? You guessed it. Good old Mel. I had no idea how he tracked me down, but I figured he had his ways since lost women were his business.

"What happened to you?" he said, feigning concern. "I've been looking all over. You must be almost out of cash by now."

"Yes, I am," I replied.

"Well, I'm still willing to help you."

"No thanks," I shot back. "You left me in that expensive place so I'd eat up my cash. If I'd stayed there, I'd have been on the street days ago."

"Oh, I wouldn't have let that happen."

"Like hell you wouldn't," I muttered.

"Well," he concluded, "you know how to reach me."

"Yeah," I signed off, "good-bye."

I figured that I must have been a real mess. Why else would Mel have been so intent on finding me? I decided to take a walk to reflect on the last couple of weeks. I was in a strange town with no resources and no friends. The one time I'd reached out for help, two guys had tried to ruin me. As I walked around, I started looking at the people. Each time I passed someone I considered poor, I did a quick comparison. Here I was with the last fifteen dollars in my pocket the only thing between me and the street and I still didn't look like these poor people. I knew I didn't feel like them either. That's when I discovered that poverty was just a state of mind, and I knew what I had to do.

I went back to the Y, found the pay phone, and made a collect call. The operator made the connection, and the party on the other end accepted. I took a deep breath and spoke one of the most difficult sentences I've ever uttered: "Hi, Mom. I want to come home."

On June 27, 1979, Muhammad Ali announced his first retirement from the ring. Funny how Muhammad was attempting to end his boxing career just as I was headed back to the ring. I didn't know it, but I was rushing headlong into the fight of my life.

10

RADIO DAZE

I was walking down the street of my old neighborhood one day, headed for the bus stop, when Miss Alice, one of the older women in the community, stepped out on her porch. "Robin," she called, squinting to avoid the sun, "is that you? Girl, it sure is good to see you. You're one of the ones that made it." I knew then that I had a job to do.

—1979

In the summer of 1979, a few weeks shy of a full year after I'd arrived in California, I climbed aboard a Greyhound bus, found an empty seat near the back, and bid farewell to the City of the Angels. As some sort of self-inflicted punishment for fucking up my life, I'd chosen the most uncomfortable form of transportation possible for my return trip across the country.

Asking my mother for the money to get back to Baltimore hadn't been easy—especially since a while back I'd asked her for the money to come home for a visit, intending all along to use it for tuition for a Summit workshop. I'd lied, and she knew it, and her only condition this time was that I really did use the money to come home. Believe it or not, I had a few conditions of my own to lay down before I'd accept the money.

"Look," I told her, "I admit that I need your help, and I have every intention of paying you back. But I don't ever want to hear how you saved me or how you knew all along that it was a mistake to go to California or that I owe you. If you can't promise, then don't bother to send the money. I'd rather stay here and live on the street."

We each gave our word, and the deal was closed. There was no way to describe the relief that swept through me as I put down the phone. The cavalry was coming. I was down to my last fifteen dollars, but help was on the way. Just like in the TV ads, I picked up the cash at Western Union the next day. To her credit, my mother kept her word—that is, until it didn't matter anymore. Just this past summer, she finally broke down and mentioned for the first time how she'd had to save me from my West Coast catastrophe.

As the bus that would bring me home pulled out of the station, and my exodus was under way, I reflected on my year in California. I had nothing to show for it, literally. No career. No furniture. No car. No money. I'd lost everything, including my credit cards. I'd even borrowed against a life insurance policy I'd taken out in the air force. Even my little retirement nest egg was gone.

I knew I was going back to Baltimore to get serious about life again. There was going to be no more fooling around. I had every intention of hitting the ground running when I got home, so I decided to treat this four-day bus trip as my last vacation for a good long while, and fortunately met up with the perfect traveling companions. There was a core group of six of us—a gun-toting Texan, his girlfriend, three young guys, and me. I even reached into my overnight bag and pulled out the ounce of pot that had been languishing there for a year. We'd smoke the marijuana while the bus was on the road, then we'd jump off at every stop, find a bar, and down a couple of beers. We caroused all the way east, holding the other passengers hostage to our merrymaking.

The last day of the trip was really sad. The pot was gone. We were all nearing home, aware that we'd left with great expectations and were returning with our tails between our legs. We'd already lost the Texan and his girl. The next member of our band departed in Ohio, another in West Virginia, still another in Pennsylvania. I spent the final hours of the trip alone, contemplating what it would be like living with my family again.

My brother, Junior, picked me up at the bus station, and as we drove through the old neighborhood, I was saddened to see that it had grown even more rundown. I didn't recognize many of the people on the street, and I didn't hear the sound of children playing. Hope had moved out, and despair had settled in. It was miserable, and it made me miserable—but not as miserable as my mother's gasp made me when she opened the front door.

"Oh, my God." She was staring straight at my head. "What happened to your hair? My poor baby looks like an orphan!"

In an instant I was back to playing by Quivers' rules. Instinctively, my hands flew in shame to cover my closely cropped Afro. I'd forgotten the unspoken rule according to which a black woman never shows her kinky hair to the world. Hadn't my mother taken that big plastic comb to my head enough to show me how awful those kinks were? Didn't I remember sitting by the stove, having my ears and the back of my neck burned by a hot iron comb she'd just taken off the heat so that no one would see what my real hair looked like? Hadn't she taken me to a dark, smelly "beauty parlor," replacing the comb with chemicals to fry my scalp?

My mother's reaction startled me because I hadn't thought to anticipate it. After all, the people I knew in California loved my hair that way. And no longer having to put a hot comb or chemicals on my scalp gave me a feeling of empowerment and freedom. With that one gasp, my mother's behavior activated years of programming that said that natural black attributes were ugly, and that it was my duty to do everything possible to mask them. I'd soon find myself in one of those beauty parlors again, applying chemicals to my tenacious kinks.

Willing to do anything to avoid sitting around my mother's house, I bit the bullet one more time, grabbed my Maryland nursing license, and started my job search with the firm resolve that it wouldn't be forever. There were two ways to go—back to the Maryland Institute of Emergency Medicine, where I'd worked in Shock Trauma before the air force, or someplace new. Someplace new was appealing because my buddies from Shock Trauma had all moved on, and I knew it wouldn't be the same. My old college friend, Kathi, was a supervisor of nursing at a Baltimore hospital, and I was sure I could work for her. There was also an opening in the Surgical

Intensive Care Unit of Johns Hopkins University Hospital. I decided on Hopkins because it was different and because they did open-heart surgery. I'd never worked in that area and, while my youthful love of the new and difficult had faded, I was curious to see what open-heart surgery patients were like. Novelty might be just the thing to get me through the ordeal of working in a hospital again.

Once I got a job, it was easier to cross the threshold of my parents' home. I was a productive citizen again. I paid rent to my mother, and as Paul would have recommended, began to settle accounts with those I'd left in the lurch. I set up new payment schedules with all the credit card companies I owed money to, and found out that it would take years to ever get another card. Then I contacted my ex-housemates and other friends in California I still owed money to and worked out deals with them. I wanted to wipe the slate clean, just like Paul had taught me. This time, my fresh start would live up to its name.

Next on the list was finding a meaningful career outside nursing. I'd tried sales and hadn't liked it. Retraining was probably a wise idea, but I didn't feel that I had the patience for four more years of college, and the last thing I wanted was a master's degree in nursing. So I picked up the Yellow Pages and let my fingers do the walking through the schools section. I thought I liked working in an office, so I wrote down the number of a business school. I loved clothes, and added the number of a fashion school that offered courses in becoming a buyer to the list. Then I noticed an ad for a broadcasting school and remembered the terrifically animated conversations I'd had with radio people while trying to sell them tapes. Radio. Radio. Why not give it a try? I made appointments at all three places. As it happened, my first one was with the broadcasting school.

The Broadcasting Institute of Maryland was located just across the city line in a large house that had been converted into classrooms, offices, and studios. The head of enrollment, Mark Clark, gave me a tour of the facility and administered what seemed to me a pretty simple aptitude test. Then we began to chat. Mark was completely entertaining, and there was something about the way he talked about broadcasting that made it really attractive. He seemed to feel exactly the way I wanted to about what he did for a living.

Mark explained that my education at BIM wouldn't be all fun. There were practical reasons for going with the program too. Many of the faculty were working broadcasters at Baltimore radio and TV stations, and other professionals visited as guest lecturers, so I'd be able to network while attending classes. The hours were ideal. I could go to school in the morning and work the evening shift at the hospital full-time. Broadcasting had hit a home run! I never even bothered to keep the other appointments.

Things really seemed to be breaking my way. I was enrolled in school and continuing my hospital orientation while waiting for classes to start. But this tranquillity would soon be interrupted by an unexpected phone call from Virginia. Uncle Leroy had just suffered a stroke and been rushed to the hospital. My parents left immediately for Newport News to make sure he was being properly cared for.

Once there, it became quite clear to them that Leroy, who'd been a widower for years, would need constant care after he was discharged. The doctors at the hospital recommended a nursing home setting, but my father insisted on bringing his brother home with him to Baltimore. That was one trip Uncle Leroy would never make. He died just as the stretcher was arriving. My father phoned to insist that I attend the funeral. That call was totally unnecessary. I would have come no matter what.

I didn't even recognize the little old man lying in Leroy's coffin and I didn't cry at his funeral. My uncle and I had said our goodbyes a year before. I knew that he had been living in misery and I was glad his suffering was over. My one lingering regret is that I didn't ask for anything that belonged to him. All my father's living siblings converged on the town and began squabbling over Leroy's meager belongings. Refusing to be a part of any of it, I insisted I wanted nothing. So I went back to Baltimore empty-handed and sad, only to find I had a new fight on my hands.

Although the rule at Johns Hopkins was that permanent shifts were only given on the basis of seniority, I had only taken the job after being assured that I'd be given a steady schedule so that I could go back to school. Now, with school just two weeks away, the new schedule had me working both days and nights. When I pointed out the error to the head nurse, she claimed that she would never have made such a deal. I thanked her for her time, quit on the spot, and was immediately given my way. After all, a hospital down the street was giving away free cars to lure nurses onto their staff.

With school and my permanent evening shift, I was out of the house from seven in the morning until midnight, which made living with my parents relatively bearable. I had to admit, though, that things had changed while I was away. For one thing, my father no longer worked. He'd taken an early retirement on disability after having had a couple of heart attacks and now suffered from chronic angina. And in the purest sense, he wasn't a drunk anymore.

While I was in the air force, he'd bottomed out one night, woken up in his car, and realized that if he didn't get help right then and there, drinking would kill him. Without even bothering to go home, he went right back to work and arranged to enter a thirty-day detox program. Once on the phone he'd told me he stopped attending AA meetings because he didn't need them to stay sober. I prefer to think that he couldn't handle one of the twelve steps—the one that says you have to ask forgiveness of those you've hurt in the past. My father had never acknowledged what happened between us. He must have had a terrible time living with his demons because as soon as he found a way to turn over his supply of booze to somebody else, he started drinking again. Like the neighborhood, he was just plain worn out. I felt sort of sad for him, and I'd occasionally let him hug me now, always being careful not to transmit the wrong message.

With the dawning realization of how far away I could fly from them, both my parents were trying hard to please me. They'd even taken to waiting with the car to drive me home when I got off work at the end of the night shift. Granted, I was giving them more than enough rent to cover the entire mortgage payment every month, but the additional money bought me additional services. All my meals were prepared for me, and my dirty clothes found their way back to my closets and drawers miraculously clean.

I thought nothing of letting the newspaper I'd been reading drop to the floor because I knew one of my "servants" would happily pick it up. An enormous anger surfaced whenever I was at home, and I used it to bend my family to my will. Finally, I was the chosen one I had so desperately wanted to be as a kid. I knew I was behaving like an absolute brat, demanding to be waited on hand and foot, but I couldn't stop myself.

When I was home, I was treated like a pampered child. During the day, though, I sat in a classroom of eighteen- to twenty-year-old kids, whose youth was a constant reminder that I had a lot of lost time to make up for. Again I turned to another lesson of Paul's and gave 100 percent of myself every moment I was in class. Realizing that maturity could give me an advantage, I used my life experience, raw talent, and discipline to attract the attention of those in charge.

Almost from the start, John Jeppi, president and owner of BIM, pegged me as a future star and took me under his wing. But he also felt that he'd noticed a glaring flaw in me that could jeopardize my brilliant career. I'll always remember him telling me, "Robin, you have the potential to be big in this industry, but you've got to get that incessant nervous giggle under control. It can only hold you back."

Mr. Jeppi's misgivings about my laugh notwithstanding, he did everything he could to launch my career. I can actually draw a straight line from where I am now right back to that school, for it was at BIM that I first met Denise Oliver. Every Friday morning, a panel of experts from a given field would convene to answer students' questions. On this particular occasion, I was chosen to moderate a group discussion of women in broadcasting. Denise was one of the guests. I couldn't even tell you who the other women were. Denise was the one I was dying to meet.

At that time, Denise was program director of 98-Rock in Baltimore, one of the most successful album rock stations in the country. For a woman to have achieved her level of success in a virtually all-male area of radio was impressive, to say the least. Because of it, she'd achieved national recognition, and in my book, this made her a need-to-know person. I planned to do the most excellent job I could that day, and the fact that I was moderating guaranteed that I would get more than just a chance to ask questions. So imagine how disappointed in myself I was when Denise and I wound up arguing about music at the brief reception after the program. The incident demonstrated to me that I needed to learn to control my compulsion to argue every possible issue. Still, I followed up Denise's appearance with a thank-you note and added her name to the list of contacts I wanted to keep in touch with after graduation.

I have to thank Mr. Jeppi for my first two jobs in radio. He had made sure to establish relations with all the small-market radio station owners in the area, and whenever they were looking for talent, those owners called the school. W100, a little station in Carlisle, Pennsylvania, was looking for a morning-drive news anchor, and Mr. Jeppi submitted my name along with those of three other students. I still wasn't fully aware that I had a major plus going for me—a good speaking voice. Aside from a couple of patients mentioning it years before, the subject never came up. But now, whenever I spoke into a microphone, people sat up and took notice. Among those who did was the manager of W100, who made me a job offer on the strength of an audition tape I had made in one of his tiny studios. Even before graduation, I'd been offered a full-time radio position as the news director of a small daytime station at one hundred twenty dollars a week. I asked for time to think about it, and spent the drive back to Baltimore mulling things over.

By the time I hit the city, pros and cons were rattling around in my head like loose change at the bottom of a purse. Granted, this was a real radio job, but it was in the middle of nowhere. I could get buried up there and never be heard from again. It was a good place to get experience, but if I was patient and waited until I graduated, I might possibly land a job in Baltimore. One hundred and twenty dollars a week wasn't much money, and I had financial commitments I couldn't ignore—like the car loan my father had co-signed with me. Even working just four days a week as a nurse, I was clearing twenty thousand a year.

Then there was the station itself. W100 wasn't just small market, it was ramshackle. The front lawn served as the parking lot, and the day I was there torrential rains had turned it into a sea of mud. The W100 sign hung at a funny angle on a broken chain above the entrance. All in all, it looked more like a haunted house than a radio station.

I had pretty much decided against taking the job when, on a

whim, I decided to drop by BIM to see if anyone was around. Spotting Tim Duff, a faculty member, I went into his office and was warmly greeted. Everyone there always seemed to be in a good mood.

"Can I talk to you?" I asked, falling into a chair across from his desk.

"Sure," he replied. "What's wrong?"

"I just got offered a job."

"Well, that's great!"

"No, it's not," I replied. When he asked why, I recited my litany of complaints. "So," I concluded, "I think I should wait for a better opportunity, don't you?"

To my surprise, he said no. I thought he hadn't been listening and asked him again. Sure enough, he was urging me to accept. When I asked him why, he answered my question with a question.

"Do you want to work in radio?"

"Yes," I said, "but—"

"Then take the job."

"Why?"

"Because," he told me, "it's a job in radio."

The next day, acting on Tim Duff's advice, I quit nursing and accepted my first radio job. The nurses in my unit who had laughed behind my back at my broadcast dreams were astonished. While I'd been at Johns Hopkins, I'd gotten an on-air internship at a local rock station. I taped two newscasts for the afternoon-drive show, and the hospital staff piped the station to the patients' rooms over the intercom, so while we all worked, we listened to me on the radio. A lot of my fellow nurses had made fun of my ambitions, but now, with just a snap of the fingers, I was vindicated.

But I was far from brimming with self-confidence. I appreciated the fact that the move I was making was risky, not to say impulsive, and I'd gotten in trouble by being impulsive. But I couldn't let past mistakes determine my future. If I wasn't going to bet on myself, who would? So I packed a bag, and on a beautiful April morn set out for a haunted house in the Pennsylvania sticks. I was on the road to Radioville.

Luckily, Ed Harris, the guy I was replacing, was at the studio when I arrived to show me the ropes. W100 was a full-service radio station which hit the air at sunrise and shut down before the sun set. In between, they played middle-of-the-road music and offered half-hourly, five-minute newscasts from 6 A.M. to 10 A.M. and a full half hour of news at noon followed by a swap-and-shop show before the afternoon-drive return to regular programming. In the two hours between my morning duties and the noon news, which would be my last broadcast of the day, Ed took me on the local rounds. We stopped at the police station to see who'd been arrested for drunken driving the night before and at the hospital to check on who'd been admitted. My original doubts about the job came flooding back when I got a clear grasp of the scope and depth of my reportorial duties.

Ed decided that we should do the noon news together that day, his last at the station before he moved on to a station in Harrisburg, so he called the afternoon newscaster and told him he could come in late. It was a W100 tradition that the morning and afternoon anchors handled the noon news together, trading stories. I had only been on the air live once in my life, and that was as a lark for about fifteen seconds during a BIM field trip to a small-market station in Delaware. The butterflies in my stomach were massing the first time Ed threw it to me. I could hardly hear myself over the beating of their wings, so convinced was I that I'd be fired the second we were off the air.

Instead, people from the sales office came running up the stairs to tell me how good I was, and Ed was so impressed, he took me aside and told me, "Robin, whatever you do, don't get discouraged and leave. The bosses at my new station in Harrisburg are thinking of expanding the news department. I think I can offer you a job in a couple of weeks." When I tried to thank him, Ed kept repeating, "Don't leave."

After spending the night at a motel outside town, I started my first day as news director and morning anchor of W100. I must have been incredibly nervous because I can't remember one single thing about being on the air that Friday. What I do remember vividly is the phone call I got from Ed, telling me his new bosses in Harrisburg wanted to meet with me that very afternoon. I barely knew the way to Carlisle, and here I was trekking to Harrisburg, capital of the great state of Pennsylvania.

Two P.M. of my first professional day in radio found me sitting in the office of Lloyd Roach, general manager of WCMB, Harrisburg, a top-forty AM station in a medium market. Again, I was told that I had potential and was offered an opportunity at sixty dollars more a week than I was making in Carlisle. I couldn't refuse. Given the fact that I would be leaving W100 after one day on the job, I wanted to give them two weeks' notice, but Lloyd said it was now or never. So I took it.

Ed was the news director and morning anchor at WCMB, but he gave me his ten o'clock newscasts so that I could sharpen my anchoring skills. The rest of the day I tracked stories at the state house, at city hall, anywhere news was happening. It was more fun than I could ever have imagined. I never stopped working, day or night, and loved every second of it.

This was a while ago, remember. Harrisburg was next to Three Mile Island, site of the worst nuclear accident in U.S. history. I got to tour the facility and report on how the cleanup was proceeding. I stood in the center of rioting Cuban refugees from the 1980 Mariel boatlift, who were protesting their internment at the army fort in Indian Town Gap. One on one, I interviewed George Bush, who was campaigning against Ronald Reagan for the Republican presidential nomination.

On the air, I worked opposite a crotchety radio old-timer named Mac, who liked to rattle me by segueing to me for the news with a question that I was supposed to respond to with a snappy reply. Initially I felt intimidated. Before long, though, I was actually looking forward to the on-air jousting, and soon listeners were beginning to respond. Once when the WCMB softball team was playing the Harrisburg fire department, a firefighter came up to Mac and told him, "She really got you with a good one today!" Mac bristled, but I knew he knew it was always a good sign when people mentioned a bit. My fear of being lost in the sticks wasn't to be realized either. Joe Templeton of ABC radio went to the effort of calling to say that he'd heard me while driving through Harrisburg and thought I had a good sound.

Not only was I testing my wings, but I was having the fun I'd hoped for. There was a real family atmosphere at the station. We all met every Thursday for happy hour at the local Holiday Inn, and I'd made a few close WCMB friends. Candy, a young deejay on our FM station, and I used to spend every Friday night watching "The Dukes of Hazzard." It wasn't that we liked the show's content, we just wanted to see Bo and Luke Duke take off their shirts. When I realized why I was addicted to the show, I knew I could never again get on a guy's case for watching "Charlie's Angels."

I never made it into an apartment in Harrisburg. Instead, to save money, I moved into the Y. It was strange explaining to the many refugees from domestic violence who were my fellow lodgers just what I was doing there, but I had my own bathroom, and anyway, I spent what little free time I had sleeping or with my friends. On the salary I was making, I'd barely managed to keep up with my bills, but whenever times were tough, I'd just tell myself that one day somebody was going to pay me what I was worth, and I'd carry on. Often I didn't have enough money for a real meal, but since I wasn't one to ask anybody for anything, I made do on candy bars until the next paycheck.

After I'd been in Harrisburg for six months, I was beginning to feel that I'd learned all I could and was about to start working on a demo tape. Once again, my luck held steady, and I got a call from Mike Majors, the news director at WFBR in Baltimore, whom Mr. Jeppi had introduced me to before I left BIM. Two weeks later, I was sitting in Mike's office, being offered a job. I had made it back to a decent-sized market in six months' time.

My hard work was paying off. WFBR, a civic institution, was the official broadcast home of the Baltimore Orioles. Johnny Walker, the morning man, was something of a legend himself, although I wasn't particularly familiar with his work. He had a reputation for being irreverent and for being a prima donna, although I hardly saw him the whole time I was there. He left immediately after his shift, jumping into his Corvette and jetting off. He was a radio star.

I'd been hired by WFBR to do midday consumer reports with a new deejay named Bob Moke on the strength of the banter Mac and I had perfected in Harrisburg. WFBR was looking for freer interplay between the jock and the newsperson after 10 A.M., and it was now my task to loosen Bob up during my four reports. Bob loved music, but he wasn't a talker. His style was to introduce me and immediately shut off his mike. To get his attention, I started planting the name Bob in my copy. If I was creating a hypothetical situation involving a man, the guy's name was automatically Bob. If it was a child, Bobby. I also resorted to an old trick of Mac's and asked him questions on air to segue into my report.

Bob's and my on-air rapport was finally beginning to develop, and things at work were generally great. Feeling like a real professional at last, I dressed in business suits, arrived on the stroke of 9 A.M., and took pleasure in working with experienced broadcasters who respected what I did. Changing careers successfully had given me a sense of accomplishment, and I could see a bright future for myself in a field I loved and was committed to. Not so the hero whose brilliant light had shown me the way thus far.

The news started like a ripple in a pond and was now rushing toward shore like a tidal wave in my head. Muhammad Ali wanted to fight again. He was thirty-eight years old and hadn't looked good in the ring for a long time. The Leon Spinks rout notwithstanding, he no longer belonged in trunks. Muhammad belonged in a suit, or a BarcaLounger, or a pool float—not in the ring. But here he was, back again.

There were whispers that something was wrong with him. Was he punch-drunk? Was there no one around him who would tell him the truth? I felt so sad for him. I was not unfamiliar with feeling as alone as he must feel. Well, I told myself, if Muhammad has to do this, I have to be with him, and I bought tickets for the closed-circuit telecast of the fight at the Baltimore Civic Center.

It probably wouldn't have mattered who was in the ring with Ali that late October night, but it so happened that the opponent was Ali's former sparring partner and the best fighter in the ring at the time, Larry Holmes. I'd never attended a boxing event before, and I dragged my brother Junior's girlfriend, Mary, along so that I wouldn't have to go alone.

It was a daunting crowd, electric with the frenzied energy of a tank of sharks driven wild by the smell of blood in the water. To me this was an historic occasion, but to the rest of the crowd it was just another fight. Some of the audience thought that they were going to see Ali perform another miracle, but most were sure they would be witnessing a slaughter and couldn't wait for the circus to begin. The mood of the crowd radically altered after the first few punches, for it became instantly clear that we were present at the passing of a giant.

Round after round, Ali came out for the bell and for three minutes endured an incredible beating. Pain was etched across that same face that had once snarled and taunted his prey and was now hidden behind his gloves. As soon as Muhammad tried to protect his head, Larry pounded at his ribs, causing him to double over. Tears streamed down my face, but I refused to turn away from the screen. I believed Muhammad would have wanted me to see this too. Losing is ugly, he was showing me, and going into a fight with no chance of winning is the worst and most sacrificial loss of all.

During the tenth round, one of Ali's trainers threw in the towel, and I exhaled at last. Now the audience had found their voices and were complaining loudly about being ripped off. I just wanted to escape. As we descended the stairs to the street, Mary started to denigrate Muhammad for his poor performance. "At least he had the courage to do it," I shouted. "You think it was easy, taking that beating?" My future sister-in-law didn't speak for the rest of the trip home.

It wasn't going to be long before I'd understand the value of knowing yourself and knowing your opponent before going into battle. Raw talent and lightning-quick reflexes wouldn't always be enough. Sometimes you have to train, and train hard, to be ready. Other times you have to fall back and develop a strategy before you can go forward. And even when you've prepared the best you can, you might still lose. It's how well you come back that counts.

All things considered, life had been relatively easy for me—no heavyweight losses I couldn't recoup, no knockdowns I hadn't been able to dodge. But I had no idea what was ahead or how much Muhammad's lessons of courage and conviction would mean to me in the future, because I was planning on staying where I was for quite a while. That's when Denise Oliver, who was now in Washington, began calling me to talk about teaming me up with an unusual new deejay named Howard Stern. From out of the blue, fate was once again summoning me on.

11

HOT BUTTONS

*A listener brought his two "sisters" down to the station to "meet"
Howard. One of the women was particularly genial, so Howard
and producer "Earth Dog" Fred Norris made love to her on the
studio floor. (Newswoman Robin Quivers, audibly upset by these
goings-on, was unable to complete one of her twice hourly newscasts.)*

—City Paper, *April 2, 1982*

Denise was so sure that Howard and I would make a great team that
following a brief private conversation with him after he and I had
talked on the phone, she extended her hand and welcomed me
aboard. In a wild reversal of what had happened to me in the air
force, I was legitimately going to be paid two thousand dollars more
than my salary was supposed to be. At an earlier meeting Denise
had said that the job paid twenty thousand dollars a year, but the
station had budgeted just eighteen thousand for the newsperson.
Since she had quoted the wrong figure, she decided that I should
get the larger amount. It wasn't like I was going to be swimming in
money, but Denise was being fair, and I considered that a good basis
on which to start our new endeavor.

Then I realized that I had to go back to Baltimore to resign from a job I liked and had held for less than six months. That wasn't going to be easy, because in my short time at WFBR I felt that I'd become an integral part of the staff. It turned out that most of the afternoon crew were genuinely happy for me, even though they were sorry to see me go. My bosses were a different story. They refused to match DC101's salary offer, but they tried to talk me out of leaving anyway. They swore to me that I'd never be heard from again after falling into the rock radio news pit, where there was little credibility and no recognition.

I had to admit that there might be some truth to their admonitions. This was another risky move. It was a spur-of-the-moment, totally impulsive decision, but if it turned out to be a mistake, I figured I'd work my way out of it. After all, hadn't Mike Wallace of "60 Minutes" once emceed a game show? And my bosses at WFBR didn't know something I did. Howard Stern was going to be phenomenally successful. I knew it the moment I heard his tape. I was going to be the newswoman on this incredibly popular morning-drive show in a top ten market.

While I thought I was going to be furiously clutching the threads of Howard's coattails and basking in the warmth of the reflected glow of his success, he was thinking he'd found a full collaborator. He had always envisioned a show in which the personality, not the music, was the draw. He wanted to be that personality, but he also knew that he couldn't do it alone. Four hours was too much time for one person to fill, no matter how talented they were, and would only lead to burnout. Now he was looking for a few complementary co-workers to help carry the ball or keep it rolling—whatever was necessary. That's what he felt he was getting from me in that one phone conversation. Although I didn't quite appreciate it at the time, I was about to become a part of Howard's grand design.

Once my private studio was completed, Howard and I seriously began to work on our on-air relationship. And that wasn't easy, because we were no longer face-to-face. My studio was right next door to his, and there was a huge window between the two, but the deejay booth was designed so that he sat at a control panel with his back toward me. He also didn't have full control of when I went on the air because I had to flip a switch before my microphone would work. I figured the best time to flip that switch was right at news time—even though I was sitting in the studio listening to the show or to music while looking over my copy up to ten minutes before I went on. I got a real kick out of Howard's antics on the air. If he noticed me laughing and reacting, he'd motion to me to turn on my mike.

Howard really wanted me to jump into the show whenever I was around, and I just didn't get it. He'd track me down in my office after the show to tell me, "Hey, Robin, I think you're really great on the air." I'd thank him profusely but in a way that said please stop because I was uncomfortable with compliments.

My tactics didn't seem to work, since he kept on insisting, "No, really. You're quick and spontaneous, and you have a great laugh. So why don't you just put on your microphone as soon as you come into the studio?" I protested that I'd only get in the way. "Oh, no," he replied. "You're great at just chiming in. Say the first thing that comes into your head. You have great instincts. And if you just think something's funny, go ahead and laugh."

Howard always thought that Denise was behind my reluctance to be on the air with him, but that wasn't it at all. In my experience, morning men were all quirky. As far as I was concerned, one day he might want me to chime in and the next day he wouldn't. That kind of erratic behavior could've sent my needle right into the red zone, so I was simply trying to avoid problems. Howard didn't know it at the time, but I was protecting him from my irrational temper. I still needed to control everything, and things were going too well to rock the boat.

In that tussle, Howard's will prevailed. He kept nagging me and nagging me until I finally started doing what he asked. I moved into the show gradually at first, turning on the mike only when I was sure I wanted to respond to something. Even this wasn't enough for Howard. He didn't want my evaluations, he wanted my spontaneous reactions. Finally, I just gave in and flipped on the switch whenever I was in the studio. Soon, he was urging me to type faster so that I could get back to the studio quicker. I had never felt so wanted before.

As we were delighting in the joys of our newfound association, the person responsible for bringing us together spent a lot of time trying to shave off our rough edges. Denise had been around and she had experienced a lot of success with the kind of radio that was on at the time, the kind of radio that fits a format and provides the listener with consistency. Howard's brand of radio was diametrically opposed to all the rules and tenets to which Denise wanted us to adhere. As a result, she wound up playing the strict schoolmarm to our wild bunch, and when her attempts to corral the two of us failed, she began to concentrate all of her efforts on Howard alone. Howard found all those closed-door sessions with Denise grueling, but he was convinced that what he was doing would work and figured if he just kept explaining himself, she'd eventually catch on.

I was relieved when she stopped including me in the meetings. Without any direct knowledge of where she wanted us to go, I was free to pick my own course and decided to become the best darn sidekick Howard could have. To do that, I needed to know everything about him, but he wasn't about to sit for hours of interviews, so I attached myself to him like a barnacle. After the show, we'd have lunch together. I'd spend my time driving home replaying that morning's show in my head, figuring out how to respond to his outrageous quips. Once I was inside the house, I'd call him and we'd spend hours bolstering each other's spirits, trading information, and discussing philosophy. It really didn't matter what the conversation was about. I got to see how his mind worked, and we began creating a history of our own. Next thing you know, Howard was no longer saying "I," but started every story with "Me and Robin."

The only possible obstacle I saw on the horizon was Howard's wife. We were already spending a lot of time together, but I needed to know everything about him, including what he was like at home with his loved ones. That meant getting to know Mrs. Stern. I was deathly afraid I wouldn't like her, which would have taken all the fun out of it. Meeting Alison Stern turned out to be much more than merely a relief. Right from the start, I thought I liked her more than I liked him. She was lively, vivacious, warm, and a lot of fun to be around in her own right. In a very short time, the three of us would become fast friends. Since they had moved to Washington just a couple of weeks before we went on the air, none of us knew more than a handful of people. We started seeing each other even on the weekends. And the audience was responding to "Howard and Robin" as a team.

Looking back, I can't imagine that anyone considered that silly show we were doing in Washington to be outrageous. But I guess it was kind of avant-garde to have "God" for a weatherman and to have him reveal that he had a gay lover named Bruce. Howard dragged the TV show "Leave It to Beaver" into the eighties with his daily "Beaver Breaks." One episode detailed the Beave being strip-searched by the Prince George's County Police. Going into the news he'd take a moment to describe my breasts, and it wasn't unusual for him to recreate the sound of some tragedy I was reporting on, as he did when I announced that Natalie Wood, the movie star, had fallen off a boat and drowned.

The show did follow a format of sorts. Every Monday was "What's Your Problem?," where Howard took phone calls and tried to deal with people's day-to-day crises. Tuesday was "Trivia and Rankouts," where we gave out prizes for the correct answers and the best "Yo Mama" jokes. Eventually we added a parody of "The Match Game" in which I played Brett Somers. We wound up with a group of regulars, three guys we found on the phones and eventually dubbed "The Think Tank," to take part in these Tuesday broadcasts. Wednesday and Thursday were sort of free-form, and Friday was "Dial-a-Date," where we matched up wackos with other wackos.

I was enjoying the whole thing, but I still had other ideas about my future until the day of the "Wedding of the Century." Howard convinced Denise to let us have a TV in the studio so that we could watch the wedding of Prince Charles and Lady Di while we were on the air. But instead of just watching it and commenting on it, we pretended that we were there. I was supposed to be in a booth above the crowd, Howard was the on-the-scene reporter, and Fred Norris, who had just joined us, was responsible for sound effects and also became any character we wanted to talk to. We pulled it off so well, people actually thought we were there. On that day I realized how powerful a medium of entertainment radio was. We could never have accomplished the same thing on TV. I was absolutely high after that show; it was exhilarating to be a part of something so creative.

I looked at Howard differently after that and thought, I want to be in this school for a long time to come. I was committed to making the radio show everything I was convinced it could be. That's when Howard and I had our incoherent meeting and formalized our alliance. From that day on I threw myself into "The Howard Stern Show" with total abandon. There was no time for a personal life—friends, men, or family. I ate, drank, and slept radio.

When we first started doing the show, I had no idea who I was on the air or how I should act. I decided I wanted to be like Barbara Walters. She could be serious and authoritative yet she wasn't above the frivolous celebrity interview. Barbara was my girl. But by the time of the "Wedding of the Century" show, I knew that I had to somehow bring more of me into the process. Howard was willing to bare his soul for the audience, warts and all. When he and Alison first decided to start a family, he instituted a pregnancy patrol, calling Alison on the air every morning to see if she was experiencing morning sickness. The more we worked together, the more I discovered I'd have to be willing to expose myself to a similar kind of public scrutiny.

I threw out all my old philosophies about radio and started from scratch. In our meetings, Denise always talked about holding an audience for fifteen minutes. I didn't see why we couldn't hold them all morning. I stopped the endless repetition of fire and accident reports. Who cared that there was a fire across town unless you were in it? I wanted everybody's ear, so I stopped repeating all but the most interesting stories. To do things my way, I needed more material, so along with the three newspapers a day I read before we went on the air, I added the *New York Post*, the *New York Times*, the *New York Daily News*, the *Philadelphia Inquirer*, the *Chicago Tribune*, and the *Los Angeles Times*. Sundays and Mondays were reading days. I scoured the huge Sunday papers and every national magazine and tabloid for things to talk about. My hands would be black from newsprint, and I had to give up nail polish because the black ink ruined the color.

Every afternoon on the way home from work I stopped at the newsstand to collect daily papers from around the country, and I listened to TV news programs well into the evening. People said that I sounded like I had been everywhere and done everything. I got a reputation for being uncannily well-informed. Even so, I had anxiety dreams that I'd forgotten to read the papers and then wound up on the air with nothing to say. In these dreams, I felt that I had let everyone down—Howard, Denise, and the listeners.

Not all my dreams portended doom, though. It was around this time that I had what came to be known as my ratings dream. The radio rating service, Arbitron, puts out what is fondly called "the book" four times a year. The first one that came out after our debut had started before we arrived, so it didn't really reflect our ratings performance, even though it indicated incredible growth in DC101's morning numbers. Everybody thought it was a fluke, and Denise was preparing us for a precipitous drop in our numbers after the curiosity wore off.

Then I had this dream in which Howard and I were called into the office of our dreaded general manager, Goff Lebar. He proceeded to ream us because he felt we were doing the wrong things to attract an audience. Howard was arguing his opinion, and I was taking his side, but when Goff claimed we had no proof, I cried, "No proof? Look at this!" I flung open the office door, and through it came pouring an endless stream of people in Mickey Mouse ears. Before long, there was no room left in the office, but they were still coming. Looking out of Goff's window, I saw another whole sea of Mickey Mice clogging the street below.

When I woke up, I was convinced that what had happened in the dream was going to happen to us in reality. Our audience was going to grow and grow. One day when Howard was feeling especially pressured from all the fighting with Goff and Denise, I told him about the dream, assuring him that we were going straight to the top. He appreciated the support but claimed that he didn't believe in dreams.

After the next book, when the ratings put us in the top five morning shows in the nation's capital, Howard started consulting me regularly to see if I'd had any more ratings dreams. He didn't understand that the one I'd had was the only one I needed.

That dream told me that we were going to be popular, but it didn't help me deal with the pressure that came with being a part of a groundbreaking show. I didn't know it yet, but I was still terribly affected by the sexual abuse I'd suffered as a child and as a result had a lot of trouble dealing with issues associated with being a woman. I knew that Howard was under attack because of the kind of show we were doing, and I wanted to support him in his fight to broaden the boundaries of language and subject matter. But my past would prove to be a huge stumbling block and threaten my ability to form a united front with him against his detractors. The first time I developed a problem, Howard made it a part of the show, as you'll see, but later the problem would be played out behind the scenes.

Because of my hypersensitivity, there were occasions on the air when I couldn't help thinking that Howard was attacking me personally. They usually occurred while he was making some broad generalization about women. All he'd have to say was something like "Women are stupid" to set off my alarms. How dare he insult me? my thoughts ran. Is he saying I'm stupid, that I don't belong on this show, or that I should just shut my mouth?

I couldn't keep my mind on the show after a statement like that. My thoughts would wander from whatever point Howard was trying to make to how hard it had been for me to leave nursing and pursue a career in radio, how radio, a few years before, wouldn't even have been an option. I finally got so angry, I stopped speaking to him off the air. I was very professional on the show. No one could detect that anything was wrong, but in the halls, I wouldn't even look at him. I suppose I thought this was an effective form of punishment because it had always worked so well on my mother. If I really wanted to drive her crazy, I just stopped talking to her. She'd finally have to go to my father and force him to make me speak. After he molested me, he could only beg and pray that I didn't choose to make an issue of it. I never did.

Since it was impossible for the listeners to tell what was going on, I was surprised one day when, instead of introducing the news, Howard announced to the world that he and I had a problem. He confessed to the audience that I hadn't talked to him for several days and that he had no idea why because he couldn't get it out of me. He figured that since his wife, Alison, was a social worker, she could get to the bottom of this, so he got her on the phone.

To my surprise, Alison didn't take sides. She was a perfect professional too, remaining impartial as she counseled her husband and me. I refused to discuss specifics on the air, but Alison extracted a promise from both of us to speak to each other after the show with honesty, openly airing all our grievances. I knew that anyone who heard this part of the show was bound to tune in the next day to see if whatever fences were broken had been mended.

The two of us convened in my studio after the show, as arranged. I have to give Howard credit for being the first one to speak, assuring me that he was concerned about anything he might have done to upset me. And I deserve some credit as well because, angry as I was, I told him what bothered me in a civil tone. I said that I was offended by his remarks about women and took them personally. When he realized that he'd hurt my feelings, he couldn't have been more sincere or apologetic. We ended the conversation with a hug and the next day, we hit the air as friends again.

Of course, Howard continued to be Howard on the air. The same guy who had Mayor Marion Barry shining his shoes in a bit and was proud to announce that he was farting into the microphone wasn't going to watch what he said about women on the air, so time and again, he would make the same kind of hasty generalizations, and I'd have the same visceral responses. I couldn't talk to him *every* time this happened, I just had to believe what he'd said behind closed doors and try not to take it personally, but it still ruffled my feathers. Once Howard invited a girl who said she had a crush on him to the studio, and he and Fred wound up under the console with her. I don't know what happened because that episode forced me right out of the room.

Then, as I was driving home one day after a particularly uncomfortable show, I experienced nothing short of a revelation. It suddenly occurred to me that the racial stuff Howard did never bothered me. He made just as many generalizations about blacks as he did about women, and they made me laugh. Why was the "woman" stuff bothering me so much? Because, just like our listeners, everything Howard said was fine with me until he hit my *hot button*. I suddenly realized that the problem wasn't Howard's, it was mine. I had come to terms with black issues years before meeting him. That's why black slurs and black jokes didn't bother me. But I still had a ton of problems hovering around my sexuality, just waiting to pounce. And each time that *hot button* was pushed, I'd react irrationally by wanting to take my ball and go home. At this moment, I saw the problem clearly and could deal with it, but women's issues would continue to plague me for years to come. Each time Howard got involved with women on the show, I'd have to relearn this lesson.

But a lot of mutual good came out of that particular sticky wicket. Once I'd conquered my irrational belief that Howard had to be what my father had not—sensitive, caring, and protective—I was free to genuinely define my role as his on-air conspirator. My job wasn't regulating Howard's opinions on womanhood or anything else. My job was to be the most articulate possible representative for my own point of view. The more I confronted who I was, the less I had to pretend that I was someone else. There was no reason in the world why I had to agree with Howard. I was right there to present my opposing view if it was warranted and would make for good radio. The birthing process was a difficult one. Labor would take years, but Howard was there for me, coaching me through the whole process.

It was a good thing we didn't air much of our dirty laundry on the program because one of our enemies' favorite tactics had always been to divide and conquer. Denise, looking for an ally in her battle to contain her morning man, often phrased her questions to me in a way that made me think she was looking for any sign of discord. "Don't you mind it when Howard talks to you during the news?" she'd ask constantly. "Does it bother you when Howard calls you Rob instead of using your full name?" she inquired on another occasion.

Even so, I felt that Denise truly had my best interests at heart and was doing the best job she could for both Howard and me. Goff, on the other hand, only seemed to care about exercising his power and was never subtle. He went right for the jugular. After the ratings came out, he called me into the office and told me he was giving me a ten-thousand-dollar raise. I was very happy to get the money. I was still commuting from Baltimore every day at two-thirty in the morning and that raise meant that I could finally move closer to work. But if he thought he was buying my friendship or loyalty, he was sorely misguided. Goff's little gesture boomeranged almost immediately when I moved to my little one-bedroom garden apartment in Rockville, Maryland. There was no longer anything keeping Howard and me apart. Now I was only a twenty-minute ride from work and a five-minute ride from Howard's apartment. We weren't just co-workers anymore, we were neighbors. The proximity had a lot to do with how closely linked we became in public as time went on.

The next thing we knew, we were causing a commotion everywhere we went. Once we even wound up blocking traffic in the middle of the afternoon in front of Channel Five. The station had announced that it was dropping its reruns of "Leave It to Beaver." After talking about it on the air all morning, we announced that we were going to the station to picket. We were shocked by the number of people who showed up to help out. Some of them almost got arrested because they refused to stay on the crowded sidewalk.

"Did you hear what Howard said today?" was the question on everyone's lips, from cabdrivers to the Capitol Hill cocktail party crowd. Even the middle-aged woman realty agent who'd shown me my new apartment was a fan. Here we were supposed to be appealing exclusively to young white males, but people of every stripe were putting up with the rock-and-roll just to hear what would happen next. The show was like an audio car wreck; people couldn't stop listening.

I was still looking for a news style that would complement the show. I did lots of different stories, but the news sounded much the same as it did on other stations. Then, one day in a convenience store, I overheard a conversation between two women and I learned how to do news.

First woman: Did you hear what Martha did last weekend?
Second woman: No, what?
First woman: She went to Atlantic City with a man who wasn't her husband.
Second woman: You're kidding! How did she manage it? What did she tell her husband?

Both the second woman and I were hooked. We wanted to know the answers to those questions—she because she knew the parties involved, I because I was getting to hear something I wasn't supposed to. I wanted my news to be that compelling, an intimate conversation about fascinating information. The headline concept of local news went out the window. I started to do longer forms of stories, and a story from the *National Enquirer* could get just as much weight as a story from the *Washington Post*. Wire copy remained important, but it was no longer the only important form of morning news.

Just because information was a few days old didn't mean it had lost its potency. If I saw an article in a week-old magazine worth talking about, I'd throw that in as well. Howard might hook the listeners in by asking me if I'd heard about the Greek guy caught coming out of the men's room with a dead pelican and then tell me the story. After a story like that, the listeners were bound to hear every other story I put in the newscast. Jerry Nachman, who was then general manager of the NBC-owned all-news station WRC, told me that he learned more from me in the morning than he did from his own station.

I really thought I had found the answers to all the questions that had haunted me throughout my life. All I had to do was be in a job I loved to calm the demons that had plagued me in the past. The restlessness and unhappiness were gone. I no longer felt compelled to wander the earth looking for something to give my life meaning. Everything I wanted and needed was right here. But just when you think you've got all the bases covered, someone steps up to the plate and smacks a line drive right into the hole in center field. And when the moment arrived for a batter to hit that line drive, he would be someone I would never have imagined, as you'll soon see.

At this point, though, nothing had happened to shake my sense of security. We were on the air every day, having fun making fun of everybody and everything. Little things began to crop up, portending trouble ahead, but I was too busy to really take notice. It gave me a great excuse any time someone questioned me as to why I never dated. "Oh, right now, I'm so busy trying to get my career on track. Maybe later, when things calm down," I'd tell them.

When you're as busy as I was and having that much fun, you miss the signs. Sure, a Congressman had read a letter of comdemnation about Howard on the floor of the House. And yes, the articles in the press had started to refer to the show as tasteless and mean, and a few parents had gotten together to mount sponsor boycotts. But, in general, the audience got the joke and the Federal

Communications Commission maintained a hands-off attitude toward the show. I thought we lived in a country with freedom of speech and never believed any of this would amount to anything.

I was feeling so good about the show and Howard that as the end of the year approached, I decided that I should do something for him. Because Howard was just a guy on the radio, people weren't recognizing him for the star that he was. Why not cook up one of those on-air birthday tributes, I asked myself, like the ones Bob Hope threw for himself on TV every year? If people like Goff heard a big fuss being made over Howard, maybe they'd appreciate him for the enormous asset he was. The idea came to me in November 1981, and his birthday wasn't until January, so I had time to plan. My only problem was that I needed help to do it and couldn't ask Howard, since it was going to be a surprise. Fred thought the show was a great idea and volunteered to help in any way he could. Then I called the members of "The Think Tank," the three listeners who'd become regulars on Tuesdays. They were excited to be in on a practical joke to be played on the jokemeister general. That was the easy part.

I didn't know how the rest of the deejays on the station would react. Some of them were openly jealous of all of the attention we got, but I underestimated their love of air time. They all agreed to create tribute messages on tape. Then it suddenly occurred to me that since Howard worked awfully hard on those live commercials in the show, the sponsors owed him something. I called in the sales department and asked them to solicit gifts for our birthday boy. Unfortunately, the sponsors immediately saw this as an opportunity to prove that they were as funny as Howard. We've always suffered from the "I could do what you do syndrome," so I had to quietly nip this little rebellion in the bud. The last thing I needed was a bunch of unfunny guys loading up the show with their stupid gag gifts.

Dealing with all these different personalities and egos was an eye-opening experience. Not that Howard didn't constantly complain about having to cater to so many people's whims, but I gained new respect for his diplomatic skills. Me, I just yelled "Noooooo," and if you didn't listen, you didn't get to come to the party. So I spent the weeks up to Howard's on-air party screaming my head off.

Those sponsors turned out to be the least of my worries. I still had to decide what we were going to do between their commercials. That was Howard's job, and I hadn't really given it a lot of thought before now. Again, my respect for him increased. I figured that guest stars would make for good filler, but who was I going to get to come in to do a morning radio show? My first score was Alison Stern. She'd never been in the studio with us before, and they'd just announced that they were expecting their first child. So far, so good. Then it came to me, a radical idea—Petey Green!

Petey was a local Washington TV personality with his own public affairs show. I had no idea why it was called "public affairs," because Petey, a black ex-con, just sat in a Papa-san chair spewing his own wacky brand of politics. Howard had discovered him channel-surfing one weekend and hadn't stopped talking about how outrageous he was because he managed to work the words "nigger" and "cracker" into every sentence. I found a way to contact Petey's people and arranged for a phone call from him on the day of the birthday show. Whatever Petey's reaction to Howard, I figured there'd be fireworks on the air. Now only one question remained—how to spring the trap.

That Tuesday morning of his birthday, Howard started the show as usual, greeting the audience and previewing what was on tap for that day. The projected highlight would be the arrival of "The Think Tank" at about seven o'clock. Howard, of course, had no idea that they were already there, stashed in a back office along with Alison, until the surprise was sprung at eight. The unwitting guest of honor started worrying at seven sharp. "The Think Tank" loved being a part of the show and were never late. Howard couldn't believe all three of them would choose the same day to screw up. He immediately jumped to the conclusion that something terrible must have happened.

"Where do you think they could be?" he agonized every time I came into the studio to do the news. I'd just shrug and tell him I had no idea. He even went to an outside window and looked out at busy Connecticut Avenue to see if he could see them. "Should we call someone?" he asked me on my next trip in. I suggested that we wait just a little longer. By eight, Howard was positive that they were all under a bus. He was so worried, I began to feel sorry for him but managed to hold out, knowing his torture was almost over.

The next time Howard opened the microphone, we all came

bursting into the room in party hats, blowing noisemakers. The birthday boy was clearly surprised and incredibly relieved to see the missing persons in one piece. He immediately loved the idea that I had played a practical joke on him, and he was thrilled that Alison was there. The show truly took on a party atmosphere, and my Petey Green brainstorm paid off too. It was a highlight and even got Howard an invitation to appear on Petey's show, which he accepted, appearing in blackface and wearing an Afro wig.

What started as a surprise special became an annual staple, relied upon by Howard and the listeners to this day. Every year I feel the pressure to top myself. The show still hasn't quite measured up to my wildest expectations, but in all honesty, I must say that it has advanced light-years beyond its humble beginnings. That Howard proclaims it one of the best shows of every year is a tribute to the increasing number of people it takes to put it together.

Shortly after the birthday show, Howard and I celebrated another milestone—in February we congratulated each other on our one-year anniversary at DC101. Neither of us had ever been at one station that long since we had gotten into radio. How much longer we'd be together was another story. We really should have been living on top of the world. By this time we had the number two radio show in town, just behind the longtime favorite old-timers' morning show "Harden and Weaver," yet we were still collecting losers' wages.

Howard had entered into negotiations with Goff, and because of the level of tension between them, I could tell that the discussions weren't going well. Finally he told me that he and Goff hadn't been able to come to terms, and that he was looking at other offers. In fact, Jerry Nachman, the general manager from the all-news station who had praised me so lavishly, turned out to be the batter who would hit the ball into that centerfield hole. He wanted us to come work for him but, the next thing we knew, Howard was no longer talking to Jerry, who understood and loved the show. He was talking to the NBC brass in New York.

These titans of broadcasting, in their infinite wisdom, had decided that Howard wasn't right for an all-news station. They saw him in the number one market in America, New York, plying his trade at their flagship station, WNBC. Howard was ecstatic. He had always dreamed of working in his hometown. Right from the start, Howard wanted Fred and me to be part of the negotiation. The smooth-talking NBC radio execs assured him that they'd "meet with his people" as soon as they'd settled with him, and that's just what they did. After Howard had signed on the dotted line, they flew into Washington to talk to Fred and me.

The day of the meeting, Fred, Howard, his lawyers, and I were all ushered into a big boardroom, complete with one of those huge mahogany tables, at the NBC offices in D.C. The place simply reeked of money and power. We were the first to arrive, but soon the door opened and a tan, balding, but very distinguished-looking man with a smile like the captain of "The Love Boat" oozed into the room. When he saw Howard rising from his chair to greet him, he flashed his ten-thousand-dollar smile, pinched Howard on the cheek, hugged him, and exclaimed, "Hey, baby!" He was then introduced to the rest of us as Dom Fioravanti, the general manager of WNBC.

Dom was followed into the room by the much less impressive looking program director, Kevin Metheny. He was bald too, but he was much younger than Dom and not nearly as distinguished. Little beads of perspiration glistened on Kevin's shiny bald pate, but he did his best to imitate Dom's shmoozy attitude. I was trying hard not to prejudge them even though they were acting just like characters from a bad B-movie. But once they started to talk, my stomach turned.

Dom and Kevin were essentially saying that they'd listened to us from their hotel rooms that morning and found us entertaining—but that nothing like our show was ever going to be heard on the air in New York. The only question they had for Fred and me was, "What will you do if we don't take you?" At this point, I was feeling pretty silly about having gone out and bought a new outfit just for this meeting. Stunned, I mumbled something about having worked before so I'd probably work again, and Fred, in the same state as me, basically answered that he didn't know.

The meeting ended with everyone smiling false smiles and shaking hands. "Oh yes, it was nice to meet you too," we all lied, then Fred, Howard, and I walked out together. Fred was the first to speak once we were alone. "What a pair of barracudas," he remarked, exhaustion evident in his voice. "Yeah," I chimed in, "real sharks!" "No, you guys are all wrong," Howard assured us. "You just don't understand."

The meeting notwithstanding, Howard kept insisting that Dom and Kevin loved the show, and we kept trying to convince him that he was wrong. "Didn't you hear them say that the show was never going to be heard in New York?" I demanded, but Howard dismissed that as a negotiating tactic. There was just no getting through to him, and what would have been the use, he had already signed a contract to work for them, so I just gave in, saying, "Okay, whatever you say." Then we split up and went home, but within minutes of getting in the door, my phone rang. It was Howard, calling a meeting with Fred and me at our favorite local Chinese restaurant.

Over delectable dishes that went largely ignored, we talked and talked. Howard felt awful that the meeting had gone so badly and swore that he was going to get Dom and Kevin on the phone as soon as possible to straighten out the whole mess. He was still sure everything would be okay. But that wouldn't be the case in a couple of weeks when Dom and Kevin stopped returning his calls.

When word hit the street that Howard was going to New York, the local news outlets jumped all over the story. It was a great "local talent makes good" item. Newspapers, magazines, and the TV stations were all calling. One of the first questions asked was, "What about Robin and Fred?" Howard dodged that one as much as possible because none of us was sure of the answer.

A few weeks before the NBC deal was announced we'd also get a taste of what it was like to be raked over the coals by a national newsmagazine. A producer from NBC News approached Howard about doing a story on the show, swearing that it would be positive. We cooperated fully, even allowing them to tape us doing a live remote broadcast from a local DC club. Imagine our surprise the night of the broadcast, when Douglas Kiker, whom we had never ever met, opened the piece by warning parents to get their children away from the set before he continued this segment on Howard Stern and "barnyard" radio. The piece aired just after the announcement that Howard was going to WNBC in New York, and we've always wondered just how much it had to do with what happened later.

Meanwhile, back at DC101, Goff made no secret of resenting Howard's good fortune and was determined to make him work every single day of the five months left on his DC101 contract. He was also looking for any way he could find to inflict punishment on his traitorous morning man. When he called me into his office, he was looking for the answer to the question everyone was asking, but *he* could get to one of the principles. I could honestly tell him that I wasn't talking to anyone at NBC. I even let him think that Howard had deliberately double-crossed me. I wasn't yet ready to burn my bridges. Goff was anxious to make sure that the team could never be reassembled, and he asked me what it would take to keep me. I told him I'd get back to him.

Things were happening at a dizzying pace. It was hard to know what to do or where to turn. Immediately after leaving Goff's office, I called Howard's attorneys, who were functioning as my silent coaches, and asked for their advice, then went back to Goff and demanded $100,000. "Well," he responded, "you're certainly not the little girl who walked into my office a year ago, are you? Okay."

Okay? He wasn't supposed to say okay. This was not part of the game plan. As a stalling tactic, I'd quoted him what the lawyers and I had decided was an outrageous price. I imagined from that response that Goff must really hate Howard and would have agreed to almost anything. I'd grossly underestimated him. Goff put a five-year deal on the table that would pay me $75,000 the first two years and the full $100,000 each of the last three.

This did not improve my situation at all. I had Goff pressuring me to sign a long-term contract for more money than I'd ever imagined making, Howard was still trying to talk some sense into the people at NBC, and I was stuck in the middle. When I told Howard about Goff's offer, he was bewildered.

"Robin," Howard began, "I was hoping to be able to make the whole New York deal happen, but I can't tell you to turn down that kind of money."

"So, I should take it?" I asked with a sinking heart.

"Yeah," he told me with obvious regret. "I guess you have to."

I had never thought in forever terms, but I just wasn't ready for this amazing period in my life to end. Yet all the signs told me that it was over. Howard had a contract with those awful people at NBC, and I had this major money offer from our enemy in D.C. What more was it going to take to convince me that the wild bunch was really breaking up?

12

TROUBLE IN PURGATORY

Shortly after I started working in Washington, my old married lover, Bradley, resurfaced. Now he was divorced, with a son, and had returned to reclaim the love of his life. "Robin," he declared, "I'm taking you to Atlanta." "Bradley," I answered, "if I move anywhere, I'm moving to New York."

—1981

As it became clearer and clearer that everything I'd worked for was crashing down around me, I started having mini panic attacks. They often occurred just as I was settling in for the night. As soon as I was comfortably ensconced between the sheets, with my head on my pillow, I'd close my eyes and search for sleep. Instead, the sound of my own heart pounding in my chest kept me awake. It wasn't just that I noticed it, the beating was so loud I couldn't ignore it. I could be awake for hours, listening to it. In the days to come, I would begin to fear that my heart would actually stop from the strain of beating so hard and so furiously.

I was sick and frantic and horrified by the tricks destiny had played on us. NBC, which had so recently seemed our savior, was tearing us apart. Just days ago, like the Three Musketeers, we had been celebrating Howard's contract as the harbinger of good times for all of us. Now it looked as if just one of the Musketeers was going to claim the glory we'd fought to win together. And, as time went on, I began to feel that one Musketeer was running off with all the spoils and didn't give a damn about the injustice of it all.

Goff had already begun his search for Howard's replacement. I'd had my participation in the selection of my future partner written into the new contract, so the weekend after we'd made the deal, Goff invited me to dinner at his favorite restaurant, Trader Vic's, to meet a prospect from out of town.

Right at the front door of the place, Goff crassly started throwing his money and his weight around, calling the maitre d' by his first name and demanding his favorite waiter. He verbally abused everyone, then tried to compensate for the abuse with lavish tips. The waiters and the busboys just smiled and endured him. At least they got to come and go. I had to sit there all evening. Goff was a big drinker, and the more alcohol he consumed, the fouler his mouth became. Dinner hadn't even arrived, and I'd already lost my appetite. There was little doubt in my mind that five years of Goff would drive me way over the edge.

I was stymied. NBC didn't want me, so in a matter of months, "Howard and Robin" would be history. Goff was offering me close to half a million dollars over five years, but that didn't make him any less despicable to me. So what did I do? What any reasonable hysteric would under these circumstances. I collapsed. I lost my voice and missed almost three weeks on the air. Goff began to get antsy. He must have assumed that I was faking the whole thing because he ordered me to get a doctor's note. So I ended up in one of those stupid paper gowns with my butt hanging out, listening to a medical verdict that I didn't want to hear.

As the doctor explained it, I was a mess physically as well as emotionally. The strain of all the fighting over the past year had sent me right to the refrigerator, and the tension showed big time on my thighs. My pounding heart was caused by high blood pressure. The doctor told me that if I didn't lose weight, stop smoking, and calm down in a month, he'd be forced to put me on medication that I would have to take for the rest of my life. When I got home, I completely broke down in tears. Here I was, not even thirty, and my body was falling apart. My heart was beating out of my chest, I couldn't sleep, and I was addicted to nicotine. Yep, definitely, crumbling under the pressure.

After I reported back to Goff, I asked for some time off to take care of myself. I called Alison and asked for her advice. She and Howard were very into Transcendental Meditation, which I had studied while trying to figure out what to do with myself in the air force. I took her advice and signed up for a refresher course. For the next two weeks, I meditated, dieted, and quit smoking. I even put on a jogging suit, deciding to start an exercise program with a good, brisk walk. My circulatory system was in such rotten shape that my legs immediately began to swell. Within fifteen minutes of leaving my apartment, I was back, lying on the floor, clutching my knees to my chest and crying in pain.

I had no idea just how much of a mess my body had become. As a nurse, I'd been on my feet, running for eight hours at a stretch. If I gained a few pounds, I'd lose them by adding a few more trips to the utility room. Two years of sitting around on my butt, talking, had taken its toll, but I vowed to make a comeback. I bought support hose to wear under my jogging suit. Then, I slowly started to work up to a mile-a-day walk. By the time I returned to the doctor's office, I had lost ten pounds, given up cigarettes, and my blood pressure was normal.

During the two weeks off, I'd come to the decision that I had to sign Goff's contract. It was the only way I was going to reap any of the benefits of the success "The Howard Stern Show" had achieved in Washington. But when I went into his office and told him I was ready to make it official, Goff informed me that it was too late. The deal was off the table. I was also informed that during my time away, he'd signed someone to take Howard's place. All the boss from hell could promise me now was a chance to try out for the sidekick job. I almost laughed. Now I had nothing.

To make things even more hellacious, the situation between Howard and Goff had burst into open warfare while I was at home getting better. Every morning on the air now, Howard tried to get under Goff's skin, lashing out at him for holding him to a contract when neither of them wanted to work together anymore. Again, I was caught in the middle. I had to do the show with Howard but was still expected to audition for Goff's new morning man. This was an impossibly stressful situation, and I felt myself moving closer and closer to the breaking point. My sanity was shredding at the edges, and screaming voices of self-loathing and recrimination flooded my thoughts. I had been a complete idiot ever to trust another human being. What did I expect Howard to do when the big money offers came—protect me? People only meant what they said when it was easy. It served me right to be in this position, my nose pressed against the glass, watching the parade pass me by.

I appreciated that what was happening to me was a reenactment of my breakdown in the air force. I could see that same black hole that had once swallowed me up beckoning me back to the darkness, but I didn't want to go. I called Alison again and tried to ask for help, but I didn't know how. She must have heard something off in my voice because she advised me to talk to my mother. I thought that was the strangest advice I'd ever heard. "Why would I do that?" I asked her.

"Well, is there anyone that you trust that you can confide in?" Alison replied.

"No."

She suggested that I call someone for crisis counseling, but I'd already stopped listening. It seemed to me that with despair consuming me, I didn't have time to develop a therapeutic relationship with a stranger. So I thanked her and got off the phone. As usual, I was going to have to be the one to find a way to save myself. I either had to take responsibility for this mess, which would have plunged me into a suicidal frenzy, or I would have to find someone else to blame. NBC was too far away to be an effective target, and I didn't really know Dom Fioravanti or Kevin Metheny anyway. That left Howard. Howard gradually became the focus for all my rage, although I fought demonizing him as hard as I could.

Three times I went to him and asked him to explain how this whole thing had gone down. Three times he repeated the exact same story. The NBC executives had told him they wanted the show and would talk to the rest of us after his deal was in place but once his negotiation was completed, they refused to take any more of his calls. He continued to insist that he knew he could change their minds given a little time. I walked out of Howard's office each time believing every word he said, but as soon as I was alone, I turned on myself with a vicious tirade of epithets and threats—just as my mother had done to me as a child. Only this time, there was no escaping that voice because I was carrying it around in my own head. I had to make a choice. Either I was going to be Howard's friend or save my own life. I chose me, and the darkness covered the sun.

From that moment on, I guess I hated Howard. In my mind, the man I knew was dead to me. He had betrayed me every bit as much as my father had, but I wasn't eleven years old anymore. Now I could do real damage. I refused to speak to him or take his calls. When he insisted on trying to find out what was wrong, I sat down at my typewriter in the newsroom and composed a letter. I called him names I knew would hurt and accused him of things I knew he hadn't done. Every other word was "fuck" or "motherfucker," and to top things off, I accused him of being a racist.

Looking back, I realize that I didn't mean any of what I wrote. I just needed him to stay away. He was the enemy, and I used my anger at him to fuel my comeback. The things I said to myself about Howard were probably far worse than anything in that letter, and they were on a loop. Once the tape had played to the end, it started over. But my rancor got me going and gave me something to prove.

I started looking for another job, using DC101 as my very own job placement center. I typed my résumé and cover letter there, made long-distance calls, and used the studios to produce and dub my audition tapes. I figured that at the very least they owed me that. I even made a call to Denise Oliver and told her I was looking for a job. In a few days, she had my phone ringing off the hook with inquiries. My anger also helped keep me on my diet and exercise program and off cigarettes. With Howard's unwitting help, I had begun to jog. I imagined that his face was under my feet every time I took a step. The faster my pace, the more I got to smash his face into the ground. I was up and running in no time.

Meanwhile, the show sounded exactly as it had before all this happened. I forgot everything that was going on outside the studio when we were working and acted as if we were still the Three Musketeers, but unless those mikes were on, not a word passed between Howard and me. Alison told me later that it was a tribute to our incredible chemistry that no one could tell we were on the outs.

Just as I had been stuck in the middle between Howard and Goff, Fred found himself caught between Howard and me. Neither one of us ever drew him into our difficulties by asking him to take sides. I never even discussed the situation with him. He continued to be the glue between us, maintaining a civil relationship with us both and behaving like a consummate professional. And I continued to look for an out.

Denise's contacts put me in touch with the news director of WCBM, the official Baltimore Colts station, which was about to go all-news talk. A couple of other stations wanted to team me up with their goofy, zany morning men, but the idea of doing one of those lame shows was like asking me to drive a Ford after I'd gotten used to a Ferrari. I just couldn't do it. So I figured I'd go back to straight news and pick up where I'd left off a year before. Planning to use radio news to get me to television, I took the job as a reporter and substitute anchor at WCBM.

As soon as the deal was struck, and I knew I'd soon be free of both Howard and Goff, I felt like one of the jumpers in a Toyota commercial. I found myself running down the hall to tell my best friend, then stopped in my tracks when I remembered that we weren't speaking. That job offer had broken the cloud that had been hanging over me, and in the sunlight, I could see that I wasn't angry at Howard, I was angry at the situation. But, in light of all I'd done to him, there was no turning back. I found Fred instead and told him my good news.

Goff was surprised when he got my letter of resignation. He really thought I'd stick around to scarf down whatever scraps he bothered to toss me from his table. He seemed genuinely sorry that I was leaving and asked how I felt about Howard. Even he couldn't tell what was happening between us. "Goff," I told him firmly, "I will never work with Howard again." I did the show through the period covering my two-week notice, and Goff and I shook hands on my last day. I said good-bye to everyone but Howard, even though I was going to miss him the most. We didn't ever speak of my leaving except to announce it during my last day on the air.

A caller asked if I was leaving because I was angry with Howard for taking the job in New York. For the first time in a long time,

Howard turned his chair to look at me as I gave my answer. "I've had fun working with Howard," I said without a hint of how I really felt, "but I really got into this business to do straight news. And, now that Howard is leaving, it's time for me to get back to it." I saved my tears for the car ride home.

Once again I was starting over, and this time I was going to have to do it carrying some pretty heavy baggage. The reputation of "The Howard Stern Show" had spread to Baltimore, and my return to my old hometown was big news. My new news director saved the article from the *Baltimore Sun* announcing my return. None of my co-workers, who were the stars of the station, had gotten such attention when they took a new job. Right off the bat, I was singled out as not just any new reporter. My return wasn't a sign of total devastation either. At least I wasn't moving back in with my parents. I found a place not far from my very first apartment and vowed to make the best of my lot. Throwing myself into the job, I resurrected the old reporting skills I'd begun to hone in Harrisburg.

My work at WCBM was basically your nine-to-five job, and I appreciated not having to get up before the crack of dawn every morning. I'd roll out of bed for a quick run, shower, eat, watch the morning news shows, and read the papers. At some point, I'd check with the station to see if they had any stories for me to cover. If not, I'd develop my own. It was a good deal if you wanted to do this kind of work, but I'd soon learn that I had lost my taste for it. Almost nothing gripped me. I was used to the total freedom of being a radio personality. I no longer wanted to pretend to be objective or uninvolved.

I admit, it was still exciting to be in the middle of a breaking story. I vividly remember covering a strike vote of angry workers, where the slightest spark could have resulted in violence. My new cohorts actually praised my call-in reports from the scene. Election coverage was fun too. I tremendously enjoyed broadcasting live from Curt Shmoke's election night headquarters when he ran for district attorney. It was his first political campaign, but everyone could see that he was a budding political star—as his eventual election to mayor would prove. Unfortunately, strikes and elections didn't happen every day, and most of the time I was just plain bored.

Even being on the air didn't give me the same thrill it had before. I filled in whenever one of the regular anchors was off the air, which meant I could be doing five-minute newscasts midday or co-anchoring morning or afternoon drive. News copy was now a straitjacket because I had to stick to the script and was constantly wrestling with my desire to blurt out something, anything, to wake people up. I kept busy, hoping that this feeling would eventually pass.

On the up side, the station itself was quite pleasant, and the new, young staff reminded me of my days in Harrisburg. Baltimore is a much smaller market than Washington, D.C., and there was less of that killer air of competition among the members of the staff. A lot of us were newcomers because of staff expansions, and I became friendly enough with some of my fellow rookies to socialize with them after hours. Even though things weren't perfect, I was finally beginning to feel comfortable and to forget where I'd been.

Then one day I walked into somebody's office to do an interview. After I'd introduced myself to my subject, the woman remarked that I looked familiar. Shrugging it off, I started my Q and A and was in the middle of asking a question when she interrupted me with, "Didn't you use to be Robin Quivers?" I really didn't know how to answer the question.

"I guess I still am," I answered lamely. Once she realized what she'd said, she blushed.

I couldn't forget that incident or ignore its significance. What was I doing in Baltimore running around with a tape recorder and alligator clips in my pocket? I was Robin Quivers. Why was I forcing myself to do something I really hadn't the heart for anymore? If I kept it up, radio would be just what nursing had become—a means to support my other habits. I had taken this job on the rebound, so to speak, never really evaluating my true situation. I'd even fled Washington, a town where I was well known, without even trying to capitalize on my name recognition or my success. I'd just declared defeat and left the field. The glare of the spotlight and the rejection by NBC had undermined my confidence to such a point that I hadn't even fought to get what I deserved.

That was the first sign of life I'd shown since this whole episode began. The second would be much more public. I was filling in for one of the afternoon anchors, trading stories back and forth with my partner, taking my turn introducing other elements and reading commercial copy. When it was time for me to throw it over to our sports announcer, I was caught off guard. Unable to think of anything novel to call him, I simply said, "Here's our sports guy" and gave his name. As soon as the red on-air light went off, my co-anchor and the rest of the staff ripped off their headphones and dissolved into hysterical laughter. "Sports guy!" they repeated, still laughing. "She said 'sports guy'!" It was like the funniest thing they'd ever heard—and all at my expense. But they all fell silent as an incredibly powerful and commanding voice filled the room. Mine.

"One of these days you're going to tell people you worked with me!" I announced as they all sat and stared at me. I wanted to crawl out of the room. I couldn't imagine what had possessed me to say such a thing. Thank goodness the sports report finally ended and we went back on the air. But I have to admit that after that little outburst, I felt better.

I also sensed that whatever happened, I wasn't long for WCBM. I needed something new, challenging, exciting. Maybe it was time for me to make the switch to TV. In fact, I'd run into a certain TV reporter on a number of stories, so I called him and asked about openings at his station. From there I started to investigate the industry. My decision was made. And as soon as it was, the most unbelievable thing happened!

Without my knowledge, Howard had continued his lobbying efforts to get me to New York as soon as he reached WNBC. He really scared the station's powers that be with his outrageous antics, and each time they reprimanded him, he claimed that the reason he'd broken the rules was because I wasn't there. In no time at all, he had them convinced that they needed me. The next thing I knew, I was talking to one of Howard's lawyers on the phone. It seemed to me that the call had come right out of the blue. But if I found just getting the call shocking, what the lawyer was about to say next should have knocked me off my seat.

"Robin," the attorney began, "Howard wants to know if you'd ever consider working with him again."

*   *   *

"Yes" sprang from my lips, and I was already on to my next thought. Even television, my former ultimate goal, paled in comparison to the rush of doing that show again. My mind began to race with possibilities, but the lawyer, applying the brakes, said, "Slow down a minute, it's not a done deal. Howard still needs to talk to you."

Oh yeah, I was overlooking a few things, wasn't I? After all, I hadn't left Howard on the best of terms. Of course we needed to talk. Howard was already on the air in New York by this time, and was working afternoon drive from four to eight at night. That meant he wouldn't be able to talk to me until after he got home at around nine. That left me with the rest of the day and all of the evening to reflect on where things stood.

Howard and I had spoken since the breakup, but only a couple of times. The first was shortly after I'd arrived in Baltimore. I'd been shanghaied into giving an interview I really didn't want to give, and it wound up on the second page of the *Washington Times*.

Before I'd left DC101, a reporter we considered a friend, Dennis John Lewis, called me at home and extracted a promise from me to discuss my breakup with Howard after the whole thing was over. I left the city without ever giving him a call because I was trying to avoid this very thing. But Dennis John, whom people always referred to by both names, was like a bloodhound and tracked me all the way to my new station. When I showed up at the WCBM company picnic, Dennis John was there with his little tape recorder. The first thing he did was show me a copy of *Washingtonian* magazine with Howard on the cover in a devil costume, wrapped around the current Miss Maryland, a young black woman. I just wanted him to get the magazine out of my face, so I waved it away. It wound up in print as, "She wouldn't even accept a copy of a magazine with Howard on the cover."

Dennis John claimed to know that Howard and I hadn't been speaking to each other the last two months we'd worked together and demanded to know why. I claimed back that Howard was trying to control what I said on the air by turning down the volume on my microphone—an out-and-out lie, but what was I going to say? I also alleged that Howard had betrayed a verbal agreement when he signed the contract with NBC without me. I summed up the whole matter by likening it to a divorce in which the exes were not on friendly terms.

Even though I'd exercised as much restraint as I could summon for this interview with Dennis John, the article definitely had bite. A few weeks later, I called Howard to pass on a message from a businessman interested in proposing a deal to him. I wasn't going to give out his home phone number, but I didn't want to prevent him from making a deal either, so I made the call myself. I gave him the information, expecting that to be the end of the conversation. Instead, Howard said, "I saw the article. It really hurt." "I know," I told him, "it hurt me too. I'm sorry."

That was all that was said before we both hung up. Recent events were still too fresh in our minds for either of us to have any real perspective on them, so talking was impossible. Any other necessary communication, which wasn't much, was handled by attorneys. Then, one afternoon when I'd gotten home early because I was filling in on the morning shift, Steve Chiconas, one of "The Think Tank" guys, phoned.

Through giggles, Steve told me that Howard and Fred were with him, and because his wife was out of town and Alison had already gone to New York, the guys were having a male bonding session complete with pot. Fred later told me that in the midst of their tribal bonding, they had suddenly missed me and decided to give me a call, figuring the worst I could do was hang up. It was both funny and sad listening to them babble incoherently into the receiver.

Eventually Howard must have taken the phone into another room, because he got serious. He confessed that he had reservations about going to New York without the team intact and kept insisting that he would still make it happen. I was resigned to the idea that it was over at that point and simply reassured him that he didn't need anyone to become a hit. I knew he'd be just fine, and I figured I would too. This moment of sobriety was short-lived, as the conversation dissolved back into the bacchanalian revelry that had greeted me when I first picked up. Then they were gone.

In that phone call, I learned that Howard had somehow finally convinced NBC of Fred's value, and Fred would be making the trip to New York with him. Once I hung up the phone, I thought that

I'd spoken to both of them for probably the last time. New York was a long way from Baltimore. At first, I had attributed Howard's candor to the booze and the pot he said he was smoking, but later I was struck by how courageous he'd been and how he was still keeping the faith. I had given him every reason to distrust me, and yet he had no fear of disclosing his feelings to me. If the situation had been reversed, I knew that I would never have been so generous. That Howard, he was always full of surprises. Now, after he'd been on the air in New York for less than a month, he wanted to talk to me.

I wasn't very successful at distracting myself that evening as I waited for his call. The TV was on, but I wasn't really watching it. I tried to go through the papers but couldn't concentrate. So I wound up sitting around fantasizing about what he was going to say. Finally, at eight-thirty, the phone rang. Though it was right next to me on the sofa, I let it ring twice before I answered. To my surprise, the voice on the other end was Alison's.

"I hope you know now that he was always fighting for you," she told me, passing right over the formalities.

"I know," I said, choking up.

Alison had called to let me know that Howard was going to be late and wanted to make sure I'd wait up for him. That wasn't a problem. I wouldn't have been able to sleep anyway. Alison and I were still chatting when he walked in and took over.

"Look," Howard plunged right in, "here's the deal. I want you to come to work here. I think I've got NBC to agree, but I can't go through what happened between us in Washington ever again. I don't want to talk it through. I can't discuss it. We've got to wipe the slate clean. So, if you take the job, it has to be just like it never happened and we're starting from scratch. If you can't do that, don't come."

"I can do that," I said, meaning it.

Taking me at my word, Howard began to talk to me just as he had the day before everything fell apart. "Don't give notice yet," he advised me. "There are still a few things to work out. We'll let you know when." So I had this incredible news, and I couldn't tell anybody. I was so excited, it took me hours to get to sleep.

Suddenly, WCBM didn't seem so unbearable. I had a secret that made even the most mundane task more exciting. It took about two weeks to get everything together, and I would have burst in that time if I hadn't told someone. I just shouldn't have told someone in the newsroom. My confidante was a young producer who had started at the station a week before me. We shared a love of movies and often attended the little art theater downtown together. I don't know why I chose her to tell, but I do know she immediately told everyone else at the station. They all began whispering that I must have known this was happening all along. Eventually the rumor got back to my news director before I could tell him myself. He called me into his office and said he was sorry to hear I was leaving because he thought I could go far there.

In the meantime, I had to meet with Dom "The Glad Man" Fioravanti again, and a new player, the news director of WNBC, Mary Beth Janus. Mary Beth was an anxious, chain-smoking, bottle blond with bug eyes who appeared to be really putting a lot of effort into liking me as we sat across from each other at dinner in the restaurant of the first hotel to open in the Inner Harbor, Baltimore's newest attraction.

Mary Beth's face appeared frozen in a permanent smile. She assured me that her specialty was developing raw talent, and that she was going to mold me into a top-notch NBC newswoman. This sounded fine, but all evening I sensed something nasty simmering just below the surface. When Mary Beth split for the gift shop to buy more cigarettes, Dom and I had time for a minute alone. "Mary Beth is a little uptight about this whole thing, but it'll be okay," he assured me. I didn't know what to think when I finally hit the street, but I decided to ignore the queasiness in the pit of my stomach. Once the Three Musketeers were together again, things would be fine, or so I thought.

Once I gave my notice, I had to think about moving to New York. Howard and Alison offered to help me find somewhere to live, insisting that I stay with them the weekend I flew up to look for a place. They even picked me up at the airport. After the first hugs, the ice was broken and we again nonverbally committed to setting our lives on the same path. I couldn't have been happier to see them. Maybe the painful endings were really behind us. Maybe a marvelous new beginning had arrived.

My commitment included a pledge of honor I made to myself. I resolved to be a better friend to Howard than I had ever been an enemy. What was important to him was now important to me. The people he loved, I loved. What he wanted for himself, I wanted for him even more. And if you wanted to hurt him, you were hurting me. At the time, I had no idea where this vow would lead me, but I made it from the heart, and while I might have broken a few of these vows along the way, no one has ever been able to get to Howard through me.

Apartment hunting in New York is on a whole different level than anywhere else in the country. Everywhere else, you check ads in the paper, see something you like, and make a deposit. In Queens, where we all wound up living at first, I spent interminable hours in real estate offices filling out applications and being driven around to dilapidated fixer-uppers even though I wanted to pay as much as $600 a month in rent.

That was more than I'd ever paid in rent before, and I certainly wasn't going to build someone's apartment while I tried to work a full-time job. In one apartment the cabinets were sitting on the floor, the plumbing was incomplete, and the agent, with a straight face, smiled and said, "It needs a little work." It seemed that all the finished apartments had dried up when the agents discovered that I was the client. I found nothing that first weekend and would have to fly up again.

The next Saturday, the story was the same. There just wasn't anything in my price range. Finally, Howard hit the ceiling and started screaming right in the middle of the real estate office, "Is it because she's black? This is bullshit! She's offering a decent price, and you're telling us there's nothing. Just give it to us straight!"

Alison and I exchanged glances of disbelief, but when we got back into their car, he continued, "I'm telling you, this is a race thing! You don't know these people. How dare they treat you like that. You're better than most of the white assholes they rent to every day. Those bastards!"

It turns out that he was right. Howard and Alison were taking me to the same agencies they would go to, but Queens is a very segregated borough. Even our affiliation with WNBC didn't help melt the ice because, since the young agents taking us around never listened to it, we were embarrassed to even tell them we worked there.

The next morning, when we resumed our search, Howard immediately told the agent, a kindly, gray-haired old man, of our predicament and suggested that the guy not waste our time. The man said it wouldn't be a problem and showed us a newly renovated unit not five minutes from where the Sterns were living. I liked it, the deal was finally made, and I began to write out the obligatory checks. At this point Howard piped up and asked if I could handle the outlay of this much cash on such short notice.

To be honest, not expecting to be moving again anytime soon, I had recently purchased a new bedroom set. I'd had to pay cash because I still had no credit. It put a serious dent in my bank account, and I admitted that I could cover all but about a thousand dollars of the expenses. Without hesitation, Alison whipped out a checkbook and asked how much I really needed. I assured her that the thousand would do it and thanked them sincerely. Now I'd be able to start my new life with a little less anxiety.

Back in Baltimore for my final week prior to the move, I went to my parents' house to tell the family I was moving to New York to work with Howard again. "That no-good bastard," my father started to grumble. In all fairness, he'd heard me say some pretty awful things about Howard during the bad days at DC101, but when he continued, "You're not going to work with that son of a bitch again," I attacked.

"Excuse me," I told him in no uncertain terms, "don't ever mention Howard's name again!"

"But I was trying to defend you," he sputtered, attempting to explain.

"Look," I replied, "all I know is that working with Howard in Washington was the best time of my life. And now he wants to try to do it again in New York, and I'm going. Okay?"

"Okay," he capitulated, and the conversation turned to preparations for the move to New York the following weekend. NBC was footing the bill for the move, but I needed my family to supervise things because I'd already be gone when the movers arrived.

My final evening in Baltimore, the phone rang. It was Howard.

"Robin," he said, "you'd better hurry up and get here. They just suspended me again." They had sent Howard home from work for an irreverent recorded bit he'd played the night before. "I don't know how long it's going to last," he concluded, "so you better get here soon!" Things were sure different in New York.

I was still driving the used car my father had helped me get when I was in broadcasting school. It had taken me to Carlisle, Harrisburg, Washington, and Baltimore again and again. It was showing all the signs of old age, but I thought it had one more big trip left in it. This time when I packed a suitcase and threw it in the car trunk, I felt full of hope and excitement.

I was going to New York to rejoin my team. Things were back the way they should have been all along. I imagined that my very presence would smooth over any roughness that Howard was experiencing with our new bosses. I had never really thought I'd live in New York City, but if that was where the show was, that's where I belonged.

13

CITY OF DREAMS

"Where are you going?" the man inside the ticket booth screamed.
"To Queens," I replied.
"Then you want the F train!" he bellowed at me as if I were an idiot. "Go right through there," he yelled, pointing to the turnstile.
Just as I was about to enter the subway, a train pulled up. Hundreds of people came rushing through the same gates he had just told me to go through. I stood there in shock with all those people rushing by as if I weren't even there.
"Go ahead. Go ahead," the man in the booth urged me in a more sympathetic tone, "they won't hurt you."

—1982

"See you Monday" was the last thing I'd said to Howard the night before I left for New York because he and Alison had an event to attend the Sunday I was arriving. Since they wouldn't be around, WNBC had assigned Kevin Metheny, the short, bald, squat program director who had been riding shotgun with Dom Fioravanti in Washington, as my one-man welcoming committee. I was to meet him at the station around four on Sunday afternoon. I felt good about this trip. Good enough, in fact, to just point the car north with no specific directions to New York City. I knew that if I headed straight up I-95, I was bound to find it.

As my poor old car stuttered and sputtered toward Manhattan, I thought back to the crazy New York streets that had frightened me so badly when I'd visited before. I couldn't believe that I was actually considering taking a car into the city, but appreciated that a true test of my love for the show would be to face my fear of Manhattan traffic and conquer it. I probably had things way out of proportion anyway. Just how bad could New York be?

Like many of my other fears, everything I knew about the Big Apple I'd learned from my family. According to them, New York was a wild place with dangerous people. It routinely ate you up and spat you out. New York was so mean that no one ever lasted long there, always running home just before it totally consumed them. Violence and corruption lurked everywhere. It was on the street, where young girls vanished after being sold into white slavery. Fourteen-year-old hookers prowled the avenues in the freezing cold wearing nothing but lingerie. Almost anyone could be a purse snatcher or a pickpocket. Why would anyone ride the subway knowing you could be shoved onto the tracks at any moment for no apparent reason? My vision of New York was straight out of the movie *Taxi Driver*. I guess I had spent all my time in New York in Times Square.

Crossing the George Washington Bridge, though, I was like a wide-eyed kid on her first roller coaster ride. Everything was brand new. I had always flown into the airport and then experienced the rush hour traffic from Queens. In the back of a taxi, I never knew where I was, and my anxiety was so intense, I guess I'd never actually noticed the Manhattan skyline. Now here it was, spread gloriously before me, just like all those photographs. Wow.

Once I was on the West Side Highway, I hit a snag. I had to get to Rockefeller Center, and I had no idea where it was. I decided that the wisest course of action was to get off the highway, find a store, and invest in a guidebook. As it turned out, I'd gotten off the highway at the 56th Street exit. Rockefeller Center was between 49th and 50th on Sixth Avenue. I had landed right where I needed to be—another good omen.

The Sunday traffic was tame compared to what I'd remembered, and I found a parking place right on the street in front of 30 Rock. I was a little early, but I decided to go up to the station, hoping that Kevin would already be there, waiting. Rockefeller Center was huge, but I wouldn't notice that for months. I found the NBC elevators and was impressed that I was going to be working in the same building as the network itself. The radio station was on the second floor, but I was going to have to get past two security guards before I could get there. The security guard called and asked for Kevin, then told me that he wasn't working that day. Once my predicament was explained to the person on the other end, he agreed to be responsible for me while I was in the building, and I was allowed past the desk.

As I stepped out of the elevators, I saw the on-air studio right in front of me and knew I'd hit the big time for sure. It was beautiful and huge. There was a big round console in the middle at which the disc jockey sat, and there were chairs in front of microphones all around the outside perimeter. This studio could accommodate a lot of people comfortably, but now the room sat empty. I was buzzed through a security door by an engineer who introduced himself, but I couldn't have told you his name five minutes later. He was working with a very heavyset deejay who was doing a weekend countdown show. He introduced himself by his air name, Big Ron. Neither of them had heard from Kevin, but they assured me that it was okay if I wanted to wait around.

Suddenly I was gripped by the dreadful certainty that my car would be towed away if I left it on the street, so I decided to move it to a lot and give Kevin a bit more time. When I returned to the studio on the stroke of four, he still hadn't shown. After I'd sat around the lobby a little longer, Big Ron gave Kevin another call. There was no answer, which we all hoped meant that Kevin was on his way.

To pass the time, I opted to go for a stroll. Unfamiliar as I was with the territory, I thought it best to stick close to the building and headed toward Sixth Avenue. As I rounded the corner, I noticed a homeless black man sitting on the edge of a box in which a tree was planted. Don't look him in the eye, my urban combat training told me, just keep walking. Unfortunately, I miscalculated and looked up just as I was about to pass him, and our gazes locked. "BIIIIII-ITCH!" he screamed as I looked away.

"BIIIIIIIIITCH," he continued as I picked up my pace.

"BIIIIIIIIITCH," he bellowed for as long as he could see me. People on the street turned in our direction and stared at me, obviously wondering what in the world I'd done to get this guy so upset.

I rushed right back to the safety of the radio station to find that Kevin still wasn't there and couldn't be reached. Too shaken to stay in the city any longer, I picked up my car and drove back over the GWB, found a little motel over in Jersey, and settled in for the evening. It was about six by then and already dark. After I got to my room, I called the station and was told that Kevin had never shown. What a sweetheart. What a welcome.

My first day in the city had been disappointing, to say the least, and I didn't know how to begin to interpret it. I had trouble sleeping that night but got up early the next day, vowing to give New York another shot. I showered, dressed, and made it to my car by seven-thirty that morning, figuring I'd have enough time to grab a little breakfast before getting to the station at nine. It had only taken me fifteen minutes to get to the motel from the city the day before, but that wasn't in rush hour traffic. Now there were so many cars backed up on the George Washington Bridge, I thought there had been a major accident. It took me forty-five minutes to cross the bridge, and when I couldn't spot a major pileup, I realized that this was everyday traffic. I only just made it to the station on time.

When I ran into Kevin, he didn't offer an explanation or an apology for standing me up. Coldly and impersonally, he simply said that he'd forgotten, then shuttled me off to personnel for my corporate orientation. I filled out a lot of forms and was given a whole folder full of information on my rights and benefits as an NBC employee. Then, I and a group of other new employees were shown around the NBC facility. When I got back to the station, Kevin gave me a cursory tour of WNBC, ending with the newsroom, where he delivered me into the hands of Mary Beth Janus.

Mary Beth greeted me with that same tight, bug-eyed smile I remembered from our meeting in Baltimore, but she was friendly, gave me a tour of the newsroom, and introduced me to the staff. The newsroom was big, open, and noisy, with a module of workstations in the center of the room. Three huge wire machines sat on counters that ran the length of the wall next to the door. Paper from the machines spilled to the floor behind them as they ceaselessly rattled off the latest local and national news. Floor-to-ceiling-high banks of electronic equipment, including reel-to-reel tape recorders, commanded the opposite wall. TV monitors hung at either end of the room tuned to Channel 4, the local NBC station, and the sound from the radio station was piped in over speakers. It was an impressive sight. In fact, it looked like how I had imagined the city room of a newspaper would.

Everyone seemed busy. Judy D'Angelis, the midday anchor, was preparing for her next newscast. An editor stood at the ready to check her work. I was told that every piece of copy and every sound bite had to be checked by an editor and approved for the air. Judy and the engineer who sat by that huge bank of equipment were cutting what's called an "actuality," a short statement from a news maker, for her next newscast.

Neal Seavey, a graying, middle-aged man and longtime WNBC news anchor, was on the phone. While he was holding, Mary Beth introduced us. When I heard his name, I realized that I was shaking the hand of the guy I was replacing. Neal had been doing the news for Howard since he and Fred had gone on the air. I felt strange facing him without addressing what was going on, but he smiled when he welcomed me. Later, Mary Beth assured me that he'd be reassigned. Past Neal's workstation sat a young black man who, Mary Beth informed me, was about to leave the station. The newsroom was budgeted for only five newspeople and since I had come, someone had to go. The news hit me like a blow to the stomach. This young black man was losing his job because of me. I was astonished that he could smile and shake my hand, knowing that I was the reason he was out.

By that time, Howard had arrived for work and I was shown to his office, which was on the same side of the building as Kevin's. I was happy to see him, but I was even happier to see Fred, whom I hadn't laid eyes on since DC101. To my surprise, Fred was rather cold and standoffish. He acted as if he were meeting me for the first time. Later I would realize that Fred had many unexplainable traits such as this, and we'd eventually explain them by saying that he was from Mars. But just then, I had other things on my mind.

"Howard," I said, "I just met the guy they fired to hire me."

"Robin," he replied, "they did the same thing to me when I got here. They introduced me to the guy who was working afternoons."

"But he's a black guy," I protested.

"Robin, we didn't make the system," he said, now understanding fully why I was so upset. "It's not your fault that he's losing his job."

"Yeah, but it probably really meant something to him to work at NBC. It means nothing to me."

Howard shrugged his shoulders. "Well, what are you going to do?" he answered. "I wanted to work with you, and that means that somebody had to get the ax. It wasn't easy to tell Neal I didn't want him. He was a nice guy, he just wasn't you."

I felt like Typhoid Mary in that newsroom. Neal Seavey had really wanted to keep that job on the show with Howard, and the black reporter was going to have a hard time finding a job as good as the one he'd just lost. Crossing the bridge into New York City the second time was beginning to look like a big mistake.

There were all kinds of undercurrents in the WNBC offices. Everybody had secrets. No one spoke above a whisper. Conversations ended and people scattered when I walked into a room. There was no denying that the people who worked there were an unhappy lot, suspicious of anyone new. I was to discover, too, in that first day, that Mary Beth wasn't going to win any popularity contests despite her assertions of how loyal her staff was to her and how beloved she was by them. She claimed credit for the news department's every success and award. Her staff was so superb, they were uniformly coveted by the other local stations, and she took full credit for making them that way because she possessed all the secrets of becoming a great newsperson. These she promised to impart to me.

Once Mary Beth left the room, it was clear that things were not exactly as she had described them. As I approached Mary Beth's secretary and Judy, who were now huddled in a corner of the room, I overheard them sneering at Mary Beth's claims of responsibility for the quality of their work and mimicking her demeanor. When they noticed me, her secretary freely admitted that she was leaving and was glad of it, though no job was waiting for her. She implied that she just couldn't take her boss any longer. Then, second-guessing

herself, she told me that things weren't really that bad and everything would be okay. Practically every time Mary Beth walked out
of the room, someone mocked her. What a strange place WNBC
was turning out to be.

I was relieved to be able to escape the newsroom at four and join
Howard and Fred on the radio. At DC101, the studio had always
been our oasis in a desert of insanity, where we would at least be left
alone to do our job on the air. Unfortunately, that wasn't the case at
WNBC. Howard sat in the center of the big console, speaking into a
microphone. Directly across from him, behind a huge window, was
an engineer who sat at a control panel. The engineer ran all of the
equipment. Fred sat in the room with the guy, telling him when to
open microphones, hit sound effects, and run commercials.

I wasn't doing the news that day, just observing, and I noticed
right away that Kevin's shiny bald head was practically pressed
against the glass. Howard began the show with a brief hello and
introduced me as a new member of the staff. Then he said the call
letters, "WNBC," and signaled the engineer to hit commercials. As
soon as he stopped talking, I heard a loud thud, as if something had
hit the wall.

"What was that?" I asked.

"Oh," Howard sighed. "Kevin probably just threw another
phone."

"*Another* phone? Howard," I demanded, "what have you gotten
me into?"

With an impish grin Howard replied, "I said it wasn't going to
be easy," then signaled the engineer to open the mikes.

I was beginning to understand all too well what he meant. At
least there had been a honeymoon period at DC101. Now I was
being told that there would be no such period of pleasantry at
WNBC. It was war from day one, and I had just been brought up to
the front line. I wanted to go to the bathroom, but I didn't dare
open the studio door with Kevin on the other side waiting to
explode each time he thought Howard had done something wrong.
It didn't take much to set him off. When I asked Howard why
Kevin had hurled the phone, he said that he probably hadn't liked
the way he'd said "WNBC." Who knew when the next phone-
hurling offense would occur? We were boxed in, and there was no
safe place.

Since I'd come in at nine that morning, I left the air early and checked in at the Warwick Hotel on Sixth and Fifty-fourth, where the station was putting me up until my apartment was ready. One of the women from the sales staff had to check me in because I still didn't have credit cards. Being shepherded around was embarrassing, but I was exhausted and anxious to get to my room. I was standing behind her like a child, clutching my NBC employee folder in my arms as she took care of the paperwork, when I heard the slurred speech of a man behind me saying, "Oh, we work for the same company."

Before I could turn around, his arms encircled my neck and his head found my shoulder. I stood there, tired and shocked, not knowing what to do but wanting to scream. Then the voice of a woman obviously assigned to take care of the guy piped up, "No, you work for ABC," she insisted, pulling him off me.

Once unfettered, I could look my attacker in the eye. To my astonishment, I recognized the face. I had watched him, in fact, had been quite impressed by his performance on the TV show "Bosom Buddies." Tom Hanks was still relatively unknown then. He hadn't yet made *Splash*, the movie that would launch his phenomenal big-screen success. New York really was like no place else on earth. Even the bum giving you a hard time could be a star. Tom has since admitted to a brief dalliance with marijuana and cocaine, which he quickly ended when, according to an article in *Vanity Fair*, he determined that a good father wouldn't carry on this way.

All the events of the day whirled past on the movie screen of my mind as I sought out sleep between the fresh hotel sheets. At least the room was nice and warm and clean. I wasn't even aware that I had drifted off until I woke with a start. I was panting and terrified, but I couldn't remember why. I guess that was a nightmare, I thought, and I haven't even been in New York a week. New York had won the first two rounds, but I was still going to answer the bell for rounds three and four and five. I didn't care how much the place scared me, I wasn't going to let it beat me. There had to be a way. Millions of other people lived in New York and loved it. I had to stay in the battle long enough to figure out how to do it too. But, I had to admit, I hadn't found any soft spots yet.

Tuesday brought more bad news. Sitting in on the show the day before, I'd realized that Howard was trying to sandwich a little entertainment between lots of music, news, traffic reports, and commercials. WNBC was so tightly formatted that there was hardly room to breathe. When he did talk, he was supposed to do it in two-and-a-half-minute chunks and no more. Here was a performer, a humorist who often needed ten to fifteen minutes to develop a story, being told to dilute and refine everything he wanted to say into two and a half minutes. No wonder other deejays sounded so dumb and wound up giving themselves goofy names as a substitute for entertainment; there wasn't time for anything else.

If Howard wanted to do a recorded bit like "God Weather Forecasts," a staple of the DC101 show, it had to conform to the two-and-a-half-minute rule, and he wasn't allowed to talk and play a bit in the same break. Talk time was a precious commodity at WNBC, and Kevin was right outside the door, keeping count of every second. Now Mary Beth informed me that I'd be similarly constrained while doing the news. There were four newscasts in the afternoon-drive format; the first two were two-and-a-half-minute headline lead-ins to the five-minute network news at the top of each hour. My job assignment was to tightly construct and deliver four to five stories with sound in that amount of time leading into the network news. This was called meeting the network. How creative.

We were back to square one. All the ground we'd fought to clear at DC101 was a memory. I was doing a traditional newscast with local fire and accident stories, and Howard was doing a traditional deejay job, giving the time, temperature, and a couple of yuks between songs. When I wasn't in the studio with Howard, I spent the rest of the week learning to write a newscast to time and practiced reading my copy to time with Mary Beth sitting across from me holding a stopwatch.

Getting my personal life together was another ordeal. I had to go before a co-op board to be approved before I could move into my new apartment. In the meantime, I had to let the movers in even though I couldn't legally take possession. That meant a trip on the subway because I didn't want to take my car out of the hotel garage. Just making it there and back without getting killed, I thought, was an accomplishment.

Owing Howard that thousand dollars was also beginning to

bother me. Howard and I had just gotten over a terribly difficult experience, and I didn't want something as trivial as money rocking the boat. I still didn't know him well enough to understand that there wouldn't have been a problem, so I turned to my parents for help. I tried to explain the situation to my mother by phone, but she just shuttled me off to my father even though she always handled the money. He started yelling as soon as he picked up the receiver, which let me know that she had already briefed him as to the nature of the call. "I'm sick and tired of having to always bail you out of trouble. Why do you have to drag us into everything?"

He sounded as if he was just getting revved up, but my blood was already boiling. I wanted to crawl through the phone and stuff the words right down his throat. I couldn't believe he was making such a stink. Hadn't I always been good to them when I had money? I was the one who'd put the fence around the backyard. I had bought them their first color television set, and had kept my promise never to miss a car payment even when it meant I had to go without food. I never borrowed money without paying it back, and I didn't intend to argue. "Excuse me," I interrupted in mid-sentence, "put my mother back on the phone."

"Either you want to loan me the money or you don't," I told her calmly when she picked up. "So just say yes or no. I'm not listening to that noise."

"Oh, you can have the money," she quickly replied.

I was on a short tether. Although my parents didn't know it, their relationship with me was already down for the count. Right then, I swore to myself that I would get their money back to them in record time, and then I'd give them their wish. I would never drag them into my life again.

I couldn't help but contrast the Sterns's response to my needs with my parents' reaction. Alison and Howard had known me only a little over a year, yet they trusted me more than my parents ever had. I decided at that moment that I'd rather live on the street than ever again ask my mother and father to help me with anything. The doors between us were slamming shut, and my parents couldn't even hear them. They had never known who I was, what I wanted or needed, or how to offer me support. I wanted so much out of life, but they didn't seem to feel I deserved any of it. If I had always been a burden, now was the time to absolve them of it.

I moved into my apartment a week later and lived in the dark, without a phone, so that I could send them most of my first paycheck. Within the month, I'd repaid the loan in full. My mother even had the nerve to say that I didn't have to rush after the last payment. I have never asked them for anything since that day.

My new place was smack in the middle of a working-class Queens neighborhood, but even though the buildings were literally smashed against each other, it was a perfect place to withdraw from the world. There was no hallway, stairway, or neighbors to contend with. The front door was my front door. Somehow, right away, I craved solitude. I never even saw my next-door neighbors.

Back at work, I was beginning to learn what it must be like in hell. Mary Beth became an ever-present demon at my shoulder, whispering to me that I was incompetent and didn't deserve to be at NBC. I was terrible at meeting the network right from the start. I never seemed to be able to talk fast enough to get all the news in before the network anchor started to speak. Each time I missed, whether by an inch or a mile, I wound up in Mary Beth's office being verbally pummeled. Never once did Mary Beth offer constructive advice. She only criticized—and loudly. I felt that everyone in the newsroom was aware of Mary Beth's dissatisfaction with my performance, and even the engineers started to razz me when I'd come off the air, clucking their disapproval at my latest near miss. I couldn't have cared less about tarnishing the good name of NBC News, but I felt bad about letting Howard down.

While Mary Beth was needling me in the newsroom, Kevin was making himself a thorn in all our sides on air. The NBC brass, who had actually hired Howard as insurance against the loss of their already out-of-control morning man Don Imus, now regarded him as a maniac who might jeopardize their FCC license with his loose tongue. Kevin's job, while we were on the air, was to sit with his hand on the dump button, a seven-second delay that would delete any words he felt didn't belong on the air. He sat across from Howard for the entire show with his arms folded across his chest, a permanent smirk etched on his face. It wasn't easy trying to entertain listeners with that sourpuss glaring at us while we worked. To make things worse, he'd sometimes actually come into the studio. The first time was quite a shock.

It was my second or third day on the air. He walked in, stood in front of me, and said, "Hey, Howard, what am I doing?" Once he had Howard's attention, he placed his hands in front of my chest and started rubbing the thumb and index finger of each hand back and forth. "I don't know," Howard said and shrugged, annoyed.

"I'm tuning my radio." Kevin snickered, then fled.

I stared at Howard in wide-eyed disbelief. "And they're worried about what *you* might do!" I said, shaking my head.

A few weeks later, I was carrying food back from the commissary when I felt something hit my behind as I passed Kevin in the engineer's studio. Rather than make a big deal out of what I suspected was a slap on the behind, I simply upended the tray down the front of his shirt and into his lap. As he was mopping up catsup and picking off French fries, I apologized by explaining that something had brushed against me and made me lose my balance. There was never another problem.

Kevin was also bent on reinventing Howard as a true announcer in the NBC tradition. He had to report to Kevin's office each afternoon for instruction. It seemed that Kevin preferred jocks who spun records and pronounced the call letters just right to the kind of personality radio Howard made so well. It was hard to miss his disapproval. If there was an NBC management course in humiliation, Kevin and Mary Beth had graduated at the top of the class.

On the heels of Howard's last suspension, Kevin had also been put in charge of all recorded bits that were played in the show. The most recent offending bit was an episode of "God Weather" called "Virgin Mary Kong," which had been played the week before I'd arrived. It featured God telling Howard about this new pinball game, the object of which was to get Mary through a singles bar without getting pregnant. Howard and God played a round, and Mary failed to make it to the door intact. The Roman Catholic Archdiocese of New York City had called to complain. As a result, every recorded bit had to be previewed by Kevin. Again he refused to confine himself to censoring the material to make sure it met broadcast standards and insisted on giving us his unsolicited critique of the humor.

Within weeks of my arrival at the station, Dom, the general manager, called me into his office to ask why I thought Howard was having such a hard time adjusting. I told him that I could sum up the problem in one word—Kevin. A saint couldn't have done any better with that ogre breathing his foul, hypercritical breath in our faces. To my surprise, Dom actually took my advice. Before long, a red phone, which was a direct line to the studio, was installed in Kevin's office. In order to tell the studio engineer to hit the button, all he had to do was pick up the phone. He didn't even have to dial. Those unnerving daily meetings were cut back to once a week. Kevin still got to approve every recorded bit, but at least we were spared his grimaces. It wasn't much, but it was an improvement.

There was no such respite for me personally. Mary Beth's relentless criticism of my work had a devastating effect on my self-esteem. I actually began to feel that I'd never be able to do a news-cast to suit her. Each time I sat down at the mike to do the news, I froze, my anxieties so high that concentrating on my work became impossible. All that kept running through my mind was that if I screwed up again, I'd wind up right back in Mary Beth's office and invariably, I'd stumble. Walking down the narrow hall back to the newsroom after yet another fiasco was like walking to my own execution.

Everything I tried failed. Having trouble fitting in four stories, I decided to give myself a break and did only three. It worked, and I managed to meet the network perfectly. I figured once I got comfortable with this routine, I could eventually graduate to four, but Mary Beth wanted perfection right away. As soon as she discovered what I was up to, she demanded that each cast contain no less than four different items. Her reasoning was that people felt more comfortable with four stories. I didn't bother to point out that a full five minutes of news followed my brief newscast. I assumed that Mary Beth, like my mother, didn't take kindly to being challenged. In fact, Mary Beth was reminding me a lot of my mother, and as a result, her words sliced through me like a knife. I found her humorless and moody. It appeared to me that the entire news staff felt that humoring her was a part of the job. They never failed to take notice of what she was wearing and always complimented her latest hairdo. Soon I found myself falling back into line, complimenting Mary Beth's impeccable taste in clothing and accessories in an attempt to pick up brownie points.

One evening when I was preparing for my last newscast of the night, an alarm sounded in the newsroom that signified that the network was going to break into regular programming with a bulletin. Kevin was still in the station and came over to help me get ready. I had to go on the air and basically ad-lib until the network announcer began to speak. Afterward, Kevin was very enthusiastic about my performance and said he'd call Mary Beth to tell her how well I'd done. The next day Mary Beth called me into her office to ream me out for not calling her at home when the emergency occurred. That I had done a good job never came up.

I was at a complete loss. What could possibly please this woman? Once I figured out how to meet the network requirement with four stories and started to do it on a consistent basis, she started to criticize my copy. Now, all of a sudden, I couldn't write, and all my copy had to be approved by Mary Beth before I went on the air. I had to sit across from her desk as she tore apart my scripts with a red pencil. Either the words were wrong or the story selection was wrong. No copy ever passed muster without a few red slashes.

Mary Beth made me feel so bad about my work that I couldn't even look the other newspeople in the eye. I was so demoralized that I couldn't get engineers to work with me when I needed to cut tape. The only person who showed any compassion at all was Bill Mahr, the afternoon editor. He often harumphed that I should just ignore the old witch after approving the same stories she was about to rip apart.

Having been the victim of unrelenting torture for two months, I felt that any break at all would be a relief. I was grateful that Christmas was right around the corner and that I could just get away from all this, even if for only a few days. I worked right up to Christmas Eve. That afternoon before I went to work, I had packed a suitcase and put it in the trunk of the car. As soon as that last newscast was over, I was going to go home.

I jumped in the car and headed straight for that same bridge that had led me into this awful place. Though I was tired, the night driving was easy. I felt the pressure lift as soon as I was in New Jersey, and the farther south I drove, the better I felt—until I reached 3034 Grantley Avenue, Baltimore.

As I pulled my suitcase from the trunk, I envisioned what was waiting for me behind the door of this supposed refuge. Nothing. This was not a place in which I felt safe or at peace. It was not a place where I could let down my guard. I would have to expend as much energy keeping up my defenses inside that house as I did at NBC. Suddenly, I realized I had not come here to rest, I had come here because I was supposed to. It was a holiday, and holidays are supposed to be spent with your family, like it or not.

I rang the bell and waited. Both my mother and father came to the door. Standing there looking at those expectant faces, I felt a profound sadness. Here was another group of people who wanted something from me, and I was utterly tapped out. The well was dry of everything but tears, so I grabbed my bag and headed for the stairs, shouting behind me that I had to get some sleep. I just managed to close the door before those tears burst into rivers, coursing down my cheeks. I threw on my nightclothes, climbed into bed, and as I cried myself to sleep, wondered who I was doing this for.

It wasn't for me. I hated Christmas at home. All I ever remembered was waking up, not getting the toys I had wanted, and then looking for my parents all day as they went from house to house in the neighborhood getting drunk and forgetting to feed us. To top it all off, as I got older, they left me alone to clean up the huge mess in the kitchen after we finally did eat.

So I must have been doing it for them, my family. The people who failed to believe in or support me, who had abused and neglected me, and had left me wandering alone in the world afraid to trust another living soul. The same people who had raised me to do my duty without ever teaching me to love.

Robin, I said to myself as I drifted into tear-filled slumber, you don't have to do this anymore, not for them. It was the last time I would ever go home for Christmas, and, although I didn't know it then, the last time I'd see that house for ten years.

When I got back to New York, I knew that I had no choice but to figure out how to make my life work. There was no mother or father to encourage me, no man to soothe me, no friends to bolster my resolve. There was just me. I had to learn to take care of myself because no one else was going to. But I had no idea how gargantuan a task I'd set for myself.

14

DEAD AGAIN

I wonder if the movie The Devil and Daniel Webster *is any good. It's an old black-and-white movie, and I only saw it once, but you couldn't really call it seeing the movie because I was in a sort of insomnia stupor, that point at which you're not asleep but not truly awake either. I remember lots of elves and demons and thought it must have been quite scandalous in its day. I've never seen it when in full control of my senses.*

—1983

There was only one reason for putting up with all the Kevin Methenys and Mary Beth Januses, and the living embodiment of it was ensconced right down the hall from Howard's office. Dom Imus, the WNBC morning man, proved that real radio stardom had its rewards. Imus was rumored to make a million a year. He had a whole suite of offices, a staff of writers, and his own secretary. His limousine was on call twenty-four hours a day.

For all his success, Imus was a real asshole. Management wouldn't dare suggest a meeting between their great morning man and their new afternoon talent. Aside from Dom and Kevin, it appeared that no one at the station was at liberty to address him directly. Even Charles McCord, his main writer and on-air partner, seemed to tiptoe around his temperament.

When we first got to New York, I tried listening to Imus to see what all the fuss was about. I thought something was wrong with my radio because Imus sounded muffled, and I kept trying to tune in the station properly. Later I learned that he had a substance abuse problem at the time, and I gave up trying to decipher his mumbling.

The first time I saw Imus he was wearing one of those parachute-cloth jumpsuits. It was so dirty, it looked like he'd had it on for a week. His eyes were hidden by the wide brim of his cowboy hat, and the only visible part of his face was his witchlike nose. I could swear I saw scabs. This, I thought, is the only bum in the city who gets limo'ed to his park bench. Kevin and Dom revered Imus. As far as they were concerned, there was no one better. They wanted Howard to be like him, and they wanted my on-air relationship with Howard to be like Imus's and McCord's.

Despite them, by the winter of 1983 we finally began to find our way around WNBC's restrictive format. "Beaver Breaks" gave way to weeklong takeoffs of other TV shows, movies, and miniseries. There was "Hill Street Jews" and "Das Love Boat," "Planet of the Gay Apes" and "Gaystoke: The Legend of Tarzan, Lord of the Gay Apes." We began to chat about current events outside of the newscasts so that Howard and I could actually have a back and forth about what was going on.

That banter often inspired some of our most outrageous bits. After I reported that Jesse Jackson had referred to New York as "Hymietown," I suggested that we change the words to the song "New York, New York." A day later, Fred, as Frank Sinatra, sang the new parody, complete with orchestration. After a couple of plays, there were so many complaints that Kevin removed it from the studio.

Discussing current events with me seemed to be the most dangerous thing Howard could do, judging by Kevin, who by now had been affectionately dubbed Pig Virus. The day Princess Grace died, Pig Virus burst into the studio just before the news to forbid us from making any comments outside of simply reporting the event. Sometime later we would finally get hold of a news story we could really sink our teeth into without even Kevin objecting.

A Howdy Doody puppet was stolen. After I reported the story in the regular newscast, we turned it into a special event, with bulletins and updates. Eventually we dubbed the show "The Day Doody Died." Kevin showed up in the studio during a break to tell us how entertaining he had found the show that day, but he couldn't resist throwing in a few criticisms. We hadn't played much music, and while he was letting us break format repeatedly that day, this was a special occasion and not something to be indulged in every day. Characters created in Washington really came into focus now.

"Outofthecloset Stern" and "Mr. Blackswell," two gay men played by Howard and Fred, became regular fixtures. They'd work up a script and then I'd interact with the characters, never having seen what they intended to say. Somehow, like magic, I always managed to find my way through these interviews.

One of my favorite characters, "Momalukaboobooday," was barely written. Moma was actually Howard doing a very broad caricature of a streetwise black man. I really enjoyed interacting with all these pretend people and seeing what I could make of the interchange. Howard and Fred created these characters and then put them into some situation. I was the clean-up person, making sure we got out of them with a laugh.

Howard had even begun to assemble a troupe of players. Al Rosenberg had been one of Imus's writers and voice men. When they wanted to give him the boot, Howard agreed to try him out for a while, and it was working. Al did a very broad caricature of a black woman whom Howard called "Sue Simmons" after the local Channel 4 newswoman, and Al used that same voice when he sat in for me on sick days as my sister, "Ophelia Quivers." Jackie Martling was a Long Island comedian who had sent us some of his albums, and Howard, hearing something he liked, invited Jackie to come in on Tuesdays. Martling was the start of a new and improved "Think Tank." Because of him, "The Match Game," "Trivia," and "Rank Outs" returned.

But even though things on the air were coming together, there were still battles on every front. Imus started saying rotten things on air in the morning about our show. When we answered back in the afternoon, we were told that we were not allowed to talk about

Mr. Imus. Howard demanded the same treatment, agreeing not to mention Imus if Imus didn't mention him, but the truce didn't hold.

Now that Kevin wasn't meeting with Howard, he was trying to memo him to death with list after list of his on-air transgressions. And just when I thought I was going to survive the newsroom, Mary Beth mounted a new attack on a different front. She had convinced the powers that be that I needed a speech coach because I just didn't sound right on the air. First, I couldn't meet the network time limits. Then, I couldn't write, and now, I couldn't talk. Mary Beth presented this new plan to me as if it were a gift. I was going to get to work with the same woman who had coached Oprah Winfrey, and the station would be picking up the tab. She failed to mention that they'd only committed to bankrolling the lessons for six weeks, at which time, if there was no improvement in my speech problem, I would be replaced. She really had me this time—or so she thought.

The speech coach, who proved to be even weirder than Mary Beth, was a short, older woman whose affect was never quite right. Her studio was in a small, crowded midtown apartment shared with several big dogs who had trouble maneuvering around all the clutter. She worked in one little corner with a stool and a desk. A video camera and monitor were prominently displayed because her primary focus was on-air presentation. She constantly raved about the on-air talents of her favorite client, CBS newsman Charles Osgood.

According to this coach, I had two major problems. One was the letter S. The other was that I didn't emphasize just a few key words when I read a news story. She gave me exercises to practice at home, and when I was with her, she had me read news copy into a tape recorder. Then she gave me her critique. I never even finished the series because before the six weeks were up, Mary Beth got her wish. The afternoon-drive newscasts were handed to someone else. I was no longer Howard's newsperson.

As you can imagine, all of this was taking its toll on my fragile psyche. I was just barely holding on to my sanity before the ouster. My fuse was super short. Old problems that had plagued Howard and me in Washington returned with a vengeance I couldn't control. Howard would say something or do something on the air that I misinterpreted or didn't quite understand, and I'd just leave the studio and take a walk around the building to cool off. He'd turn around to say something to me only to find me gone. Eventually Howard felt the need to say something about my behavior. "Robin," he pleaded, "either you're doing the show or you're not. You just can't get up and walk out."

I was either okay or I was mad as hell. It was as if I no longer possessed any of the other speeds. The least little thing, like getting the wrong lunch order, could set me off, and I'd just start screaming about everything that I imagined had ever been done to me. Nothing ever went away. Grievances kept mounting up, one on top of another. I hated getting angry because my anger was so great. I was afraid that one day it would get away from me and I'd do something terrible. This only served to double my fury at whatever person lit the spark.

It didn't help that intellectually I knew I sounded just like my mother. My nerves were shot, and those little jaunts around the building helped me blow off steam. When I stopped doing that, I could think of no other alternative but to lash out at the person who cared about me the most. After the show harboring some ridiculous resentment over some petty thing, I'd hunt Howard down in his office, corner him, and proceed to conduct a very loud discussion. Usually even I could see that my screaming was about nothing once it was all over, but at the time it seemed critical. Howard, who was fighting constant battles with WNBC to keep the show on the air and to keep me employed, did not enjoy being repaid with shouts and insults. At first he tried to make sense out of my eruptions. Later he just started yelling back.

Hours later, I'd follow up an outburst with a call of apology and a promise that it wouldn't happen again. Howard was always receptive and understanding, again attempting to determine what the problem was. He tried to explain how he was trying to thwart WNBC's attacks on all of us and give me a pep talk in the process, but time and again, I lashed out at him irrationally as if he were the cause of my grief.

There had already been a million fights and a million apologies before Judy D'Angelis was named newsperson on the show. This was more humiliation than I could bear. I wasn't being fired, mind you, because the station chiefs had determined that I was Howard's security blanket. Those were their exact words. It wasn't as if I did anything. For some stupid reason, Howard just liked having me around, and they agreed that he worked better that way. If they had only known what was going on behind the scenes.

Trying to put the best face on WNBC's latest intrusion into the show, Howard kept saying I should be glad that I didn't have to worry about meeting the stupid network anymore and could concentrate exclusively on the show. I still had newsroom duties, though.

I was a reporter again, and I had to stick around to do the last newscast of the night, the one at nine o'clock, an hour after the show was over. This was another slap in the face. That newscast had been a part of the job when I was the afternoon-drive anchor, but when Judy took over, she only worked until the end of the show. I had to hang around an extra hour to do this one, largely unheard, news report. Mary Beth was really in her glory. She actually had visions of sending me out on stories. That's where I drew the line. I was not going to run around New York all afternoon and then dash back to be on the air. Any time the subject came up, I always came up with some excuse to stonewall her.

The head brains at WNBC chose Judy because they assumed Howard liked working with women. Maybe the plan was to use Judy to replace me altogether, but I'll never know. It's not like they discussed this stuff with me. Judy was a perfect newsperson in the NBC mold, and just as with everyone else in the studio, Howard included her in everything that was going on. Being taken off the news was one thing, but watching and listening to Howard working cheerily with Judy was intolerable. It pushed me even farther into that ditch of despair I was digging. Ethel Merman, the Broadway star, died shortly after Judy joined the show, and Howard discovered while talking to Judy that she did a Merman impression. Every time she came in, he asked her to do it again. I smiled, sitting there in the studio, but I was dying inside.

I went for Howard like a screaming banshee after the show. It must have hurt terribly to hear me accusing him of betraying me once again when he was working so hard not only to make the show a success but to withstand my incredible volatility. At that point, he, Fred, and I always traveled to work together. We used the subway to get to and from work and believed we were safer traveling in threes. Even though I had to do another newscast an hour after the show ended, Howard and Fred waited for me, using the time to write. But on this particular night, Howard was so disgusted with me, he walked out and made his way home alone. Fred stayed behind to make sure I got home safely.

I couldn't hold it together anymore. I managed to be okay when the show was okay, but as far as I was concerned, the show wasn't working. It didn't feel the same as it had in Washington, and my losing my place in the lineup meant I wasn't working either. I felt that I had broken my promise to Howard and that my instablity had left our relationship in tatters. As far as a life outside of the show was concerned, I didn't have one. Once again, I'd put everything into the show, and again I felt it slipping away. After we got off the subway in Forest Hills, Fred drove me to Howard's apartment to pick up my car. I cried all the way there, trying to explain to him that I was trying as hard as I could to hold on. I wanted someone to know I wasn't being wantonly destructive. I just couldn't help my behavior. I don't think Freddy had any idea that I was talking about my sanity.

I was experiencing full-blown regret by the time Howard called me that night and started apologizing as soon as I heard his voice. Howard hadn't called for an apology though, he'd grown tired of them. I tried to explain that it was the whole Judy thing that had set me off this time. Right away, he assured me that he'd much rather be working with me but we needed ratings if we were ever going to gain full control of the show and that meant doing the best show possible regardless of who was doing the news. All it would take was time according to Howard and he urged me to pull it together so that we could make it work.

I knew that night that my relationship with Howard was hanging by a thread, but my rage was out of control. A few weeks later, I was in his office screaming again. I had become incredibly insecure, and the only way I'd ever learned to determine if people cared was to make them fight with me. In my family, fighting equaled love. But Howard and I didn't fight well. Every fight left its residue. The air was never cleared afterward, it only got heavier.

This time Howard put it all in perspective for me. He looked me squarely in the eye, making sure he had my full attention, and announced, "Robin, you're getting crazy on me again, just like you did in Washington." I couldn't deny that he was right. The way Howard remembers it, he told me that he couldn't take much more, and darned if I didn't get better!

But I didn't get better, I just took my problems underground. I stopped fighting with him because it wasn't working, but that rage had to go somewhere, and when Howard refused to be my punching bag anymore, I turned it on myself just as I had in the air force. Only this time, because my descent was more gradual, I was able to keep my breakdown a secret.

I had already seen the signs. I was withdrawn, had no energy, and was eating everything in sight. My ice cream addiction returned in full force. I had already become familiar with all the Friendly's restaurants in Queens and had discovered a few supermarket brands of vanilla chocolate chip that I liked. After the arguing stopped when Howard refused to be the enemy, I began to blame myself for my predicament and the voices in my head started to pick me apart.

Now, with Mary Beth's constant criticism coupled with my own, there was no letup. Morning, noon, and night, I was wrong. Inside my apartment and outside it, I was worthless and didn't deserve to be around. I had always been able to escape in sleep, but now even that became impossible. I spent all day fighting Mary Beth, and at night when I settled down and lowered my defenses, I'd start on myself. It was as if my mind was more active when I was lying down. As soon as I shut my eyes, I'd rerun everything that had happened that day at sixty miles an hour, with a negative spin. Maybe Mary Beth was right about me. Maybe I didn't belong there. Maybe Howard liked working with Judy better than he liked working with me. Maybe I was crazy. As time went on, I spent every night sitting on the living room couch watching "Joe Franklin" and the late, late-night black-and-white movies on television. I was getting by on almost no sleep at all. What little energy I had went into doing the show. Even getting to work became a chore.

Howard's twenty-seventh-floor apartment was our common meeting ground; from there the three of us set off for work each day. It was all I could do to face the high-rise's army of doormen, bellmen, garage attendants, and security guards. Once inside his place, the real act started. I had to appear normal, not like a person who sat in the dark and peeked out through her curtains at life. And the act had to last until the end of the evening, when I could finally get back to my apartment and collapse on the floor or resume placing the tiny odd-shaped pieces in the thousand-piece jigsaw puzzle that lay spread out on the bare living room floor.

The puzzles took me out of my head and gave me some relief. I sat for hours, holding myself up by leaning on the heel of my left palm. When I began to lose sensation in the fingers of my left hand, it took me a while to realize that the way I was sitting was causing the problem. After I figured it out, I changed positions to prevent permanent nerve damage. On the weekends, I'd sit in darkened movie theaters. The massive screen and the loud volume blasted me out of myself and I could trade my problems for those of the huge people in front of me for at least a little while.

I lost track of time and forgot to pay bills. I didn't have the strength to go through the hassle of getting a New York driver's license and was still using my Maryland one. I couldn't even handle ordinary everyday transactions. When tax time rolled around, having to file forms for both Maryland and New York overwhelmed me. I took all the forms and shoved them into a drawer and forgot about them. When the show went on vacation, I was afraid to leave the city because of an irrational fear that I wouldn't be allowed back in.

I was feeling so rotten, there was no way I wanted to deal with my family. I sat around the house listening to the phone ring but refused to answer, afraid that my mother or father would be on the other end. Later, when I was wallowing in the depths of self-pity, I'd imagine that my friends had stopped calling me because they no longer liked me. But even these precautions failed to protect me from my family. They caught up with me. It happened one Saturday night during what for me was a pretty good weekend. I suppose that's why I answered the phone. I hadn't spoken to anyone in Baltimore in months, and I had no idea what my reaction would be— and I didn't want to find out. But there he was, my father, on the other end of the line. Tears streamed down my face at the sound of his voice. "Daddy," I croaked, "I'm sorry, but I can't talk."

"That's okay," he said in a cheery voice, ignoring my obviously hysterical state, "I'll talk for the both of us."

There must have been one small vestige of sanity somewhere in my head, because at that moment I said to myself, These people will kill me. They won't do it on purpose, but they'll do it just the same, and I've got to protect myself from them. How could my father just carry on a normal conversation when I was sobbing hysterically? Only a nut could have ignored the state I was in.

After that, I gave up answering the phone altogether. I worked out a code with Howard. He had to call and ring once, then hang up and call right back to get me to pick up. I wasn't taking any more chances of running into good old mom and dad until I could handle it. Howard, of course, had no idea what I was up to, but he went along because he needed to get me on the phone.

They weren't through fucking with me at work, either. After Judy started doing the news, Kevin and Mary Beth had to come up with a way to justify my salary. They decided to base part of my pay on the number of times I spoke on the air. This also gave Kevin another way of controlling Howard. It worked out something like this: Howard could talk to me three times an hour, but he had to choose to talk to me either going into a commercial or coming out of one. That ruled out spontaneous conversation. Howard had to look at the show and decide where he wanted me and where he could do without me. Fred, meanwhile, was given a chart, and it was his job to keep track of every time I opened my mouth.

Working with Dom, Kevin, and Mary Beth was making me all too familiar with hate. Love and hate were said to be a lot alike, and I now knew why. Just as you become obsessed with the object of your love, you can't stop thinking about the people you hate. And I hated the three of them with more passion than I had ever managed when in love. As far as I was concerned, they were all trying to destroy us, but I hated Mary Beth most of all because I felt that she knew what she was doing and she enjoyed it.

I began to fantasize about creative ways of torturing Mary Beth to death. I wanted her to die slowly, painfully, and to know that I was the reason she was suffering. It became a nightly ritual to find out just how I planned to kill off Mary Beth. Howard, Fred, and I would all pile into one of our cars after leaving the subway for the ride back to Howard's apartment, and the first question asked was, "How are you going to do it tonight, Robin?"

Then I'd impart my latest morbid desire. Looking back, only two of my more inspired death dreams come to mind. The first, Howard's favorite, involved stripping Mary Beth and strapping her to a wall, then with a pair of stiletto heels, I'd stab her to death through her nipples.

The second, Howard actually got me to reveal on the air one day when Mary Beth had been particularly loathsome. He has always been exceptional at judging when people are about to blow, and he could tell that day that I was ripe. Like an expert attorney, he led me right to the edge and then I shouted, "I want to do the Bic pen test on Mary Beth's head!" When Howard prodded me, I explained the process in graphic detail.

"The Bic pen test," I told him, "is the one where they load a Bic pen into a rifle and then shoot it at a board. I want to replace that board with Mary Beth's head. After I fire the pen through her skull, I'll check to see if I can still write 'Bic' on the wall while it's still stuck in her brain." As I spoke, a saleswoman who had become a friend, Paula Schneider, stood at the studio window pale with terror, giving me the cut sign. But it was too late. I'd already said it. I was sure the price of that outburst would be instant termination.

Howard thought the whole thing was hysterical and went right to a commercial right out of my exuberant outburst. I, on the other hand, was waiting for the footsteps in the hall. They were coming rapidly. The heavy wooden door of the studio flew open with such force that it hit the other wall. In the doorway stood Kevin—grinning. "Oh God," he gasped in delight, "I wish I could have said that!"

That's when I realized what Howard already knew: that the WNBC triumvirate of management was not such a cohesive group. Kevin hated Mary Beth as much as I did, but I was the one who had to go straight back to the newsroom and face her. When I sat down at my desk, Mary Beth calmly looked up from her work, flashed her pearly whites in an evil Jokerlike grin, then immediately returned to what she was doing. I knew I was dead meat as far as she was concerned and that I'd better really watch my step.

Just as I'd thought, Mary Beth stepped up her campaign. She was at me every chance she got. So anxious was she to kill and gut me, she often overlooked the obvious. One day I had to park ten blocks from work in the pouring rain. When I finally reached the building, I was soaked to the skin. My shoes were squeaking, my hair was dripping water into my eyes, and my clothes were stuck to my body, but to Mary Beth all that had happened to me was that I was late again. She called me into her office before I could even remove my coat and started to lecture me.

"Excuse me, Mary Beth," I interrupted her, "but can I dry off first?"

"Oh," she said, puzzled, "is it raining?"

"No," I replied, feeling rather flip, "I just poured a bucket of water on my head."

"Well, go dry off and then come back," she said with a perfectly straight face, "I need to talk to you."

I went to the women's room and dried myself as best I could with paper towels, then wrung out the hem of my skirt to stop its dripping. My shoes were history. Then I returned to the snake pit we called the newsroom, feeling strangely brazen. When Mary Beth launched into her lecture about chronic lateness, I interrupted by asking her, "You really don't know what you're doing, do you?"

"What?" she asked, shaking her head in disbelief or just to hear it rattle. I wasn't sure which.

"You really don't know what you're doing, do you?" I said again.

Apparently surprised, she asked if she was getting to me, and I told her, "Yes!"

"Okay, fine," she said. "Then I won't speak to you for thirty days. No matter what you do, I won't say a word to you for a month."

Now I was confused. Could she actually be giving me a chance to recover when she had me on the ropes? I was so stunned, I just stood there gaping at her.

"Go," she said, waving me away with the back of her hand. "Go on! I'm not talking to you for thirty days," she said and continued shooing me away.

For the next month, Mary Beth kept her word. Whenever I did something that usually brought a swift rebuke, she'd just look at me and smile after glancing at the wall calendar behind her head. She didn't comment on my work. She didn't say hello. She didn't say a word, but she remained a glowering presence. Every day when I walked into the newsroom, she waited until she saw me looking and then made a point of marking off another day. They really could have used her in Vietnam, I thought. Prisoners of war wouldn't have stood a chance!

Thirty days. Thirty days without Mary Beth at me every second I was in the newsroom. Thirty days to work on myself. I was miserable and thought about quitting constantly, but whenever I did, I remembered what the show had been like in Washington. How I'd loved the show. At its best, it was like being on drugs. That's how transporting it was, and I knew it could be that good again if they'd only let us do our thing. Then my voices would taunt me with, "Why should you let Mary Beth win? You'd just better stick around until they fire you or you kill her."

Murder definitely had its appeal. For one thing, she wouldn't be around to gloat. But could I really kill another human being? The answer was no. I couldn't have lived with the knowledge, and I didn't want to sit around in jail for the rest of my life either. It seemed that I was stuck in an unsolvable dilemma. Then I figured it all out.

The way things were was killing me, and I felt that NBC's strict rules were strangling the show. A shake-up was definitely in order and since I wasn't being of much help on the air, I figured I was the best person to provide one. Despite Howard's certainty that we'd eventually get the ratings we needed to ease the pressure on us, I knew I was running out of time and probably wouldn't make it to that day. I decided to sacrifice myself for the sake of the show. I'd go down in a burst of flames after one gigantic confrontation with NBC, and then I'd be free. Thirty days without Mary Beth on my back would give me just enough energy for one last offensive.

At three o'clock the next day, I walked into the radio studio, took a seat, and leaning back, put my feet up on the console. As soon as Howard started the show, I started talking to him. I talked to him every break, before commercials, after commercials, during commercials. I spoke up whenever I felt like it, and I never left. In just a few minutes, I had broken all the rules Kevin had set down when he and Mary Beth took me off the news. I sat there waiting for someone to notice. I stayed in the studio for the whole show.

Nothing happened. Okay, so I got away with it for one shift, but they'd get me tomorrow, I thought. Howard was the first to notice what I was doing. "You're talking an awful lot today," he said the next time we were on the air. "Keep it up. Nobody's stopping you." What he didn't know was that I wanted them to try and stop me.

Fred had been dutifully marking his chart every time I spoke, and on the third day, he hit the talk-back button to warn me that I was stepping over the line. "Robin," he said over the intercom during a commercial break, "you've used up all of your speaking allotment for the whole month in the last three days."

"Whose fucking side are you on?" I yelled back at him after pushing my talk-back button. Like I said, I was a loose cannon and I yelled at everybody, friend and foe alike. Freddy was just trying to do his job and protect me. He couldn't have known that I meant to do this, that I was trying to get myself fired. I had made my decision in private to openly revolt, and now all I needed was for everybody else to just do their jobs and leave me alone.

I figured once Freddy's charts were filed, I'd be home free, but little did I know that Howard would swoop down and save me once again. He had offered to make up for all the times I'd spoken over my limit from his own pocket. All the while, I thought Kevin and everyone else in the front office had gone to sleep on me. So there I was doing the show full time when the ratings started to go up. Eventually Mary Beth did notice that I had disappeared from the newsroom, and she came to the studio to retrieve me. I had been breaking the rules for months by then, and Howard felt perfectly within his rights to solicit Kevin's help to rescue me. And to my surprise, he did. Kevin burst into the newsroom and informed Mary Beth she was no longer allowed to speak to me during the show.

This all would have been very funny and very rewarding had I not been in such bad shape. I really wanted to go, but I just couldn't quit. And now that my great plan had backfired, I was being held hostage to the show. I didn't know how much longer I could muster the energy it took to do it, and I didn't know what would happen once that energy ran out.

I was at a place I'd never been before—total mental exhaustion. Since there seemed to be no earthly escape from my pain, I started considering suicide. It started as a fleeting thought, but when I realized I was stuck, it became an obsession. I thought about it in every way possible—how to do it, what people would say afterward, what my funeral would be like, how big my obituary would be in the paper, how long it would take to find me. What really pissed me off was that I knew life would just go on. I had to stay around until I could make people really sorry for what they'd done to me. In my imaginings, no one ever suffered enough.

That still didn't prevent the nocturnal tours of my apartment to see if I had anything to do it with, or that daily question that sprang to mind as soon as I awoke: "Is today the day?" I asked myself that every morning. I wouldn't even keep aspirin in the house. I didn't want my death to be an impulsive act. If I was going to do it, I was going to have to get the supplies when I was genuinely ready. I'd had thoughts like this before, but never so strong and never so persistent. Just like the insomnia. It certainly didn't help that I spent all my time off the air alone. I had a galloping case of agoraphobia on top of all my other problems. Soon it would inflict another wound on what I considered was my foundering relationship with Howard.

In the summer after Howard and Alison had their first child, they decided to throw a little party to introduce their new arrival to the world. The big bash was going to be held at his parents' home. I checked the guest list every day to see if Howard was inviting Dom and Kevin. He finally decided that he couldn't invite anybody from the station if he didn't include them, so I told him that I wouldn't be there. He must have thought I was kidding.

The day of the party I tried as hard as I could to make myself leave the house, but the very thought of encountering Dom and Kevin paralyzed me. So I didn't go, and I never even phoned to say I wasn't coming because I was too filled with dread to make the call. I spent the afternoon sitting in my apartment with the curtains drawn. Ironically, Dom and Kevin never showed.

Howard was extremely hurt by my behavior, and, since no excuse was acceptable, he didn't even want to bother hearing one. So the whole subject was relegated to a growing list of things we just never discussed—a black hole in a conversation. Someone would mention the party to me, then realize that the person they were speaking to, the first person aside from Howard's actual family they'd have expected to be there, hadn't been, then would abruptly change the subject.

Fred too would fall victim to my disease. One night after he'd gotten home from work, he began to experience chest pains. He thought he was having a heart attack and decided to turn to his friend with the medical background. He climbed back into his car without calling and came to my door. I couldn't even get off the floor to see who it was. I lay there in the dark, praying that whoever was pounding at my door would just go away. Fred wound up in an emergency room that night. He had strained some muscles in his chest that weekend chopping down a tree in his grandfather's yard and was fine, but I had been no help at all. I didn't even know it was him until I showed up at Howard's to go to work the next day.

I felt pretty sorry for myself, sitting in my apartment alone on weekends and holidays, double-ordering Chinese food to hide the fact that I was by myself. I cried a lot. I cried because no one called, even though I wouldn't have answered the phone. I cried because everyone in New York seemed to be yelling at me. I cried because I didn't have a mother or father to go home to, and I cried because I was in terrible pain and couldn't sleep and was having strange thoughts. I was too tired to live and getting less and less afraid to die.

Things came to a head for me during my week off. Everybody on the show went on vacation at the same time so that none of us would be stuck alone at that god-awful station to fight the hoards of assholes who wanted us to fall flat on our faces. So there I was, idly roaming the streets of Manhattan with all the time in the world to kill, wondering if I'd take my life when I got home. I was crossing Columbus Circle when, from out of nowhere, tears started to stream down my cheeks.

I was crying this time because it was all over. I couldn't take it anymore, and I knew it was never going to stop. I felt very sad that such a good and loving person couldn't find a place in this world. I wasn't even angry anymore. If I'd been angry, maybe there would have been some hope, but all I felt was exhaustion.

I was determined to give myself every shot possible, though, before I put out the light. That afternoon when I reached home, I pulled out a book that had always been magic for me—the Yellow

Pages—just to see if I had spent all my wishes. After all, when I needed a place to live in Los Angeles, it had been the key. And when I needed a new career, it had provided the answer. In all the fairy tales, there were always three wishes. This was my third.

Now, with my very existence hanging in the balance, I went to the well and looked up Psychologists. I had no idea where to start. Did I expect to find an ad I liked or see a name that appealed to me for some unfathomable reason? But I opened the book anyway, and my eye went to a blocked-in ad for a referral service. Steeling myself, I dialed the number, and when a calm female voice answered, I found myself confessing to a total stranger, "I need help."

PART THREE
BREAKTHROUGH

15

IN THE BELLY OF THE BEAST

Happy Thanksgiving to me. I'll wish it to myself. No one else who knows me has. I don't regret spending the day alone since the only invitation I received was from my parents. I had some pumpkin pie and apple pie to celebrate the holiday and went to see a couple of movies. First I saw Terms of Endearment, *which made me cry, and then I followed it up with a terrible movie about a rat. Maybe next year I'll be able to celebrate the holidays with someone.*
—my diary, November 24, 1983

A day after making that phone call to the referral service, I sat in a small room waiting for a therapist, wondering what was going to happen next. I thought I knew a little about the therapeutic process because of the psychology courses I'd taken in nursing school, and walked into the waiting area expecting to find a room full of mixed nuts there to see the doctor. Instead, here I was, alone with my anxieties.

Not having much faith in the field, I was anxious to get the session over with so that I could move on to something else. But just as I was mentally writing off psychotherapy, a door opened on the far side of the room, and an average-looking, middle-aged man with sandy hair appeared. "Hello, I'm Dr. Dornan," he said. "Won't you come in?"

Beams of sunlight poured through the bare windows of Dr. Dornan's office. Two cloth-covered occasional chairs sat across from each other in the center of the carpeted floor. The room was done in different shades of green, with neutral-colored wood accents. It was so peaceful that its appearance alone relieved some of my tension.

The doctor motioned me toward one of the chairs, then settled into the other. He picked up a legal pad and a pen from a little table next to him, asked my name, and immediately began to take notes. Just like a medical doctor doing a routine examination, he asked, "So, what brings you here today?"

Mental exhaustion had made me reckless, so without hesitation I said, "I'm thinking of committing suicide!"

"Have you thought about suicide before?"

"Yes," I admitted, "but this time the thoughts won't go away."

"Do you have any idea why you want to kill yourself?"

At this question, I took a deep breath and realized that I couldn't hide anymore and that I didn't have time for games. Looking down at my hands resting in my lap, I told this man, this stranger, what was bugging me.

"I'm tired and I can't sleep. I spend my time putting together huge jigsaw puzzles or watching TV way into the night to take my mind off my problems. I think about suicide constantly because I'm so tired and it seems to be the only way to end the pain. I can see everything I've worked for slipping away. It's always the same old thing, just when I'm about to get what I want, I seem to do something to screw it up. I love what I do and worked really hard to get here, but I'm about to blow it. I've ruined my relationship with my co-workers and I hate the people I work for. I feel like people expect things from me that I just can't give anymore. Everybody thinks I'm happy all the time and I'm always supposed to be laughing, but it takes more and more energy to keep up this façade and I don't know how much longer I can. It's all people want from me, and once I can't do it anymore, I'm afraid they won't want me at all. I have no friends, no family, and nowhere to turn. I was sexually molested by my father as a child, and I don't trust anyone."

▲ Junior and me in front of my mother's "dream house" in 1958.

▲ My mother and father, circa 1956.

▲ The Quivers family. *From left:* my cousin Shirley, my older brother, Charles Junior, my mother, my father, and me at four.

▲ Uncle Leroy, I love you. You gave me my first lessons in pride.

▼ Jimmy at eighteen months. He came to us as a newborn and saved my life.

▲ Me at nine, with the first two foster kids my family boarded.

◄ High-school graduation, the only time I've ever worn a long white dress.

► High school graduation. Don't I look like a black Breck girl?

▲College graduation. Pinned, capped, and conked.

▲ A senior in college and no longer a prisoner in my parents' house, I know I'm going to make it.

▲ Graduating nurses getting our caps. Me *(left)*, my friend Kathi *(second from right)*, and pals.

► Kathi *(left)*, me *(right)*, and fellow graduates after yet another elaborate nursing ritual, the pinning ceremony.

Why is this air force
inductee smiling?

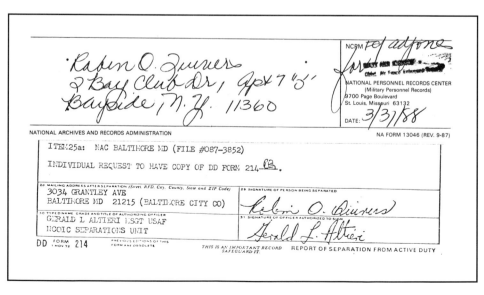

Two years and a nervous breakdown later—my discharge papers!

▲ Clowning around on hallowed ground. The workshop room at Summit, site of many self-revelations, San Francisco, 1978.

▲ Out of work, out of workshops, and almost out of California, 1979.

▲ Headed for radio, jheri curls and all, 1980.

▼ ▶ The young King and Queen of All Media.

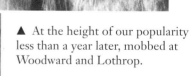

▲ At the height of our popularity less than a year later, mobbed at Woodward and Lothrop.

▲ At a radio promotion in Washington soon after Howard and I teamed up, 1981.

▼ In our first foray into the New York public, the whole show escorts a dateless girl to her senior prom.

▲ The King and Queen of All Media surveying their domain . . .

►. . . . are resplendent to the multitudes from the Jumbotron in Times Square.

◀ Howard, me, and Sugar Ray Leonard, heir to my hero, Muhammad Ali.

▶ Joe Frazier stops by to say hi.

◀ Joan Rivers makes an appearance to wish Howard a happy birthday.

▲ The move to
television gave us
untold opportunities
to act up.

◄ Prebirthday confab
before Howard arrives.
From left in front row:
Fred, Jackie, me. *Back
row:* "Stuttering John."

▲ We broadcast from L.A. with Pat Benatar.

▲ 1984: The stress at WNBC was driving me to ice cream, *lots* of ice cream.

◄ 1985: The show took off, and the pounds went with it.

◄ 1986: Hiding in plain sight. The publicity shot of me nobody recognized.

▲ 1986: The real me.

▲ 1994: Me, today and together.

▲ Gary Dell'Abate, producer.

▲ The King of All Media.

▲ Fred.

◄ Al Rosenberg, aka "Ophelia Quivers."

► Jackie Martling (left), John "Stuttering John" Melendez.

▼ Steve Grillo, intern.   ► Cathy Tobin, secretary.

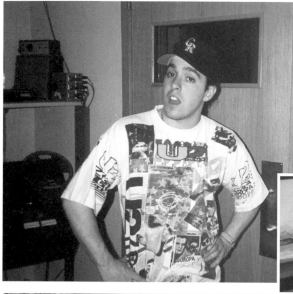

▲ Richard Christenson, intern.

▲ Kathi, my friend
since nursing days, and
me in Paris.

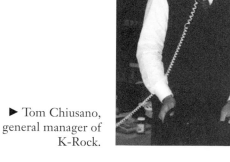

► Tom Chiusano,
general manager of
K-Rock.

▲ Alison Stern.

◀ I'm showing my good friends the Zimmermans and their daughter, Becky, around when they visit me in New York.

◀ Don Buchwald, "Super Agent."

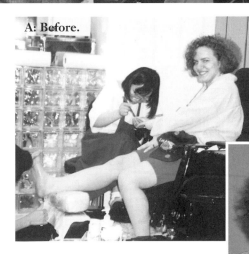

A: Before.

▲ Mike Gange, intern.

▲ ▶ Lea, my former Little Sister, getting spiffed up for her senior prom.

B: After.

▶ One picture of Muhammad
isn't enough. He's in every room.

◀ My most prized
possession.

Connecting the dots between Jimmy's three-year-old face and the one he has today.

▲ Jimmy and his mom and dad.

▼ Just like I always imagined it would be!

My mother and father in the late eighties.

I went on for what must have been fifteen minutes, hardly taking a breath between words. I wasn't proud of my background or
my inability to overcome it. I had to get it all out in one fell swoop
or I wasn't going to get it out at all. I went on and on, not even listening to what I was saying. I whined like a punctured balloon until
I was out of air, then collapsed in silence against the back of the
chair, waiting for a response.

"Wow!" Dr. Dornan exclaimed, leaning forward in his seat.

At this point, I couldn't tell if the doctor's reaction was a good
thing or a bad thing, wasn't sure what the look on his face meant.
But when he finally spoke, his words gave me enough hope to make
it through another day. "Has talking to me today helped you at all?"
he asked.

"I don't know . . . yes, I guess so."

Then came the letdown. Doctor Dornan explained that since it
was July and he was leaving for vacation in three weeks, he couldn't
take me on as a regular patient. Before I could resign myself to
defeat, though, he said he knew of someone he thought would be
good for me. The other therapist was a woman whose office was in
the same suite as his, but she wouldn't be back from her vacation for
three weeks.

"So," he suggested, "if you found talking to me today at all
helpful, you can come in for half an hour once a week for free until
she gets back."

I didn't think I'd be able to do what I'd just done all over again,
and I wasn't up to conducting some meticulous search for just the
right person, so I took this handout. After making an appointment
for the following week, I peeled myself out of the chair and headed
for the street. Once outside, I was immediately conscious of how
different I felt from when I'd entered the building. I'd taken my
first baby steps toward breaking the chains that had been holding
me back. I had, after all, violated a Quivers' taboo simply by making
an appointment with a therapist.

When I was thirteen, I'd begged my father, the only one who
should have fully understood, to please let me talk to a psychiatrist.
He'd made it clear that he didn't approve, claiming I just needed to
get out of the house more. Psychiatrists were for crazy people, not
people like us, he insisted before stalking angrily from the room.

Well, maybe this present act of defiance meant that there was hope for me yet. But any hope I might have had was far from evident at work.

As the French say, the more things change, the more they stay the same. To our glee, Dom Fioravanti announced that he was departing WNBC for the greener pastures of MTV. His last day at the station he made a point of visiting everyone to offer a personal good-bye—everyone, that is, except me. My feelings for Dom and the rest of NBC management were well known, and when Dom appeared in the doorway of the newsroom, flashing that expensive smile and waving his manicured hands like a politician, I bristled. My disgust must have registered, because his smile instantly faded, and he never ventured farther into the room. From the door and with not a hint of mirth, he called to me, "Take care of the big guy," to which I replied just as soberly, "I always do." That was the last I saw of Dom Fioravanti.

Kevin "Pig Virus" Metheny couldn't move into Dom's office, but he certainly moved quickly to take over the duties that went with it. It appeared to me that he became so preoccupied with being the boss that he forgot about the show. The ratings were going up anyway, so he had already begun to take a more hands-off attitude. Mary Beth, unfortunately, was also aware of the power vacuum created by Dom's departure and once again began to assert herself where I was concerned.

I still had to provide reporter stories for the afternoon- and morning-drive newscasts. With no more newscast to tear into me about Mary Beth focused her attention on my scriptwriting. She'd listen to every wrap, calling me in afterward to give me her critique and then ordering me to do the piece over. When I was unable to complete my assignments before I went on the air, she'd complain that I was too slow. The engineers also helped delay me by refusing my requests for assistance, so I commonly missed the deadlines she'd imposed on me.

The time was nearing for me to begin treatment with my new therapist, and it couldn't come a moment too soon, because life was already getting difficult again.

*   *   *

Three weeks of seeing Dr. Dornan had given me something to look forward to, and I must admit, just having someone to tell my troubles to was a relief. Those weekly visits were like life preservers keeping me afloat in rough waters. Now, here I was again in that same waiting room, about to meet another stranger to whom I'd have to spill my guts. I didn't know if I could do it again, and I had few expectations that it would help even if I managed to. I must have felt a little better to seriously consider backing out of the whole therapy thing because the thought wouldn't have occurred to me the first time I'd sat here. Only Dr. Dornan's recommendation could have made me take a chance on door number two, behind which sat a stranger who might be my savior.

When I finally stepped into Dr. London's office, I met a large, round woman whose kind face was framed in red curls that tumbled to her shoulders. She sat in a large Naugahyde chair. Bookshelves lined the walls, and some tables, a couch, and a cushioned, cloth-upholstered chair completed the decor. Unlike Dr. Dornan's light, airy office, this one had an air of heaviness about it, the only light provided by a lamp with a low-wattage bulb behind Dr. London's chair. With a wave of her hand, my new therapist motioned me to take a seat. I spotted a Van Gogh–like painting of a yellow flower on the wall directly across from me. It was to this flower I would eventually tell all my secrets, but on this first day I returned my attention to Dr. London as she lit a cigarette and began her interrogation.

"Dr. Dornan told me a little about you, but I'd like to hear you tell me what you think your problems are."

I drew a deep breath before starting my story. By now, I had reduced it to a brief summary of "Just the facts, ma'am." Dr. London refrained from speaking until I had completed my entire spiel. After I'd finished, she looked at me with a twinkle in her eye and said, "Well, we have our work cut out for us, don't we?" Then she dived right in.

"I want to see you twice a week. Whenever you are scheduled to be here, I expect you to be here. If you're not, you'll be charged just the same, and I expect payment at the end of each session." The rules were not a surprise to me, but her attitude was. "Let me warn you," she continued, "I'm very good at what I do, and I'm very expensive. My fee is seventy dollars a session."

Remember, this was 1983. Dr. London wasn't kidding. Her services came at a very high price for that era, and I wasn't making a lot of money. Coming up with one hundred and forty dollars in cash every week wasn't going to be easy, but I was impressed with the woman's self-confidence. It occurred to me that I had medical insurance through my job. The notion that it might help pay her fee was the determining factor in my accepting her terms. Dr. London and I agreed that we'd meet on Tuesdays and Thursdays before I went to work.

Once I'd signed on, I decided to ask a few questions to let Dr. London know that she wasn't dealing with a total neophyte, but she was not impressed and played her hand close to her chest. First I asked if I'd have to lie on the couch and she, to my relief, answered that it wasn't necessary. Then I inquired as to what we'd be talking about, and she told me that it was up to me. As to what kind of therapy she practiced, I was informed that she had her own brand, based on a variety of methods.

I walked out of Dr. London's office aware that the true work would begin at our next meeting. I had no intention of spending the next twenty years staring at a yellow flower and wondering why my life was so screwed up. I promised myself that I'd work hard. At Dr. London's prices, I knew that was a promise I was more likely to keep.

I was still having trouble handling the simplest kind of everyday transaction, so even if my insurance would have helped cover the cost of therapy, I wasn't in any shape to apply for it. I never even bothered to try. I paid Dr. London's fees right out of my pocket, which was difficult at times. But therapy fast became a priority. After all, I was trying to save my own life. This was no time to bargain hunt.

Since Dr. London had told me I was running the show, I decided that I'd talk about the present. I'd seen all those movies about therapy in which couch-bound clients spend every session whining about what had happened to them in childhood. Screw childhood. I couldn't change that. It was the present that was bothering me. I needed some sleep and to learn to control my emotions.

In those first sessions, I spent my time listing for Dr. London the number of sleepless nights I'd had since the last time I'd seen her, how many blowups I'd had at work, and what I did in my spare time. It all added up to a pitiful bunch of symptoms of just how uncomfortable my existence had become. One day, she decided to interrupt the cataloging of my despair to ask what I wanted out of therapy.

"I want to feel comfortable again about going to work," I told her, "and I want to be totally self-reliant. I don't want to need another human being."

"I can help you with the first," she said and smiled, "but I don't know about the second."

"Well, that's what I want," I pouted.

"But why?"

"Because people are a problem," I answered as honestly as I could. "If it weren't for people, I wouldn't be here in the first place. They've never meant anything but trouble to me."

"What kind of trouble?"

"People are selfish and self-centered," I hissed. "They're cruel and don't care about others. You can only trust them so far, and they always let you down."

"Aren't there any people you like?"

"Children are okay," I said firmly. "They're not like adults at all. They're honest and don't have ulterior motives. I just don't know what happens to them when they grow up."

"And there's not one adult you know who has any of these qualities?

"No!" I roared. Sometimes I'm so loud, I scare myself, but Dr. London was unmoved. She demanded a list of the people who were causing me problems. Mary Beth was at the top, followed by Kevin, Dom, Howard, Fred, everyone else who worked at WNBC, my parents, my brother and his wife, and all my so-called friends. The doctor was curious as to why even my friends had made the list. "Because they abandoned me," I explained, beginning to feel a little sorry for myself. "They only needed me when they didn't have anyone else. Now that they're married, they've gradually eased me out of their lives."

"Have they told you this?"

"No!!" I hated her for probing like this, but she kept right on going.

"Then how do you know?"

"Because they don't call," I admitted, reaching for a tissue from the box next to my chair.

"Have you tried calling them?"

"No!" I'd found my shield of anger again. "If they wanted to talk to me, they'd call."

"And just how did you decide that?"

I was really beginning to detest this woman. I had barely managed to hold back the tears that still threatened to break loose, yet she kept poking at the same sore spot. Thank goodness I hadn't discarded that tissue. "I don't know," I sobbed. "I'm just afraid that if I do call, they won't want to talk to me."

Dr. London urged me to test my theory right away, but I was already in such bad shape, I couldn't afford to find out that I was right. The ignorance of silence was preferable, so I resisted her pressuring me for two more months. I constantly sat by the phone and thought about picking it up, but didn't find the courage until one Saturday night. Lifting the receiver off the cradle and dialing may seem simple to you, but for me it was like having vertigo. I was that terrified of the outcome.

The first people I called were my old air force friends, Linda and David Zimmerman. When I heard the call connect, I thought I was going to faint, but I didn't hang up. I was rewarded for my courage. Linda and Z were so obviously happy to hear from me that I was shocked. They hadn't heard from me for almost a year and had been worried that they'd done something to me that had made me stop calling.

This was my very first therapeutic breakthrough, and I was anxious to get to my Tuesday session to share the good news. Dr. London was proud of me but typically wanted more. She urged me to call another friend right away and see what would happen. It took another several weeks, but when I finally did call Kathi, my old nursing school buddy, I got another warm reception. This second success gave me reason to feel that just maybe Dr. London knew what she was talking about. Still, dealing with my friends was one thing. Learning to talk Howard was another.

Week after week, I spent my sessions screaming and cursing him. The little irritations I was carefully keeping track of had grown into a mountain by now, one that seemed impossible to climb. After listening to my protracted griping for some time, Dr. London correctly concluded that many of my grievances held very little weight. She advised me not to react the next time Howard seemed to be stepping on my toes.

"Count to ten," she recommended. "Do whatever it takes to keep from blowing up at him. Give it twenty-four hours and then see how you feel."

The flare-ups between Howard and me were coming quite frequently at this point, so it wasn't long before I got to put this advice to the test. One evening during the show, Howard dismissed an opinion of mine by saying, "That's stupid!" Normally, it would have been more than enough to set me off, but I forced myself to table my resentment and go on with the show. Later, when I got home, I could really have done a number on myself and my relationship with Howard from that one statement. I could have repeated "That's stupid" over and over until it made me sick. I could have added the incident to the long list of alleged offenses I kept in my head so that it would be right at the end when I'd finished running through it from top to bottom. By the time I got ready for bed, I'd have been so disturbed I wouldn't have been able to sleep. This time, I refused to give the matter another thought until morning.

In the cold light of day, I was amazed at how little Howard's inane remark affected me. I could barely remember why I'd been so upset. All my anger had dissipated in less than twenty-four hours. Could it be that just a simple night's sleep would have prevented most of our fights over the past year? Clearly, my reactions to Howard came from somewhere else and had nothing much to do with what was happening now. On Thursday, I revealed this latest discovery to my therapist, who then explained a bit more to me about my faulty wiring.

"Robin," Dr. London began, "as you were growing up, you developed an incredible number of defenses to protect yourself from all the danger you saw around you. These defenses were necessary then, but now it's as if you have a body full of buttons that are always being pushed. The people closest to you can't possibly avoid pushing them, especially Howard."

I didn't believe Dr. London at first, but time and again I found that twelve to twenty-four hours later, something that would have made me blow my stack prior to entering therapy no longer upset me. But just when I was beginning to think there had never been any real problems, I came across one that was still bugging me a day later.

I'm from the South and was used to Southern manners. When I was growing up, we were taught that it was rude to interrupt a speaker no matter how they droned on, and if you did, it was only in an emergency, and an apology was always offered before the person interrupting made their statement. Howard often caught me off guard with his quick uptake on the air. In his anxiousness to express himself, it's not unusual for him to just jump right into a conversation while a speaker is in the middle of a sentence. When he interrupted me, it set off what I called my "disrespect" radar detection system, which alerted me to any attack on my pride or self-esteem. Howard's outbursts set alarm buzzers screaming, "Warning! Warning! He's treating you like you're nothing."

It was my job to offer the audience the facts, but Howard often charged the gate before I could even blurt out what was happening. I had learned to speak very quickly, but there were times when he just couldn't wait to put in his two cents. I had Mary Beth on my back all day, Judy was now doing my job, and the moment I got to open my mouth, Howard interrupted me.

I had promised myself and Dr. London not to blow up and I didn't. But the problem had survived the twenty-four-hour waiting period and became the first topic of conversation in my next session.

"Well," she said, "if his interrupting bothers you, you're going to have to talk to him about it."

These were not the words I wanted to hear. "Howard and I only fight when we try to talk," I whined.

"That was before. This time you're going to speak to him without the anger. Why don't you just go in, calmly tell him what the problem is, and then see what happens?"

"Oh, I can tell you what's going to happen. Nothing," I said, challenging her. "People don't change for other people. Talking to Howard is a waste of time. It'll only lead to more fighting."

"Just try it," she persisted. "Haven't some of my other suggestions worked out?"

I was paying Dr. London a lot of money, so I figured I might as well take her advice for a test drive. But it wasn't with a light heart that I walked out of her office that day. I'd made some headway in my relationship with Howard, because the fighting had stopped. Working with him had become easier because there was less tension. I had no desire to take a giant step backward, but if it was going to happen, I figured I might as well get it over with quickly.

When I got to the studio, I went straight to Howard's office, closed the door, and told him calmly, "Howard, I need to talk to you." Before I could finish the sentence, Howard gripped the edge of his desk with both hands, leaned forward, and started yelling at me. My God, I thought, look what you've done to him. He thinks the words "I need to talk" mean "I want to attack you!" It was then that I realized I'd been beating up on Howard, and I didn't want to do that anymore. This time I would set it right.

"Howard," I interrupted him, "I haven't even told you what the problem is." My reasonable tone must have been quite a surprise, because it immediately stopped his shouting. Settling back in his chair, he prepared himself to listen. Then I explained as simply as I could just what was bothering me and offered a possible solution. ". . . so if you could just let me complete my sentence before you start talking, I'd feel better."

"Oh. Yeah, I can do that," Howard agreed with obvious relief. "No problem."

"That's it." I ended the discussion with, "See you on the show."

I couldn't wait to tell Dr. London how successful our little talk had been. This was the first time Howard and I had ever discussed a problem without having it turn into a screamfest. Not only had I been heard, it appeared that I had been understood, and there had been no blowup, no hurt feelings, and no further erosion of our relationship. When I shared with her what had happened, she said the most amazing thing: "That's how people treat you when they love you."

I wasn't quite sure I knew what she meant. "People who love you want to help you, Robin," Dr. London went on. "They want you to feel okay. They aren't looking to irritate you."

"Well, I think it's nice that he said it," I replied, "but I really don't think he can do it."

It turned out that I was wrong. A few days later we were in the same situation. I was doing a story that Howard was chomping at the bit to jump into, but just as he was about to interrupt me, he caught himself and waited for me to finish. Only then did he burst forth in typical "Howard" fashion. I don't know how I managed not to cry right there on the air when it struck me that he was the first person to ever keep his word to me.

My therapist was overjoyed. "You see what I mean, sweetie?" she said after I'd related the story to her.

For all the time I'd been seeing Dr. London, I thought I'd been deep in therapy when I was still in the honeymoon stage. Now the process really began. She had won my respect and my trust. Now I could get down to the business of figuring out what made me tick. When I realized that this meant dredging up the past so that I could discover how it was affecting my present, I became afraid. The last time I'd tried to do this, I told her, I'd lost my voice, and I couldn't afford to do that now.

"This time you'll be doing it with professional guidance. Maybe it won't be the same," she answered. So, together we went on.

From my childhood stories, Dr. London surmised that I had grown up surrounded by emotionally immature people whose own lack of self-control and inconsistency had forced me to feel the need to control every situation in order to feel safe. They had been my only examples of adults, and with a child's mind, I had based all my rules about life on their model. As a result, I believed that I had to be bigger and stronger than they were to stop them from hurting me, and that I had to scare the piss out of them to make them leave me alone. I was still playing by these same rules even though the game had changed. I was still treating Howard and everyone else like the scary, unreliable adults I'd known as a child.

Dr. London's theory didn't go down easy. It had a bitter taste. She was telling me that my mind wasn't working all that well, that same mind that had gotten me pretty far without much outside help. But Dr. London insisted, "Robin, you grew up in a strange place around a lot of strange people. You have to understand that the world isn't necessarily the way you see it. I don't mean that you're not in touch with reality, but have you ever heard the term 'rose-colored glasses'?"

When I nodded yes, she continued. "Well, growing up the way you did, you're bound to see the world in a different way than most people, as if you're looking through lenses of a different color. It's going to be my job to help you see the world the way it really is."

"Okay," I countered, "maybe I'm not seeing the world like it really is most of the time. But what about Mary Beth?"

"I don't know," she told me frankly. "With Mary Beth, you may have a real problem. We'll have to see."

To get just this far had taken six months. I looked back on the days before therapy and compared them with the way things were now. I still had bouts of insomnia and suicidal thoughts. I still spent most of my time alone and had anxiety attacks about going outside. But things at work were getting better, and even when they were bad, instead of suffering in silence, I could run to Dr. London and tell her what was wrong. She had become my first really trusted adviser, and the advice she gave me actually led to solutions that guided me forward. The lessons I was learning from her would become the tools of my eventual success. But there were going to be many dark days before I'd see the light.

Just as I thought I was making all this progress, the bottom dropped out. Overnight, therapy became torture, and things seemed to be getting worse. For a while I had even been making friends and going out a bit. I had started to fix up my apartment to make it more livable and had made measurable progress at work. But throwing open the door to my past sent me spiraling back into the depths of depression, and once again, thoughts of suicide haunted me day and night. My bed became a battleground. Every night I wondered how long I'd lie sleepless before getting up to watch television on the living room sofa. As the number of sleepless nights mounted, the weird thoughts that had surfaced in the last of my California days came back with them.

Out west, I'd barely cracked open the closet door behind which all my skeletons lay. I hadn't even attempted to clean the closet, yet I'd managed to find myself in some very dangerous situations. Psychotherapy was tantamount to flinging that door wide open and releasing all of my repressed sexuality with it. I still harbored thoughts that my body was essentially evil and felt that it must be kept under strict control.

At the same time, I felt that I possessed incredible power over men when we were having sex. Just as many prostitutes report, men seemed to be under my spell in that context, totally subject to my will, and that's the way I liked it. The only time I'd ever completely lost control in bed was the first time I slept with David, my beautiful, pot-smoking air force boy toy. I fell so far into the moment that time lost its meaning. I had no idea how we'd gotten where we were, or what I'd been doing, when I came back to my senses. I made sure that never happened a second time. I didn't want to enjoy sex too much and risk losing control.

In California, when I determined that relationships weren't my thing, I'd tried turning to the sex trade for an outlet. Fortunately or not, I managed to rein in these urges before I could get into any real trouble. Now, when I started rummaging through my emotional baggage in therapy, I became a cowardly version of the Diane Keaton character in *Looking for Mr. Goodbar*. I'd spend entire weekends in bed masturbating, which was difficult because I could no longer conjure up the image of a naked man. It had been a long time between romances, so I turned to *Playgirl* for inspiration. I'd drive to out-of-the-way magazine stores to avoid the embarrassment of having the corner deli owner who sold me the newspaper know what I was after. Once armed, I could stay busy under the covers for hours until I passed out.

Occasionally masturbating wasn't enough. On those nights, I'd find myself climbing into my car with the intention of going to a bar and picking up a stranger. I didn't get out, just cruised around arguing with myself about whether I should actually make a move. I never did because what I really craved was sex, not human companionship, and I knew that no matter who I picked up, I'd have to deal with a personality. That notion always sent me home alone.

I might never have disclosed these details to my therapist if my compulsions had ended there, but I found that even this problem had escalated to the point where I feared I'd no longer be able to keep it a secret. On my nighttime prowls, I'd drive by sex shops and want to go inside. It became harder and harder to just keep driving. Then I was gripped by another compulsion. I almost acted on the

urge one day as I crossed a street not far from my apartment in
Queens. There was only one car on the street, and it was stopped at
a red light. As I was about to pass it, I felt an overwhelming desire
to rip open my shirt at the driver's side window. It took an incredible effort to resist and just keep walking.

That episode scared me into telling Dr. London about what was
going on. I began to wonder if I wasn't going crazy. I didn't think I
needed more proof. I was just about resigned to the notion that one
day I'd be living out of a shopping cart on Third Avenue or sleeping
in the ATM office of a bank. I became fearful of homeless people, as
if merely seeing them might make that eventual reality come
sooner. I didn't see how I was ever going to be able to fix everything
that was wrong with me, and I was ready to give up.

I often characterized my sessions at this point as cursing
tantrums. I'd sit with my eyes closed or staring directly at the painting in front of me and see how many times I could use the word
"fuck" in the same sentence. If I wasn't screaming, I was crying, a
tissue wadded up in my hand like a little knot. Sometimes I didn't
make the session at all, just forgetting that I had an appointment or
oversleeping. That's when Dr. London decided that we should meet
three times a week.

"Am I nuts?" I asked her.

"I don't answer questions like that."

"Well, then, tell me what's wrong with me. Give me a diagno-
sis."

"I don't think that's the point," Dr. London told me. "The point
is, are you making progress? Is work going better? Are you sleeping
better? Are your problems less severe?"

The answer to all of these questions was a qualified yes.

"Then let's go on," my therapist told me, and we did, but I
knew without her telling me that I must have been in pretty bad
shape. Two more days and I'd have been seeing her every day of the
week.

I was becoming a difficult patient. I was sick and tired of being
sick and tired, and sometimes I blamed Dr. London for what I considered my lack of further progress. I also felt sorry for her having
to listen to me rant for forty-five minutes three times a week as my
buried anger began to surface. Sometimes I'd wonder what she was

doing while I sat there cursing like a sailor. I thought she must be horrified, but when I sneaked a peek, she was just sitting there listening and not judging me at all. Then I'd say to myself, You're here for you, not to worry about what she thinks, then go back into my zone.

In one session I was grousing about everybody I knew. Finally Dr. London piped up and asked, "Is there something about me that irritates you?"

Normally, I would have lied and said no. I didn't think anybody cared about what I did or didn't like, and if I wanted to keep them, the last thing I could afford to do was tell the truth. But inside Dr. London's office, I wasn't normal. "Yeah," I heard myself say, "I hate your smoking!"

I felt really bad when she began to stamp out the cigarette in the ashtray next to her. I just wanted to articulate my feelings. I didn't expect a response. But she never smoked in my sessions again, and to my surprise, she never held it against me.

At this point in treatment, I was discovering that no matter where I started my sessions, they all seemed to end in the same place—my parents' home. Every time I thought I'd finally put a ghost to rest, I'd wind up right back at the same spot, wrestling with it yet again. It was amazing to me how many decisions derive from one single incident and how many times that same episode can produce tears. The crying sessions were the worst. Sometimes when they were over, I felt too drained to go to work. I'd step out into the street and wonder what to do. Finally, I'd just start walking and somehow always wound up at 30 Rock. Since I was already there, I'd go up to the second floor and do a show.

I'd made no secret of going into therapy. Alison Stern was supportive and just wanted to make sure I was seeing someone I liked. But, of course, I had to put up with a lot of "Are you sure you need a shrink?" and "What do you think you're getting out of it?" from Howard and Fred and some of my other friends. I'd just smile and tell them all that I thought it was a valuable experience. Clearly, no one knew how badly off I really was. One thing was for sure. I wasn't seeing Dr. London to be trendy. The bottom line was that my life hung in the balance, and I was not only dedicated to trying to save it but to putting Humpty together again better than ever before.

In the midst of all this, my parents, whom I'd been trying to keep at bay, began calling again. Junior and his girlfriend, Mary, who was now his wife, came to visit me. When they returned to Baltimore, my parents picked them up at the train station. As soon as they got home, Mary decided to call me to let me know they had arrived safely. Being unaware of the situation between us, she threw my parents on the phone. My mother and father mistook my civility that night for a green light to start pestering me and began calling me again after having laid off for some time. It really steamed me because they never even bothered to check to see if it was all right. Finally, I decided to let them know just how angry I was in a letter.

"I asked nicely the last time that you leave me alone," I began, "but now I realize that without knowing it, you would kill me, and I don't want to die. So, I'm taking matters into my own hands. If you call me again, I will hang up as soon as I hear your voices. I don't want to hurt you, but I'm going through a lot here, and it's going to take some time to sort it all out. I need you to stay away for a while. I can't say how long, but I have to have some time."

After this, they did stop calling, but my mother started writing long, rambling letters about nothing, which never acknowledged that there was even a problem. As I went deeper into therapy, even these letters began to infuriate me. Here I was trying to put some emotional distance between them and me so that I could see my problems with some clarity, and my mother just wouldn't let go. At the beginning of therapy, I'd assumed I could work out my problems with them in a short while. Now I was learning that just the opposite was true.

I was furious all right, furious at them. All the cursing and crying in session after session was to vent feelings I'd had to suppress as a child. While my parents did whatever they liked with impunity, there had always been rules to cover whatever I was experiencing. If my feelings were hurt, I was told that I was too sensitive and wore my feelings on my sleeve. If I was sad, I was warned that these were the best days of my life and that children had no problems to be sad about. If I was angry at my brother, that was wrong, brothers and sisters shouldn't fight with each other. And I was committing a sin that would force God to cut my life short if I directed at my parents any but the most pleasant of emotions.

All my life, each and every one of my feelings had been system-

atically invalidated. Nothing I thought or felt was ever right or
merited discussion. It was amazing that I knew how I felt at all and
completely understandable how I'd become so pent up. Whenever I
did manage to express myself, it was in an explosion of emotions
because I'd held them back for so long. My anger was venomous,
eroding relationships, resulting in bad judgment, and ultimately
consuming me whole. When I couldn't find any other outlet, I'd
turned it all on myself.

I still didn't have control over that fury, but at least I was beginning to understand it. When I'd written that letter to my parents,
I'd actually managed to channel some of my rage in the right direction. It was the insane conditions they had forced me to live under
that had made me so volatile and confused. I had needed that anger
to protect me as I got older in their home, but in this new world, I
was like a tiger out of its cage.

I was finally beginning to realize that I was the one who was out
of sync. But getting back on track would be an agonizing and often
embarrassing ordeal that would put to the test both my inner
strength and the devotion of those around me.

16

THE RETURN OF
THE GUNFIGHTER

Even though therapy was going okay, I still thought of suicide. Then I saw Marsha Norman's play, 'Night, Mother, starring Kathy Bates, on Broadway. Bates's character tells her mother that she has decided to kill herself because she's tired of living with uncontrollable epilepsy. The mother spends the rest of the play trying to talk her daughter out of it. I started to cry from the moment I realized what the play was about. Right to the end, I wanted the mother to win. That's when I knew I wanted to live.

I'd now been in treatment for a little over one year but still couldn't see how this therapeutic examination of my childhood was helping me as an adult. I certainly wasn't feeling all that much better, and Dr. London and I seemed to be going around in circles. Eventually I did stop screaming and started talking. When I did, I knew I had to do something about my relationship with my parents.

I had just barely managed to deal with them before I started treatment, and reliving my childhood traumas hadn't exactly helped the situation, because now I wasn't talking to them at all. "Honor thy mother and father so that thy days may be long" was the phrase my mother repeated over and over again as I, her willful child, was growing up. Now I replayed it over and over in my mind. Did it mean that I had to keep these people in my life even if it killed me? I was beginning to think not. No God I could serve would demand that of me. I was coming closer and closer to the conclusion that I would have to abandon my parents completely.

The Stern family, on the other hand, has always been very close. Howard, from the beginning, made it an on-air practice to call Alison, his mother, and other relatives if he had a question or needed advice. When we came to New York, it wasn't unusual for him to phone his mother and ask her about her sex life. He even enlisted Alison's aid in re-creating the birth of their first child on the air. People were horrified at the thought that he'd actually brought a tape recorder into the delivery room. Sometimes the Sterns would call in on their own when they heard him talking about them.

Howard also used to call my mother when we were in Washington. Shortly after we started at WNBC, I'd asked him to forget about phoning her for a while, and he'd agreed. But a few months later, he casually commented that he wished I'd resolve whatever was going on with her so that he could start calling her again. "She was good on the air," he concluded. I just smiled and replied that I was still working things out.

I'd managed to avoid my parents for quite some time now. On holidays I still sent cards, making sure the messages weren't overly effusive. Of course, they continued to send me the gushiest cards around, complete with sugar-coated verses and pictures of warm, loving relationships. I even managed to have my two younger foster brothers, the boys Social Services had placed with my family after Jimmy was taken away, come for summer visits without actually speaking to either my mother or my father. All the arrangements were made by letter. But even though I wasn't talking to my parents, my rage toward them increased. Their letters and cards only served as nagging invitations to take up the mantle of lies that had been smothering me, and I resented them for it. So one day, I announced to Dr. London that I was severing all ties. "Are you sure that's what you want to do?" she asked, concerned.

I'd thought about it for a long while and felt that I'd reached this conclusion objectively. In all the time that I had been out of touch with them, I hadn't once missed anything about them. I had never thought of anything I missed doing with them or any time we'd spent together that was worth re-creating. In over thirty years there wasn't one tie binding me to them except duty. I went home because I was supposed to, called because it was expected, wrote because that's what everybody does. I never shared my secrets with them. They were far from the first people I thought of when something wonderful happened. When things were bad, I became deathly afraid of them.

Dr. London protested again. "Don't you think that you'd just like to speak to them sometimes? After all, they are your parents. I know you can't believe this yet, but on some level you must still love them."

"I don't think so," I sighed. "If I saw people like my parents walking down the street, I'd cross to the other side rather than pass them. I don't see any reason to spend time with people like that."

"Well," she said, relenting, "I guess you've made your decision. But don't let pride stand in the way if one day you want to change your mind."

I knew right away that I'd done the right thing. As long as my parents were in my life, I'd always be alone instead of with people who could love and support me. I'd still be crying for the kind of mother who would hold me in her arms and tell me everything was going to be all right and a father I could trust to protect me. By severing all ties, I was acknowledging that they could never fill those roles. I was free to go out and find what I needed. Still, Dr. London wasn't the only one to question my action.

Howard and Alison were the first people I told that I was never speaking to my parents again. I was out for a drive with them the day I chose to break the news. I remember the scene distinctly. Howard was driving, and Alison was beside him in the passenger seat of their new Cutlass Supreme. I was sitting in the backseat with their baby daughter, Emily. Now that Howard was a father, he tended to identify with parents in general. Maybe his reaction wasn't this overblown, but this is how it appeared to me at the time. He began screaming and banging on the steering wheel with his fists. "You call your parents and talk to them!! They couldn't have done anything that bad. What you're doing is wrong!!"

Howard didn't even know my parents. Why was he defending

them? I was crushed that he was taking their side over mine. His
words played into my self-doubt. I turned into a jellyfish and started
to ooze off the backseat with every harangue. Then, calmly but
firmly, Alison spoke up. "Howard, Robin doesn't have to talk to her
parents if she doesn't want to." With that, Howard just stopped
talking. The subject changed and was never brought up again. I
found my backbone and sat up in my seat. I will always be grateful
to Alison for that statement. She was the first person to confirm
that I had a right to my feelings and a right to act accordingly.

A few years later, Howard surprised me by admitting on the air
that he thought it was awful when I rejected my family but went on
to add that, hard as it was to believe, I'd actually gotten better since
I'd made the decision.

With my parents out of the picture, I began to rebuild my life in
earnest, but I'd be less than honest if I claimed the process was
painless. Sometimes being with people made me sadder than being
alone. I hung out a lot with the Stern clan, but my times with them
were painful reminders of what my family was not. Watching a
group who loved and supported each other, and enjoyed being
together, often made me feel that I was on the outside looking in on
something I might never know. What I really wanted to do was cry
at those moments, but as was my habit, I'd continue to smile and
refuse to let the sadness overwhelm me in public. The energy it
took to maintain my façade required frequent sugar fixes. On the
way home, I'd head right to the nearest place that had candy or ice
cream.

When my friends Linda and Z found out that I was, in effect,
divorcing my family, they invited me to spend Christmas with them
in Pittsburgh, and the first year I'd had a great time. The next year,
though, I convinced myself that I'd be intruding and stayed away. I
spent the day alone, wallowing in self-pity and nursing a cold, but
Linda had made me promise to call her mother's around dinner-
time, so I did. To my amazement, the entire family gathered around
the phone to sing Christmas carols to me and insisted on talking to
me individually so they could each tell me how much I was missed.
The following year I didn't hesitate to accept their invitation. They

are an open and loving family who took me into their bosom and made me feel like a member.

With Dr. London's help and encouragement, I was discovering that just because I wasn't blessed with my own set of loving parents didn't mean I couldn't have all the things they could provide. It was simply a matter of determining what I missed and then replacing it with an acceptable alternative in my emotional and personal life. Therapy also continued to help me with my problems at work.

The more I understood how the past affected the present, the better I was able to cope with the daily grind of working at WNBC. I discussed every move Mary Beth made with Dr. London, who would devise strategies to minimize, even thwart, her assaults. With every victory, my job performance improved, while an increasingly frustrated Mary Beth started to get sloppy.

I sometimes filled in for the midday news anchor when he was off and had to do network joins. With the pressure off, I had figured out the whole system and now managed without fail to deliver my four stories before the network anchor spoke. I was at the top of my game, feeling comfortable on the air again.

Since I'd been complaining about Mary Beth almost from day one, things had gotten to the point where no one in the front office even noticed anymore. I guess they all thought it was a simple case of incompatible personalities, not a calculated campaign to undermine my work and drive me out of WNBC. Granted, I was paranoid, but this was a paranoid's worst nightmare because somebody really was out to get me. I had the feeling that this was the case because each time my job performance improved in one area, Mary Beth appeared to shift her attack to another. This time she zeroed in on my reputation with my peers.

A grotesque serial murder story was breaking in the Ironbound section of Newark, New Jersey, while we were on the air one day. I still wasn't familiar with all the little towns and cities that dotted the tri-state area, and it was the first time I'd ever heard of this section of Newark. Howard asked me for the latest information on the story when I joined him in the studio after Judy had done the news. I was speaking without notes and mistakenly referred to the area as the "Ironside" section. Realizing my error, I corrected myself in the next break and continued to use the proper name for the rest of the show. But, radio listening being what it is, somebody only heard the mistake and wrote a letter of complaint to the station. I should thank this man because his letter led directly to my eventual triumph over Mary Beth's tyranny.

The letter writer carbon-copied everyone. I got a copy. Pig Virus got a copy. And, of course, Mary Beth got a copy. Pig Virus wrote me a note and left his copy of the letter for me in Howard's office. When I ran into him that afternoon, I told him that I was already aware of the mistake and had corrected it on the air. That was the end of the incident as far as he was concerned, but when I walked into the newsroom a few minutes later, I was astonished to find Judy D'Angelis reading the same letter of complaint. "Where did you get that?" I demanded angrily. Judy, caught by surprise, admitted that Mary Beth had given it to her.

I don't know what possessed me, but all my investigative instincts suddenly sprang into action. I checked my mailbox to see if Mary Beth had left me a copy of the letter or even a note to see her that afternoon. There was nothing. Even if she'd meant to alert the rest of the staff so that they wouldn't make the same mistake, she'd breached protocol by not informing me first. In fact, it seemed clear that she was trying to publicly humiliate me. Once I checked my mailbox, I knew I had her. I wasn't about to let this toothless piranha slide off the hook. I'd been waiting too long for this chance.

Mary Beth was out to lunch, and although she didn't know it, she was going to be out of a lot more before this week ended. I headed directly for her secretary. For the first time since I'd started working at WNBC, I was the one demanding a meeting with Her Royal Highness. Then I walked over to the other side of the building to request a formal meeting with Pig Virus for the next afternoon. By the time I got back, Her Majesty was standing in the doorway of her office, beckoning me.

Once inside, Mary Beth and I wrestled for control of the conversation. She wasn't about to entertain my accusations that she was trying to turn the rest of the news staff against me. Instead she resorted to her old tried-and-true tactic of disparaging my work performance. "The kind of mistake you made reflects badly on the entire department!" she screamed.

"Mary Beth, I spotted the mistake right after I made it, and corrected it on the air."

"That's not all you've done," she continued. "Your delivery still isn't satisfactory, and there are—" I ended her tirade by walking out, aware that she was trying to guilt-trip me into letting the whole subject drop. All the while she was screaming, I was having difficulty hiding how pleased I was by her response. Her very reaction assured me that I was sitting on a gold mine, but I let her think her attack was effective and never even hinted that I planned to see Pig Virus about her the next day. Mary Beth would soon find herself on the ropes, unable to dodge the barrage of blows coming at her from every direction.

The next afternoon, I asked Howard to join me in Pig Virus's office. Howard had witnessed the effects of Mary Beth's handiwork and deserved to be in on this, I thought. Once I laid out the facts, he even chimed with his own examples of Mary Beth's unreasonable behavior. Then Pig Virus asked what I have to admit was a clever question, "Why is it that you're having such a problem with straight news when your participation on 'AM66' is just fine?"

"AM66" was a weekly, hour-long public affairs show produced by the news department for which I wrote two segments per episode, one on health-related issues and the other on entertainment. My pieces for "AM66" went unchallenged, and the show always garnered awards. If I was as incompetent as Mary Beth claimed, why, indeed, wasn't I having trouble with "AM66"? Now that everything was falling into place, I could easily answer Pig Virus's question. "My stuff on 'AM66' is good because Mary Beth leaves it alone. My confidence isn't constantly being undermined, so I can still perform my duties for that show effectively."

At last both Howard and Pig Virus were beginning to believe me. Pig Virus asked a few more questions, then actually extended a sincere apology for not having taken my previous protests seriously. "I had no idea what you were going through," he said by way of explanation. "It's going to take some thought, but I'll figure out a way to handle this." As I left his office, I thanked my lucky stars for Dr. London, who had helped me find the ammunition I needed to fend off Mary Beth's threat to my career. Later that afternoon, my nemesis received a luncheon invitation from Pig Virus for the following day.

When I got to work the next day, I warned everyone in the newsroom that Mary Beth was not going to be in a great mood when she got back from lunch. They all demanded to know what I'd done, but I kept my secret safely hidden behind yet another enigmatic smile. I was getting quite good at these veiled grins. "Just watch your backs," was all I told them. When Mary Beth strode through the newsroom on the way to her office, she shot me an icy glare but said nothing.

Later, Pig Virus met me in the hall to tell me what had transpired. "I think I got through to her," he began. "She really went crazy when I ordered her to cut you some slack. I finally had to tell her that if it came down to a choice between her and you, you were much more valuable to the station than she was. That's when she started to get reasonable. It may take a while for it to show, but I think she got the message." Pig Virus was right. She stewed about the new shape of the playing field for several days before coming up with a new plan of attack.

Among Mary Beth's few cronies was a black woman named Nell who headed the public affairs department, and she decided to enlist her aid in an effort to reestablish relations with me. Nell and I had never done more than exchange greetings in the hall, but all of a sudden, she wanted to be my best friend. A few days after Mary Beth's lunch with Pig Virus, I received a luncheon invitation from Nell. I discussed this latest plot twist with Dr. London at our next session, but she refused to believe intrigue was behind every move made by the NBC honchos. She was actually encouraging me to accept the invitation from Nell to increase my social contacts.

"I may not see the world correctly most of the time, Dr. London," I pleaded, "but don't make this a test. I'm a good judge of character, and I know Nell is only doing this for Mary Beth!"

"How do you know so much?" my shrink asked, at her most shrinklike.

"I accept that I'm not right about everything," I countered, "but I'm right about this."

"Just try it," she urged me.

"Okay," I agreed reluctantly, "but I know I'm going to be sorry."

I had never trusted anyone the way I had begun to trust Dr. London, and I believed that my faith demanded she always be right. I was afraid that this mistake would destroy all that we'd built together in the past months and that once again I would have to question her guidance or, even worse, be thrown back into a state in which I only trusted myself. I begged her not to make me test my theory, but she insisted.

So I had lunch with Mary Beth's bosom buddy, inwardly cursing Dr. London the whole time. Nell wasted my afternoon by singing Mary Beth's praises and trying to convince me that I had misunderstood her motives all along. "If you could only get to know her," Nell crooned in her deep satin voice, "you'd realize she's not your enemy." Then came the bribes, invitations to Nell's house in New Jersey for great parties where I could meet some fabulous people. She started dropping names, Sammy Davis, Jr., and Harry Belafonte. She jawed about how we simply had to go shopping at the malls.

Nell was laying it on pretty thick. I sat there nodding and smiling at everything she said, but frankly I'd stopped listening to her long before the lunch came to an end. I was thinking about my next therapy session. I was angry as hell at my psychotherapist. She had watched me throw tantrums about everyone else. Now she was going to find out what it was like on the receiving end.

"Well, I was right, and you were wrong," I spat out at the start of our next session. "I had to sit there listening to that bitch defend Mary Beth for almost two hours. I told you what she was up to, but you wouldn't listen to me, so I had to waste my time sitting across from that maggot while I tried to choke down rotten food. I hope you're happy."

"Okay, so I was wrong," Dr. London admitted quite calmly. "Was the lunch really that bad?"

"Yes, it was awful!"

"I'm sorry," she told me with a slightly sheepish grin. "How was I supposed to know you were such a good judge of character?"

I couldn't even get a good argument out of this woman! Wrong or right, Dr. London was pretty cool. Even her response to her own misjudgment proved that she wasn't there to play God. She had taught me a whole new vocabulary of problem solving. She wasn't afraid to push the envelope if she thought it would help me grow. Ultimately, she wanted me to be in charge of my life, to be capable of standing on my own, and to accept the fact that I could make mistakes. And what she had helped me accomplish with Mary Beth was nothing short of a miracle.

About a week after that uncomfortable lunch with Nell, Mary Beth called me into her office and really lost it with me just as the show was about to begin. I'd already had a bad morning, and I just didn't need her hammering at me that day. I guess Mary Beth's outburst was the straw that broke the camel's back, because as soon as she started yelling, I could feel the floodgates open. I ran from the office to avoid crying in front of her, but the tears were already flowing when I hit the hall, headed for the women's room. So who do I run into? Nell. She tried to stop me, but I eluded her grasp and just kept running.

No one had ever reduced me to tears at work before, but Mary Beth was a master at that part of her job. Still, as I splashed cold water on my face, I was convinced that she had just lost the war. That outburst was the final straw. Mary Beth was dead meat. I was through being fucked with. I'd reached my limit, and since no one else seemed to be able to take care of her, I'd just have to do it myself.

I walked out of the rest room and headed for the studio, where Howard had already opened the show. It seemed like the whole station had been alerted about my tearful breakdown. I walked through a gauntlet of stares as I made my way through the hall, every eye questioning what I'd do next. I burst through the studio door, slung my chair around, straddled it as if it were a horse, and grabbed my headphones. Howard too had heard the news, and when he turned to face me, I could see that he was tired of dealing with all the bullshit. "What's going on now?" he moaned.

"Fuck it," I replied with a toss of my head, "we've got a show to do." And with that I slapped on the cans.

"All right," Howard said, grinning from ear to ear. He might not have had a clue as to what had been going on with me, but it was obvious that he was glad to have me back.

Nell must have warned her buddy that she'd better try to do some damage control, because Mary Beth called me into her office during the next break. "You're much too sensitive. You take everything too personally," she began as I stood on the far side of her desk looking down at her.

"Fine, no problem, I don't really care anymore," I replied with a dismissive wave of the hand as I turned and walked out the door. I was cool, cooler than I'd ever been, so cool that Mary Beth never even bothered trying to call me back.

Subsequently, scrambling to recover the edge, she shifted gears again and attempted to bring me into her inner circle. I'd heard rumors that she kept us all at each other's throats by taking us aside and sharing her complaints about another colleague. Now she was carping to me about one of the freelancers who was subbing on the traffic copter that day. "He's just not as good as we are," she smiled, including me among the privileged. I inquired if that was all and walked out on her.

Not long after the Ironbound incident, WNBC finally got a new general manager, Randy Bongarten, to fill the void left by Dom Fioravanti. Pig Virus, who had gotten used to functioning as GM in the absence of a real one, now found himself relegated to his old job. Since he was no longer in a position to control Mary Beth, I felt it imperative to get to Randy and explain my position. I had to make sure he was aware of everything Mary Beth had done in the past so that he'd understand when I came to him about her in the future.

I was thrilled to find Randy an enthusiastic and knowledgeable fan of the show. He had every intention of cutting the few cords still left binding us at WNBC so that we could once again do the kind of free form, avant-garde broadcasts he'd heard us do in Washington. But when I made my complaints about Mary Beth, he too chalked them up to a simple personality conflict. Randy considered himself a real "people person" who'd never met the management difficulty he couldn't smooth over. He saw fixing my relationship with Mary Beth as part of his job description and assured me that it wouldn't be a problem. Unfortunately, he had no idea how far out of control things had gotten, but he would find out soon enough.

Next, at Randy's insistence, Mary Beth entrapped me into accepting an invitation for dinner at her newly decorated co-op. Oh joy! I had desperately tried and failed to get out of it. Now I lay sleepless, finally facing the fact that there was no way I could get through the evening. The next day, I walked over to Randy's office and demanded to see him immediately. He was sitting on his couch glancing over some papers when I walked in.

"Mary Beth invited me to dinner," I hissed through clenched teeth.

"Yes, isn't that great," he responded without looking up.

"No, it's not," I replied, making it clear that I was not amused. "I'm not in the habit of breaking bread with people who have tried to kill me."

"Okay, Robin," Randy said, seeing for the first time the gravity of the situation, "I'll take care of it. You don't have to have dinner with her. I guess this problem between the two of you is a lot worse than I thought. Isn't there any way to resolve it?"

"I don't think so," I told him honestly.

Later that afternoon, Mary Beth told me something personal had come up and that she'd have to cancel our dinner plans. I almost dissolved into hysterical laughter.

Whatever Randy had said to her didn't stop Mary Beth's attempts at reconciliation. She even called me at home once to have a little chat. When I responded to her query about what I did on the show, she expressed surprise and said that she had no idea I had so many duties. She also admitted that she had done horrible things to me and had tried to get me fired, but claimed she was under orders from our old general manager, Dom Fioravanti. I never bothered to tell her that Dom had expressed misgivings about her before I had even gotten to New York or to point out that Pig Virus, Dom's protégé, had been the one to come to my defense when I finally got the goods on her.

Pig Virus left shortly after Randy took over, but no one had discovered yet what it would take to unseat the Queen of the Newsroom. Even with the intervention of a new general manager who was openly supportive of the show, Mary Beth seemed incapable of changing her ways. She still tried to stick me with all the dirty jobs.

When WNBC started carrying basketball, the games often pre-empted the show by as much as two hours, since we were on the air from three to seven in the evening. In those instances, I would have been able to leave early with Howard and Fred except for the fact that Mary Beth demanded I cover the newsroom until nine. Randy agreed that the coverage was unnecessary but didn't want to completely override Mary Beth's authority, so he came up with a compromise. Since Mary Beth wanted the newsroom covered during the games, it would be done on a rotating basis and shared by three people—me, Judy, and Mary Beth. I thought that her little bug eyes were going to pop right out of her head when she discovered how badly her scheme had backfired.

Each time it was her turn to cover the newsroom during a game, Mary Beth called me into her office and asked me, as a favor, to sub for her. Things between us had cooled down slightly, so while I resented it, I always agreed in the interests of détente. Then one day she abruptly developed a fear that somehow Randy would discover she wasn't pulling her rotation. First she asked me to cover for her. Two hours later she told me I could leave early. Then she changed her mind again. This waffling went on all afternoon. In the end she pulled her own shift.

I hadn't put up the least bit of resistance, yet the following afternoon, one of the vice presidents of the radio division confronted me in the studio. He shook Howard's hand in a friendly old-boy manner when he first came in, then he turned to me. When I took his hand to shake it, he looked me right in the eye and announced angrily, "And you, why'd you have to make her such a bitch last night?"

I was so shocked, I couldn't believe my ears. He had to be talking about my news director, Mary Beth. When I told Randy about the bitch comment, even he was floored. After that incident, Mary Beth lost all control over me. Randy informed her that any order she wanted to give me had to be submitted to him in writing first. Never again did I have to deal with her directly.

Randy was true to his word about liberating the show. He not only removed Mary Beth from my life, he reappointed me afternoon-drive news anchor and scratched the network newscasts because he wanted us to do the news the way we had in Washington. Soon, too, the wimpy sounds of Barry Manilow, Air Supply, and Toto began to fade as Howard regained full control and started to bend his artistry around the stifling WNBC format.

"Dial-a-Date" got wilder. We even set up men with other men on dates, to say nothing of interracial couples and swingers. We held the first Christmas party in which listeners had to perform weird stunts like burping out the alphabet to get in. The first naked women began to appear. And the ratings went through the roof.

We were truly beginning to have fun doing radio again. Our enemies had been vanquished, and we were pulling our own weight. Advertising on the show was sold out. Not only did articles appear about the show in the entertainment section of the paper, but in the financial pages as well. Under Randy, the station began to treat us like stars. We no longer had to travel by subway because WNBC sprang for a town car, and I got a hefty raise. We walked through the halls holding our heads high, no longer afraid to meet the gazes of engineers and salespeople. We were winners.

The Randy era marked our happiest time at WNBC. Even when he balked at some of our more daring on-air fare, Howard could charm him. If he couldn't exactly reach Randy himself, he'd call Randy's wife, Fran, during the show and enlist her aid, begging her to give Randy sex that evening so that he'd mellow out and get off our backs. Eventually our ratings outstripped even those of the venerable WNBC cash cow, Don Imus, who was now getting his butt kicked by Scott Shannon and his "Morning Zoo" on Z100. All of a sudden, we were top dogs.

Howard and I started to feel so good, we began to take a renewed interest in our personal appearance. We'd both packed on the pounds from the stress of fighting off Mary Beth and Pig Virus by consuming five or six generous meals a day. We had lunch before the show, ordered in during the show, then pigged out again once we got home. There were two signs that things had really gotten out of control.

One of our sponsors, Baby Watson Cheesecake, started sending us boxes of their product, which we'd munch on air. One afternoon, I walked around the console to hand Howard something and discovered on the floor beside him a half-eaten Baby Watson full of huge gouge marks. I could just imagine him digging his fingers into the cake, grabbing a chunk, and stuffing it into his mouth in the minutes between live commercials.

The second revelation happened one winter night as we made our way to Radio City Music Hall to see a live Richard Pryor show. I noticed that each time Howard took a step, his huge down coat made a swishing sound as it rubbed against his hips. That coat was supposed to be loose, and when I realized that it was now formfitting, I burst into laughter right in the middle of Sixth Avenue. When I told him why I was laughing, Howard replied, "Well, you're no lightweight yourself!" That shut me up. I had to admit that up until then I'd thought the cleaner was shrinking my clothes.

In fact, I'd regained all the weight I'd lost in Washington and hadn't so much as taken a brisk walk since I'd moved to New York. Even my face was a perfect circle under a mound of greasy jheri curls, a hairstyle I'd adopted, to my mother's delight, shortly after I'd come home from California. I was a real fashion disaster. It hadn't seemed to matter much before, but now people wanted to interview us and take our pictures. It was time to pull it together. So we did. In the next six months, we would get ourselves in shape and back to our fighting weights.

At the same time, therapy was becoming a real drag. I had achieved the first of my initial goals. I was no longer uncomfortable at work. The fighting and temper tantrums had ended. Howard and I had learned to talk to each other again, and while Mary Beth was still there, she wasn't a factor anymore. We were doing so well, Imus stopped drinking and started barging into writing sessions just to hang out. He'd even do the first couple of hours of the show with us each afternoon. I figured it had finally hit him that we were the new wave and he wanted to catch it before it engulfed him and he drowned. We eventually threw him out, so he started calling us on the phone. We couldn't get rid of him.

At home, the living room floor was clear, the jigsaw puzzles having been relegated to my second bedroom, which was used for storage. I had relearned to sleep through the night and no longer prowled the apartment in the wee hours looking for instruments of suicide. Even the exhibitionism and sexual preoccupation faded away. I woke up each morning looking forward to the day. I had friends and had become even closer to Howard and Alison and their daughter, Emily.

That was as far as I wanted to go, but Dr. London had other ideas. She was pushing me to expand my horizons even farther. "Don't you want to have a relationship with a man?" she asked one day. "Wouldn't you like someone of your own?"

"Nope," I said, sticking to my guns. "I only want to work and not need anybody. Maybe I'm not totally self-sufficient yet, but one day I will be."

I still couldn't handle the idea of being that close, of really needing someone else's approval. Besides, I still didn't think I deserved to be loved, so why bother? That was when I started lying in therapy. I'd decide what to talk about before I got there to make sure that Dr. London didn't accidentally stumble onto a door and open it. Eventually, I realized that I was wasting my time and hers and began to think about quitting. I was skipping sessions again and getting sore about all the money it was costing me.

I knew that if I discussed these feelings with Dr. London, she'd assure me that there was more work to do. Inwardly, I guess I knew that was true but wasn't willing to face it, so I left her out of the decision completely. I'd cut back to two sessions a week but was rarely making both. And, one day, I simply announced to her that this visit would be the last. Dr. London was obviously shocked. "Don't you think we ought to talk about it if you want to leave?"

"I've already decided," I answered.

"If that's what you want to do," she offered, "there's a process we call 'termination' that involves a certain number of sessions to wind up loose ends."

"No thanks," I told her, "I've been terminating for weeks. You just weren't aware of it," I replied without emotion.

We continued to talk for the rest of that forty-five-minute session about I don't know what, but at the end Dr. London said she was leaving my Thursday session open just in case I changed my mind. "I've already told you I won't be here!" I said angrily.

It was hard enough to break away. Didn't she know I was afraid and didn't need this added pressure? "I've learned a lot from you, and it's been over such a short period. I need some time to let it all sink in, that's all," I continued more reasonably.

"Well, I don't know if I'm ever going to see you again," Dr. London said, her eyes getting a little misty.

"What are we going to do, have lunch?" I was angry again.

"No, we can't do that."

"Then I guess you're not going to see me again."

"Well, I'll still leave Thursday open," Dr. London said as I again shot her a look. "Just in case," she said, holding up her hands to indicate that she wasn't pressuring me. "And if you ever need to come back, my door is always open. You know where to find me."

"Okay." I was fighting back tears as she gave me a hug.

"'Bye, sweetie," she said as she walked me to the door.

I shed a few tears in the elevator, but when I hit the street, I entered what seemed like a brave new world. I was about to find out who Robin Quivers was without close supervision. Could I hold it together on my own? Was I ready for prime time? Only the days ahead would tell.

17

UNFORGIVEN

One day I got a call from my old Summit friend, Kathryn Starfire. Kathryn had dropped the "Starfire" and was once again using her real name, but she was still in the self-actualization business, working for Werner Erhard's new company and living in Boston with the man she would eventually marry. We spent Thanksgiving of 1984 reminiscing about the good old days at Summit. "Robin," Katherine mused, "you really ought to give Paul a call and tell him how you're doing. You're the one who's really living what he taught."

Now that I had both feet firmly planted on the road to recovery, I found myself wanting to share my secrets with others. For years, I hadn't told a soul a thing about myself unless it was a lie. Now I babbled about my past to complete strangers. There was only one secret I kept from all but the most special people. That was the story of Jimmy, whose pictures I still carried tucked inside my wallet.

I remember telling Alison Stern about him when we were sitting at the kitchen table of her new home, and how strange it was to hear myself actually forming the words. After struggling through tears to finish the part about the adoption, I realized that Alison was crying too. So, for the first time, I let someone else see those two pictures I'd been carrying around for fourteen years.

"My goodness, Robin," Alison lamented, "you had such a hurtful childhood. Have you ever thought of looking for him?"

"No, he was only three and a half when he left. He wouldn't remember me," I answered. "Besides, how would I explain who I was?"

Although Jimmy remained a precious memory, another figure from my past unexpectedly reentered my life. Denise Oliver, the woman who had introduced me to Howard, was hired by WNBC's sister station, WYNY, as a program director. After three years apart, she was again right down the hall. Denise always took pride in the fact that she'd been the matchmaker between Howard and me and reveled in our success. Once again in close proximity, and now more friends than mentor and protégé, we started hanging out together.

Most weekends, I'd throw a bag in the car and head up to Connecticut to bunk with her or my other NBC friend, Paula Schneider. Their town houses were like camp cabins for single adult refugees from Manhattan. We'd go to the beach, barbecue on the patio, watch videos, or go to the movies in the evening. This was a kind of leisure I'd never experienced before. I couldn't have been more pleased with the way things were turning out. Work was on track, and I actually had a social life. I figured maybe the "dating thing" would just naturally fall into place and I wouldn't ever have to confront my feelings on the issue while lying on some therapist's couch. In the meantime, I just wanted to have a good time.

I'd enjoyed the beach so much that I didn't want the summer to end, but it inevitably began to slip into the dreariness of fall. As October loomed ahead, the very thought of the cold to follow finally got me on a plane and out of New York for one last dose of hot-weather fun in the Bahamas. I'd heard so many of my married friends raving about their honeymoons in the Caribbean that I wanted to check it out for myself. It was the first time I'd gotten that far away from New York in two years.

As soon as we landed in Nassau and I registered at the beautiful new Cable Beach Hotel, I started wondering what there was to do here for a person alone. First on the agenda seemed to be unpacking, jumping into a bathing suit, and hitting the beach. The water was an unbelievable aqua and so clear that you could see a natural aquarium of exotic plants and fish all the way to the ocean floor. Fascinated, I began to traipse along the shore, dodging waves. Before long I'd wandered away from the hotels dotting the beach and could hear reggae music coming from a parking lot just off the sand. Seeing people who lived on the island doing something other than working at the hotel appealed to me.

Before long some of the locals spotted me walking alone. My demeanor must have screamed naive tourist because all of a sudden, I had company. One of the young men from the gathering in the parking lot approached me, smiling too broadly and asking too many questions. He wanted to know my name, where I was staying, and where I was from. That I lived in New York really turned him on, which made me edgy. When a friend of his came up to us, I became genuinely anxious and demanded that they leave me alone.

"Oh, we're here to protect you," the first guy announced.

"Yes, I'm from hotel security," his friend chimed in.

"If you don't get the fuck away from me, you're going to make me angry!" I spat out at the two of them.

"Why are you yelling at us when we're trying to help you?" the first man asked.

"I don't need any help, I need you to get away from me!" I screamed, clenching my fists.

The first young man told his buddy to leave, then attempted to calm me down, but there was no getting around my fear. "You go too!" I demanded. He eventually turned away and headed up the beach as I walked as fast as I could back to the resort area. I was panting by the time I reached my hotel. When one of the staff said hello, I barked at him to leave me alone. Secure once more behind the closed door of my room, I finally calmed down. This was, after all, the first time I'd been anywhere on my own in a long time, and there was no denying that I still had a healthy supply of paranoia on board, which made what happened next a total surprise.

To my delight, I met a white Bahamian—who even knew there was such a thing?—while on a snorkeling trip. Philip sounded just like Sean Connery even though he looked like Jody from "Family Affair" all grown up. While I wasn't really into his blond, blue-eyed good looks, that accent was killing me. By the end of an incredibly pleasant evening together, I knew I was a goner. I hadn't made love in a long time, and I was terribly nervous, but this young man made me feel truly appreciated all night long. I have no idea where Philip got his stamina.

After he left the next morning, I was pleased that both my private parts and my womanly wiles were still in working order. Philip and I had one more bittersweet meeting before I left, and when I got back to New York, I put the conch shell he pulled from the sea for me on a shelf in the bathroom. A few weeks later I received a lovely postcard from him assuring me that I'd always be warmly welcomed in Nassau.

I held the Sterns rapt as I recounted the story of my island tryst. Howard eventually used the episode as the basis for his theory, later revealed on the air, that I was some kind of "Black Widow." He'd been working with Fred and me for almost four years, he explained, and had never known either of us to have a date during the entire time. Fred had actually been the object of many crushes among the secretaries and interns at both DC101 and WNBC, but he never took advantage of this. Howard and I would often speculate about Fred's sexual orientation when he wasn't around, and I'm sure the two of them had similar conversations about me when I left the room.

Now Howard started referring to me as a "Black Widow" who traveled to exotic places to suck the life out of young men. His reasoning went that my sexuality seemed to surface for a time, then disappear. He expounded that like Spock, the Vulcan character from "Star Trek," I had a mating season every few years. The truth of it was that I still didn't feel worthy of love and was afraid to feel anything too deeply. I wasn't sure I could survive a profound hurt, didn't particularly care for messy relationships, and had had enough of flirting with depression. Since I'm not one of those people who hates being alone, fear won out over romance. Just as, at the station, the status quo was about to win out over the new and different.

Our heyday at WNBC proved to be just the calm before the next storm once Randy Bongarten was promoted to vice president. Even as he was packing his things for the move upstairs, he promised us that the show would always have his support. But Randy was a thorough packer. When he went, he took the good times with him.

Randy's replacement, John Hayes, was a rather attractive but utterly humorless man who appeared to have something to prove and who despised "The Howard Stern Show." Needless to say, John didn't appreciate Howard's calling him on the air before he'd even gotten to the station, to inform him that he wasn't our boss and to keep his hands off the show. After John arrived a week or two later and actually appeared on the show, I knew we had a problem.

Howard was just being himself. He wanted Hayes to state on the air that he was the most talented radio personality in the country, and when he couldn't get that out of him, Howard tried to pry into his personal life a bit. In the end, Howard warned Hayes once again to forget about touching our show. John was visibly uncomfortable and couldn't wait to get out of the hot seat. I ran into him in the lobby later and mentioned lightheartedly that I thought the little encounter had been fun. "No, it was not," he replied. I thought he was kidding until I took a good look at him. He was deadly serious.

As far as I was concerned, the single good thing about John Hayes was that he had no use for Mary Beth. One of his first official acts was to have her replaced as news director. Practically overnight, Mary Beth was busted to street reporter, trying to feed tape to the station through Judy and me. The queen of the newsroom was now a commoner, and Judy and I both outranked her. It was a stunning transition watching Mary Beth trying to ingratiate herself with us.

Judy and I took great delight in making sure Mary Beth got as good as she gave. We had the newsroom declared a no-smoking area, so, old chain-smoker that she was, Mary Beth had to adjourn to a hall at the back of the station to light up. Since she needed one of us to monitor the transmission of her tape feed to the engineer, we'd make her call back again and again, claiming that we were too busy to help her until later. And we made sure that she was never included in casual office conversation. Before long, Mary Beth was history. She just sort of faded away, and no one shed a tear. Her only friend, Nell, had already left.

Blithely watching Mary Beth get booted from the train must have given me tunnel vision because I totally missed the fact that our own tickets were about to be punched. When Hayes moved next, it was to infuriate Howard even more. John felt he needed a personality-driven complement to Imus in the morning and Howard in the afternoon, and one day on the train in from Connecticut came up with what he considered an inspired choice—Soupy Sales.

Howard had actually been a big Soupy fan as a kid. While we were at DC101, Sales had been in Washington to promote the rerelease of his hit novelty dance single, "The Mouse," and had agreed to do the Stern show. Howard couldn't contain his excitement. I only remembered Soupy from "The Ed Sullivan Show," but Howard claimed that his children's program out of Detroit had been brilliant. I was prepared to be impressed. After Soupy's appearance, Howard was still raving about him in an attempt to convince me of what an incredible talent he was. I didn't quite get it. "Howard, he was a nice guy and everything," I finally said, "but calm down already." As far as I was concerned, it was Howard who was the genius and Soupy who should have been raving.

Shortly after Soupy joined the WNBC lineup, Howard's attitude changed. He didn't resent Soupy getting the job, he just wanted Soupy to have to prove himself the same way he'd had to before getting all the perks that went along with success. Yet Soupy was being handed everything before he'd clocked a minute of airtime. Among the blandishments were a town car, an office, and a producer. They even went out and bought him a piano for the studio and hired someone to play it. On the other hand, the station had balked at adding a paltry one hundred and fifty dollars a week to our budget so that we could hire someone to help around the office. Gary Dell'Abate joined us only after Howard had waged a long, exhausting siege. All Soupy had to do to collect the goodies was show up.

Before long, Howard and Soupy were at war. Hostilities commenced when Soupy's producer, Boy Lee, who was one of our former interns, refused to clean the studio after they'd used it, and they escalated when Howard jammed one of the little hammers on Soupy's piano. From that moment on, our camps stopped speaking to each other. I thought it was hysterical, but I'm sure John Hayes didn't appreciate his man being harassed on the air by Howard day in and day out. It never seemed to have occurred to him that the feud would bring Soupy a lot of attention, not to mention ratings.

Meanwhile, we had already begun to take advantage of being in the same building as "Late Night with David Letterman," "Saturday Night Live," and "Live at Five." We commandeered every one of their guests that we could, and the list of big names appearing with us included Bette Midler, David Brenner, Eddie Murphy, Joan Rivers, Billy Idol, Billy Joel, Bill Cosby, and many more. Now Soupy was also demanding guests. When the issue became another bone of contention, Howard went to management and insisted that he be given right of first refusal.

Suddenly, we were back to square one or worse, battling with Imus and Soupy on one front and on another with John Hayes, who had a thing about complaint letters. He either didn't understand or didn't care that "The Howard Stern Show" always generated lots of complaints along with big ratings. His ideal station was a bunch of nice little shows that didn't offend anyone and attracted airline commercials.

And that was before Howard tried calling John's wife during the show to enlist her aid in calming him down. Then Hayes really hit the ceiling. I honestly believe that he saw Howard as the Antichrist and feared that merely hearing his voice on the phone would put his family in danger of damnation. After that incident, we were officially informed that Mrs. John Hayes was not to be called on the air or otherwise disturbed by the likes of us. Not that we didn't feel the tension generated by these little run-ins, but we were sure we could handle them because we had the numbers as security. Howard, by this time, was the biggest radio personality in the country. He had even done a guest appearance on David Letterman's show.

And so it was that, even though he hated us, Hayes agreed to let us take the show on the road. Howard had come up with a song parody contest in which listeners rewrote lyrics to popular songs using people on the show as subjects. Each of the fifteen winners and their guests would accompany us on an all-expenses-paid trip to Los Angeles for one week. The L.A. trip was our first experience in taking listeners on the road, and we didn't have the foresight to book ourselves into a different hotel from the one where the winners were staying. Everyone ended up together at the Universal Sheraton, although Howard and I were staying on different floors and left orders that our room numbers were to be kept a secret.

Unbeknowst to us, two of the women in the group had vowed to sleep with Howard from the moment they'd learned that they were going with us. One of them even seduced Gary in order to find out Howard's room number. On the final night, they confronted me as I crossed the lobby on the way to dinner. They couldn't wait to tell me that that very night they were planning to surprise Howard in his room, wearing only their underwear. Howard, who had been flirting on the air with the two of them all week, was waiting for me in the hotel restaurant. Between the appetizer and the entrée, I told him that he would be getting some unexpected company that night. "Robin," he fumed, "you tell those bitches I'll rip their tits off if they come near me!"

Gary found the girls and headed them off before their midnight run, saving them from a painful and unsightly amputation. That's when I learned how much of a family man Howard really was. I was bowled over by his fidelity to his marriage and family, and right then and there decided that not only was he a genius, he was a hero.

I had to admit that L.A. was a blast and, yes, we could still have fun on the air despite the fact that our enemies were lined up at the studio door. Even my personal life had settled into a pleasant rhythm of working out and friendly outings, but I should have know better than to think it would last. Just when everything seemed under control, my family came tearing through my fragile veil of tranquillity.

When I stopped talking to my parents, I'd told my brother, Junior, that I wanted to keep in touch with him and the two young boys who still lived with my parents. He'd agreed, but wouldn't you know it, his very first call on family business was about my father, who had been admitted to the hospital after a heart attack. Junior seemed terribly worried that poor Dad might have to have open-heart surgery on his badly clogged arteries.

I didn't know what to say. Hadn't I made it clear that I didn't care to hear about my parents' problems? I spent a sleepless night rethinking my decision to stop speaking to them, but by morning had once again resolved that I was right. I did not want to see or

talk to my father even though it sounded as though his health problems could be grave.

Junior called again the following evening to inform me that the
doctors had indeed decided to operate. "What do you want me to
do," I asked, interrupting him, "come home and kill your father?
That's really all that I could do." My brother didn't say a word, and
I felt that I owed him an explanation for my apparent heartlessness.
So I told him as briefly as possible about our father sexually molesting me. When I finished the story, he just said "Okay" and hung up.
I stood in my kitchen listening to the dial tone, unable to believe
that this was his only response. It reminded me of the time during
my parents' worst fight when I'd come to his room looking for
comfort and he'd angrily dismissed me because, I guess, he didn't
want me to see him cry. I was just as disappointed in him now as I'd
been then.

I should have known that my mother was behind Junior's calls.
Once he failed in his mission, she wrote me a letter, calling me
names and pleading my father's case. According to her, he'd spent
his time before surgery sitting on the side of his bed weeping and
calling my name. I'm sure it was only because he thought he needed
my forgiveness to avoid hell if he died in surgery. "If you don't leave
me alone, I'll tell you why I'm not there!" I wrote back.

A few days later, another letter from my mother arrived. Quite
uncharacteristically, she wanted to know what was wrong. So I sat
down and composed an eleven-page handwritten letter, telling her
what had happened to me on some of those Thursdays when she
was out shopping. I waited on tenterhooks for a response, wondering how my mother would react to the disclosure. I didn't have long
to wait. In a few short days, I was walking back from the mailbox
with a fat, business-sized envelope in my hand. Inside was a letter
from her and another sealed envelope with "Robin" scrawled across
the front.

My mother swore that she hadn't known anything about the
abuse and told me how sorry she was that it had happened. She also
revealed that she had confronted my father with my letter and that
he had tearfully confessed. The second envelope contained his written apology to me. I picked it up and turned it over again and again,
examining it from all sides while I thought about opening it.

Finally, I ripped it to shreds, took it outside, and threw it in the Dumpster. I didn't want an apology she had ordered him to make. Then I went back inside to finish reading what my mother had to say. Something about her words touched me, and I found myself dialing the fatal phone number.

In a moment of uncharacteristic charity, I thought that maybe it was possible for us to have a relationship, but it wasn't long before talking to her had me literally shaking. She sounded exactly the same as always. We spent a few minutes talking about the letters and how long it had been since we'd spoken before she changed the subject to how my father had destroyed our relationship. In no time at all we were in full swing, both ganging up on Dad as if he were the only villain of the piece.

Even while I was engaged in the conversation, I knew we were veering off in the wrong direction. I hadn't stopped talking to my mother because of what my father had done. I'd had my own problems with her, and this phone call was reminding me only too well what they were. As soon as I hung up, I had a full-blown panic attack, complete with shortness of breath and palpitations, then spent the night tossing and turning.

It had been all too easy to lapse into that old family dynamic in which we'd make one person the enemy and then pick him apart until we were down to the bone. I was ashamed of myself for having participated, but I knew I couldn't have helped myself. It was how we spoke, how we lived, how we interacted. I had been drawn so deeply into the psychodrama, I'd agreed to let my mother come for a visit. But that was the least of my worries at this point; I was mostly concerned about myself.

As soon as I got to work the next day, I ran to Howard's office and slammed the door shut. I was in quite a state by that time, eyes red from crying and lack of sleep, tortured by my own thoughts. "Howard," I began, "I had a talk with my mother last night. I have those people's genes inside me. What if they just blow up on me one day and I become just like them?"

Most people might think that Howard is the last person to come to for reassurance, but I can tell you that he's never let me down when he knew I needed help. "Robin," he told me calmly, "you are not those people, and you are never going to be those people."

"Are you sure?" I asked uncertainly.

"Yes, I'm sure," he insisted with authority.

On the strength of Howard's belief in me, I pulled myself together and once again set out to resist being pulled into the whirlpool of strangeness in which my family spun. And that wasn't easy, because my mother, God help me, was intent on keeping the date we'd made that night and I didn't know then how to refuse her. I spent the weeks before her visit lecturing myself on what my life was like now and alerting some close friends to the fact that I might need their help while she was here.

Hoping against hope that she wouldn't do exactly what I expected her to, I drove to the Port Authority bus terminal in Manhattan to pick up my mother on a Friday afternoon. Just as if we had always been closer than two peas in a pod, she ran toward me with outspread arms, like in those hair commercials. I knew the weekend wasn't going to work when she grabbed me in a big bear hug and my body stiffened reflexively. Of course, she ignored my reaction and began to chatter on about the trip. Then, she eyed me from head to foot, completing a quick inventory.

I was thinner and more fit than I'd ever been. I worked out with a personal trainer, lifting weights three times a week, and I'd started jogging again. My hair was shorter than it had been when I'd returned from California but this time, instead of gasping in horror, she said that she liked it, I guess because it left my earlobes exposed to reveal diamond studs. When we got outside the terminal, I put her bags in the trunk of my new red Mustang. I could almost hear the cash register ringing as she took note of all that she saw. By the time we got to my new place, a cute little two-bedroom garden apartment which had just been newly restored, she could no longer contain her amazement. "Chile, you livin' rich. Diamonds all in your ears!" she exclaimed.

I was trying with my entire being to remain civil, but having been put under inspection was beginning to take its toll. "Well," I replied, "no one else was going to give me these things, so I figured I'd better get them myself." I was remembering all the tension I'd felt when I began to detect her jealousy of my achievements as a young girl. I tried to keep busy and not talk much. Why couldn't she stay in the living room while I prepared dinner? Instead she propped herself up at the kitchen table, and unable to find any topic of conversation to my liking, settled on my father. I held my tongue as long as I could, vividly recalling why I hadn't come to her after his very first kiss. I hadn't wanted to be a part of the laundry list of my father's failings and now, here in my kitchen, she was adding my name to the roster.

That's when I lost it. I just started screaming at her that she was no saint and that I could give her just as long a list of her own wrongdoing. For a while she tried to defend herself, but when she couldn't outyell me, she fell silent. Even as I turned my back to her to continue preparing the food, I was screaming out my grievances. Wheeling around to face her, I realized that she wasn't even listening. Suddenly, it hit me that I'd never be able to scream loud enough to get through to her, and that my neighbors had already heard more than enough. I stopped yelling and put the food on the table. It was impossible to eat, my throat was so tight. She started chattering about nothing again, and I just couldn't take it anymore. I ran to my bedroom, slammed the door, and threw myself across my bed, in tears.

I felt trapped inside this little room, just as I'd felt trapped as a child, and just like back then, I had no idea how I was going to get out. I picked up the phone and called my friend Paula. "She's here in my living room," I whispered, "and I'm trapped in my bedroom and I don't know how to get out."

Realizing that I had regressed to an infantile stage, Paula gave me explicit instructions. "Robin, you have to go out there and tell her it's not working out and she has to leave. Get her a hotel room for tonight, and make sure she's on a bus back to Baltimore tomorrow."

I knew that Paula was right, and I was sitting in a chair next to the door, summoning the courage to face my mother again, when, without even knocking, she burst into the room. "Come on, baby, don't you want to cry on my shoulder?" Her barging through the door like that reminded me once again of how none of my boundaries had ever been respected in her home. "No," I said quietly.

She took a seat on the edge of my bed, and burying her face in her hands, she began to heave great sobs. "Stop the crocodile tears," I told her. Instantly dry-eyed, she looked at me through her fingers and inquired, "Why do my tears have to be crocodile tears?"

"Look, Mom," I began, "this isn't working out, so I want you to go to a hotel tonight—," but before I could finish my thought, she interrupted me with an outburst much like that of a petulant child.

"I want my family back!" she screamed with bared teeth, hovering over me, her arms straight at her sides, her hands clenched tight. "Why can't you just forget it? It happened a long time ago."

Although I begged my mother to go to a hotel, she refused. When I repeated the request, she refused again but added that if I wanted her out I could call the police. At that point I went down on my knees and pleaded for her to go. "I don't live like that anymore," I cried.

Finally, she agreed to spend the night at a hotel I found for her near my apartment. The next morning, as we rode the Port Authority escalator down to the level where she'd catch the bus back to Baltimore, my mother wished me a nice life. The last thing I said to her was that I'd have one as soon as she was on that bus. Until that moment, I'd never been completely sure I'd been right to cut them out of my life. Now I was. When I left that bus station, though, I didn't know if I was free or if I was an orphan. The one thing I did know was that I could never go home again.

I talked to my mother one more time on the phone after that trip, explaining that it wasn't possible for us to have a relationship unless she got some counseling. That was a foreign concept to her, but after she said no, she asked if I thought she was sick because she really didn't see anything wrong with her life. "I can't answer that," I said. "I only know that it was wrong for me."

I realized that my mother was telling me there was a limit to what she would do. All the giving would have to be from my side, as it had always been, and I still had nothing to give, so I said goodbye. From that point on, I gave up looking back and committed myself to growing and changing. I was through with the lies and subterfuges of denial, and still couldn't see how I would ever be able to forgive them for failing me so.

This was 1985, and one more time I was painfully reminded that I was alone. None of the positive things I'd done had managed to change that one irrefutable fact. No matter how hard I had worked, no matter how much I had confronted, no matter how good I tried to be, the gods seemed to feel that there was more I needed to do to absolve myself of my sins. It was time to try something else, so I embarked on a spiritual search to see if that road offered any answers, and the first place I found myself was back in church.

I'd heard about a progressive nondenominational church called Riverside while I was still working at WCBM in Baltimore. One of my co-workers there had been a regular churchgoer. Something happened to her every time she spoke about her faith. I don't know if it was a sense of peace or that zombie look religious fanatics get that came over her, but it was awesome. Ever curious, I had attended a couple of Sunday services with her. Her church wasn't anything like the holy rollers' churches I'd grown up attending. The minister was quite human and gave thoughtful, relevant sermons that made me think, rather than feel guilty, long after they were over. He had mentioned Riverside Church to me when he found out I was moving to New York.

Three years later, I decided to give God one more try. Maybe it wasn't religion I had objected to, just the brand my parents practiced. So with an open mind, I headed into Manhattan one Sunday morning to search out God at Riverside Church and see if He had anything to tell me. While I might or might not profit from the experience, at least it was movement. Whether it was in the right direction or not remained to be seen. But while my personal and professional lives seemed to be chugging along, even picking up steam, storm winds were gathering. It was time to test my mettle and see just how strong I had become.

18

AFTER THE STORM

I'm driving my car at top speed in traffic on a superhighway, only I can't see because my eyes are closed. At first it's okay, then I become anxious, and no matter how hard I try to open my eyes, I can't. I try to slow down, but I can't do that either, yet somehow I don't hit anything. Soon I realize that there's nothing I can do but let it happen, and then my eyes open naturally, as if I could have opened them all along.

—a dream

John Hayes had a lot of plans for WNBC, and "The Howard Stern Show" just didn't seem to fit in. Hayes had Soupy doing middays, but evenings were still a problem. Now that FM radio had really come on strong, no one was going to tune in to AM just to hear music unless there was no other choice. Our show was the one entertainment format that proved people would switch back to AM. The only other venue providing any draw at all was sports.

John thought the perfect solution for nighttime was to compete with Art Russ, who did a popular sports talk show on WABC. Art was a sports authority, but John, in his infinite wisdom, challenged Russ by hiring a guy who was anything but, Jack Specter, an elder statesman of New York radio. Jack's most frequently repeated line was "I'm not a guy who knows statistics or remembers dates, I'm just a fan." It will come as no surprise that he didn't exactly set the evening radio waves ablaze.

Soupy's ratings remained soft in middays and Jack's could never be termed anything but anemic, yet Hayes, satisfied that both shows were the cornerstones of his master plan to personally imprint WNBC, moved on. Next he dealt with overnights, filling the slot with the syndicated Wolfman Jack show. Now, gazing out over his empire, there were only two programs which didn't bear the Hayes stamp, Howard Stern's in the afternoon and Don Imus's in the morning.

We've always speculated that Imus made a pact with the devil to achieve his success. He was the Teflon deejay. Nothing ever stuck to him. He managed to outlast every administration and every industry shift, continuing to prosper, if not thrive. We, on the other hand, have never been able to figure out why our karma makes us the inevitable target of every bad manager and news media assault. So even with dropping ratings, Imus's show escaped John's interference because it continued to make money and not waves. We, on the other hand, were not to be so lucky.

John Hayes saw our show as the next thing that needed fixing. Once again, the enemy would attack Howard from my side. Hayes felt that he could get Howard to follow format by reintroducing network news to the show and claimed we stuck out because we sounded different from the rest of the daytime lineup. He never realized that uniqueness was the key to our success. Hayes wanted to reverse the clock, bringing back the network news that would lock us into the format again and prevent Howard and me from engaging in our lengthy discussions.

Once again we found ourselves being called to meetings, sometimes individually and sometimes together, in which Hayes would attempt to enlighten us with his vast radio knowledge. "I could make some money on the show if I could sell advertising to the airlines," he'd repeat like a mantra. But we weren't budging. In fact, as the meetings increased, Howard, in a ghostly reprise of his last days at DC101 with Goff Lebar, started taking his fight with John to the airwaves.

To our listeners, Hayes became known as "The Incubus." As time went on, Howard began every show by lampooning The Incubus's most recent intervention. People loved it. Everyone could relate to having an overbearing, impossible boss and couldn't resist the vicarious thrill of hearing Howard turn the tables, taking the boss to task for his incompetence with seeming impunity. When he railed at Hayes, he was screaming for all the people who had to swallow their pride and just take it.

The day The Incubus and Howard got into an on-air shoving match marked the collapse of all pretense at civility. Howard was demanding to talk to him in the studio, but The Incubus now refused to appear on the show. We tried calling him, only to be told by his secretary that he was out, but we didn't believe her and dispatched Boy Gary, our producer, to his office to see. As we thought, The Incubus was in hiding, with his door closed.

As impish as ever, Howard refused to take no for an answer, and grabbing a wireless mike, he set out for John's office. On the way, he primed the audience for the confrontation by telling them that he planned to riffle through John's desk to discover what everyone at the station was being paid. The Incubus, in his utter humorlessness, took him seriously. When Howard tried to get into the office, the ensuing scuffle went out over the air. Howard carried it off with macho bravado but later, when we were back in the studio and had gone to commercial, he expressed genuine amazement. "John was really pissed," he told me. "I think he really wanted to hit me!"

A few weeks later we were in John's office once again, listening to him whine that he needed us to sound more like the rest of the station. We were only too familiar with the argument by now and tired of listening. So as John laid out his concerns, Howard and I made eye contact, rose in unison, and walked out of the office, leaving The Incubus in the middle of a sentence. A brief moment of sanity possessed me once we were back in the show office. "Howard," I asked, "do you think we might be going a little too far? I mean, we just walked out on the general manager while he was still talking."

"Naaah," he replied after a moment's reflection. "After all, Robin," he continued with a shrug of his shoulders, "what are they going to do, fire us?" He had a point. We were sitting on a 5.7 rating. We were number one in the afternoon and the highest-rated show on the station. What did we have to worry about? We were WNBC's top guns. They needed us.

That's why we couldn't understand when, a few weeks later, the new program director, Dale Parsons, tried to talk us out of working the Friday afternoon Hurricane Gloria was supposed to hit. Dale called Howard several times, urging him to tell us all to stay home, but we decided we could make it despite the threatening skies. That Friday show turned out to be genuinely pleasant. With none of the stuffed shirts around, we had the station to ourselves. What made it even better was that because The Incubus hadn't ventured in from Connecticut, we were spared a meeting we were supposed to have with him. It had been rescheduled for Monday at noon, but at the time, Monday seemed a long way off.

Over the weekend Howard, who had become a jogging fanatic in the course of losing all the weight he'd gained, tripped over a fallen tree branch and sprained his ankle. So Monday began with Howard in pain and on crutches. Somehow this new glitch made us forget all about the meeting, and we didn't get to the station until one. Dale was frantic. "Where have you been?" he shouted, gesticulating wildly. We just pointed to Howard's crutches, then went our separate ways.

A few minutes later, I was summoned to Hayes's office. Expecting to see Howard, I was surprised to find The Incubus alone. He was sitting on the couch, not at his desk, and he motioned me to one of the occasional chairs opposite him. I figured Howard would be along presently, so I was puzzled when Hayes told his secretary to close the door behind her. As soon as she was gone, The Incubus threw back his head and began massaging his temples. He was frowning as he told me, "This has been one of the worst days of my life."

"Oh, John, nothing could be that bad," I moved to reassure him. "Why don't you tell me what the problem is?"

"The radio show has been canceled," he intoned, staring straight ahead while avoiding my eyes.

"What are you talking about, John?" I asked quizzically. "This is radio, not television. Radio shows don't get canceled."

He tried again to get his point across by telling me, "The radio show is no more."

"Are you telling me that we're not doing a show today?"

"Yes," announced The Incubus with obvious relief.

Then I understood. We weren't doing a show today or tomorrow or in three weeks. We were never doing the show again. We'd been sacked.

For some reason, my only response was to ask him why he hadn't phoned me instead of making me brave the Manhattan traffic just to get the bad news. My calmness seemed to stun him into silence momentarily, but he soon went on to explain that NBC would pay my salary for three full months as severance, but was under no further obligation to me since a contract we'd been negotiating hadn't been signed. And that was it. I headed for the rest room in a state of shock. Once inside, I found myself face-to-face with Judy D'Angelis. "I just got fired," I said out loud for the first time.

It was a real massacre that day. Once I'd pulled myself together, I walked back to the main office and found Donna Feducia, our traffic copter reporter but hardly a member of our team, distraught. For some unfathomable reason, The Incubus had fired her too. Once I returned to the show office, Gary, who hadn't heard the news, wanted me to sign a bunch of publicity photos. "Get those things out of my face," I barked. At the time, Gary and I barely knew each other, but he could sense that something was wrong. When he asked what was happening, I told him that he'd have to wait for Howard.

Howard wasn't saying much when he reappeared, but he seemed to be in better shape than I was. He quietly walked into his office and shut the door. A few minutes later, the door opened and he called Gary, Fred, Al Rosenberg, and me inside to announce that there was no show that afternoon because we'd been let go. No one knew what to say. Then Howard told us that he'd put in a call to his new agent, Don Buchwald, who was on his way over. Don had negotiated Howard's most recent WNBC contract, and though I'd become familiar with his name, I'd never met him.

Once he arrived, the doom and gloom instantly lightened. Don was a vision of nonchalance, his overcoat slung capelike over his shoulders, a fedora perched on his head, and a broad smile illuminating his bespectacled face. He veritably swept into the room singing "Happy Days Are Here Again," a bottle of champagne cradled in his left arm. Gary was commanded to find cups, the cork was popped, and drinks were poured. Then Don and Howard adjourned to Howard's office to talk privately.

I had to wonder what I was celebrating, but at least sitting there sipping champagne made us look undefeated when The Incubus finally appeared. Howard had gotten the news from our old friend Randy, but Hayes was clearly anxious to witness the results of his handiwork for himself. When he'd repeatedly called to request a meeting with Howard, he'd been refused, and he finally just showed up. While he waited for Howard's office door to open, he attempted to make small talk with me. "I know you guys are just going to go across the street and beat the pants off us," he schmoozed.

The Incubus never did see Howard that day. The inner-office door remained closed the entire time he was there. It soon became glaringly obvious that Howard was ignoring him, and he eventually drifted off without making a peep or getting satisfaction. He should have seen us half an hour later when Howard, propped up on crutches, and I were standing on the street in front of 30 Rock, surrounded by a wall of boxes and pitifully trying to get a cab. Our car had already left, and although we called, we couldn't seem to get another one to come. Between Howard's crutches and our boxes full of tapes and scripts and our sound effects carts, we were a sorry sight.

In the wake of the initial massacre, The Incubus had told Gary, Fred, and Al that they were being kept on the WNBC payroll for the time being, so Howard and I were on the street, fleeing WNBC without our troops, when our old friend Jerry Nachman happened by. Jerry, who had gotten us involved with NBC in the first place, was now running the local television news department. When he heard about our misfortune, he suddenly remembered that he was in a rush. "Call me," were his parting words as he scurried into the lobby.

The next morning, I was scheduled to do a voice-over job in Westchester and felt good that I had someplace to go. But it didn't account for the lightness I felt when I awoke. At last, I was fully aware of the tension I'd been carrying in my body all the time I'd been at WNBC. My chest was no longer tight. I didn't have to do daily battle anymore. I decided I'd just enjoy my first day of freedom and not think about getting fired. But as I was driving through the tollbooth at the Triborough Bridge, I spotted a huge picture of Howard, Alison, and Emily on the front page of the *New York Post* proclaiming the news that NBC had sent us packing. There was no escaping what had happened to us. Everybody knew.

Riverside Church hadn't turned out to be as warm and friendly as I'd expected, but I'd still decided to join in the hope that I'd eventually develop a feeling of belonging. In order to be a member, I had to attend classes and meet with one of Riverside's dozen ministers. It just so happened that my meeting was scheduled for the Wednesday after I'd been fired. The minister's name was Pat DeYoung. I'd heard a couple of her sermons, liked them, and was glad she was conducting my interview.

Pat ushered me into the office and motioned me to sit with her on a couch across from her desk. When I told her about losing my job, she was sympathetic and asked me if I was going to be okay. I then filled her in on the situation with my parents because there was a question I needed to have answered. "I know I'm supposed to be able to forgive my parents," I explained, "but I just can't. I don't know how. Is that wrong?"

"You may not be able to forgive them," Pat replied, "until you've experienced some of the love you feel you never got."

"So it's okay that I can't forgive them?"

"You can strive to make forgiveness your goal," she said, "but God wouldn't require you to do something you aren't capable of."

Before I left, Pat also advised me to touch base with my old therapist, since I was facing a crisis. For a change, I didn't resist. I could tell that I wasn't ready to handle something this big alone, and frankly was on the brink of wanting to tackle bigger challenges. I hadn't admitted it to anyone, but I was beginning to feel that it might be all right to get close to someone, to need another human being. It occurred to me now that if I cleared away some more of the cobwebs, I might just be strong enough to figure out how to do it.

Not being the most forgiving sort myself, I wondered just what kind of reception I'd get from Dr. London. I hadn't exactly left under the most congenial of circumstances, but, as always, she was gracious and sounded happy to hear from me. After I filled her in on the latest news, we made an appointment. This time, I knew, therapy would be even scarier. Since I was no longer desperate, I'd have to find some other reason to burrow deep inside. I'd have to find out if I loved myself enough to face all my fears and do whatever it took to get better.

Dr. London was surprised to see who was standing at her door. "Look at you," she said and smiled. "You're so thin."

I'd left therapy still overweight, jheri-curled, and with no particular concern for my attire. But I'd meant it when I told Dr. London that I needed time to absorb all I'd learned from her. My physical appearance testified to the fact that I was still making progress during our hiatus. Dr. London hadn't ever seen my new short Afro hairdo or my new trim physique. I'd even completely revamped my wardrobe with the help of a professional shopper. I'd had a slight panic attack when I'd gotten the four-thousand-dollar American Express bill (yes, I'd even managed to get a few credit cards), but that's what happens shopping at stores in Trump Tower. I discovered that clothes don't make the woman, but people did treat me differently when I was fashionably turned out. Suddenly, I had no trouble catching a cab, and men rushed to open doors for me. So here I was, forging ahead with therapy and wearing designer clothes. You'd never have thought I was unemployed.

Actually, we were only out of work for a month, but a lot happened in that short period of time. Howard was in every paper and did every news program in the first few days following the big headlines, but there was a problem. Most of the media was unconvinced that the firing was real. It had to be a hoax, they reasoned, because nobody had ever heard of a top-rated deejay being canned for no apparent reason. That phenomenon was a John Hayes invention. But no matter how much Howard protested, the reporters all assumed we'd reappear on WNBC in a few days, none the worse for wear. When that didn't happen, the story died.

Before that first week ended, Don Buchwald called me into his office and pitched himself as my agent. "I don't approach people," he said, "unless I truly believe in their talent and feel that I can help them further their careers." I didn't know what else to do and Howard seemed to really trust him, so I agreed to let him handle me. That's how the man whom Howard eventually dubbed "Super Agent" wound up representing me as well.

Although Howard and I were desperate to get situated, Don ordered us to go home and sit tight. Waiting for the big phone call was driving me crazy. All of a sudden, all my conversations began to include game show references. Howard was going nuts too and came up with the idea of doing live shows in clubs to keep busy. I finally begged him to let me do some of the legwork just to get out of the house, so I scouted locations and picked up props to pass the time.

Our first live shows were filled to capacity, but we were really out of our element and it showed. I'd always heard of people crying after bad performances. Now I was actually doing it. The worst part of it all was that the reason we'd taken them on in the first place no longer pertained. By the time we hit the stage, we were on our way back to the airwaves.

Don wanted to continue to sit back and let the offers come in. He's a master at the game of timing, and he constantly assured us that the cards were falling our way. He hadn't been kidding when he walked into the office the day we were fired singing a happy song. The first thing we had to do was to decide if we wanted to stay in New York or move to Los Angeles. NBC was offering Howard money to go to the West Coast. They clearly wanted us out of town. Having seen the luxurious house of Rick Dees, a Los Angeles deejay, I was also lobbying to go west. I knew the only reason we weren't living like that was because Hollywood couldn't hear us. "But don't you want to stay here and pay back all these assholes?" Howard demanded. I had to admit that sounded awfully nice too, so we chose New York.

Don wanted us to wait it out until we'd been off the air for about two months, calculating that the money offers would continue to mount, but Howard and I couldn't take the sitting around. In one of my diary entries I wrote, "Rock Hudson died today, and we're not on the air. John Hinckley, Jr., is engaged, and we're not on the air. The Mets are in a do-or-die race for the playoffs, and we're not on the air." I really love doing the show, and it kills me when things happen and I'm not there to comment on them.

Howard and I were good to each other during the hiatus. We stuck close together and used the free time to do some much-needed soul-searching. I remember walking into his house one morning on the way to a meeting and having his daughter, Emily, greet me just as she had every other day she saw me, with a big smile. That's when I realized how nice family could be. I was just Robin to her, not the person who had been kicked out by NBC.

Meanwhile, the world in general acted as if someone had died. "Are you okay?" was the way people greeted me now, and they never believed it when I said I was fine. I started hiding from my neighbors again to avoid the stares and the questions, and I was feeling a little jealous of Howard. He had his family for support, but what did I have? It was a good thing I was in therapy, where I could talk out thoughts like this instead of letting them fester.

One evening after a meeting in which Don had talked us into biding our time, Howard phoned to ask me if I thought waiting was a good idea. "Look, I always want to work," I answered. "Then I'm going to call him and tell him to just make a deal," Howard replied. A few days later we were sitting at a press conference in the Beanstalk Restaurant announcing that "The Howard Stern Show" was moving to the new rock station WXRK to do afternoons. So here we were, spending a weekend a month torturing ourselves doing these live shows while working on the air again at K-Rock, as our new station had dubbed itself.

The first time I met my new bosses was after the deal had already been set. Once again we were going to work for a station that needed us. WXRK was trying to recover from the disco era. The station had been known as Disco 92 in the heyday of the dance craze. They'd had great ratings then, but disco had died an untimely death and the station had suffered the stigma of its quick demise. They had tried to hire us to do mornings, but we preferred the casual pace of afternoons. Jay Thomas, now the leading man on the TV show "Love and War," was the morning man, which was just fine with us.

Jay hadn't had much luck in the morning, and by February 1986, K-Rock was going to dump him anyway. They approached us again about mornings, and Howard said no. We'd vowed to never work those hours again, but that night, as we climbed into the car to go home, something occurred to me. "Are you sure we're not just being lazy?" I asked Howard and Fred, who were sitting across from me.

"You want to get up at four o'clock in the morning again?" Howard asked.

"No, but don't we want to go up against all those idiots in the morning?"

"We're already number one. What's the big deal?"

"Yeah, but the papers always qualify it by saying that sure, we're number one, but we have no competition."

"Yeah, that's true," Howard replied, beginning to catch fire. "And I could really stick it to that bastard Imus."

We talked about the move to mornings the rest of the car trip home and ultimately decided to go for it. But before we left each other, the guys made me promise that, since it was my idea to do mornings again, I would never complain about the hours. Every time Howard moans about getting up early, I remember this promise and it kills me.

The first day we took over mornings at K-Rock, I scratched "#1" into the wall below my studio window. That's where we were headed, and we were taking no prisoners. In the deal to go to mornings we got the station to spring for another writer, and that's when Jackie "The Joke Man" Martling went from sitting in one day a week for gas money to becoming a full-time paid employee. The early hours were awful, but morning drive is prime time in radio and it meant more money and more opportunity. Every great move has its trade-offs, and this one meant going to bed at nine in the evening and having great difficulty in keeping up a social life.

The new hours, the new situation, and therapy made for an interesting amalgam. I found myself right back in the throes of depression as Dr. London and I once again agitated the bats in my belfry. The changes created an instability that unearthed some old defense mechanisms, not the least of which was my paranoia. I believed I was being attacked on all sides. Unfortunately, Gary and the interns bore the brunt of most of my white-hot anger without realizing that it wasn't due to anything they'd done. I was just angry in general. And on top of all this, as Christmas of 1986 approached, I experienced a full-blown case of the holiday blues.

At K-Rock we'd reverted to the separate studios arrangement we'd had at DC101, and Howard and I were able to see each other through a window that connected the deejay studio and the news studio. I watched him, Fred, and Jackie cavorting happily with each other during the show and felt left out. It wasn't long before I had myself convinced that all their levity was at my expense.

The gang was beginning to irritate me on the air too. Now there were three people to compete with for talk time, and whenever I got cut off, my blood pressure would rise. I began to hate all of them. Everyone who sat on the other side of that glass became my enemy. And then Gary started pestering me to make decisions about Howard's birthday show. January 12 comes up right after the holidays, so all the planning has to be done before we take our vacation. That year we planned to take the show to another location for the first time and really make it a big blowout. Gary needed my help but, in my state of mind, I was in no shape to deal with it.

I had a sneaking suspicion that my problems had more to do with the holidays than with my co-workers and did everything I could to keep my nuttiness from causing problems, but sometimes I failed. Gary was calling me on the phone and trying to find me at work. He finally figured out my moves and cornered me one morning right after the show. I'd had a bad time that morning and was about to have a blackout from rage when he found me in the newsroom.

"Gary," I warned him, "you'd better leave."

"No, Robin," he refused, angry, "you've been avoiding me, and I really have to get some questions answered if we're going to have a show."

"If you don't leave now, I can't be responsible for what happens next," I begged, to no avail.

"You do whatever you have to do, but I've got to go over this list with you," he said, pointing to a legal pad.

That's when I lost it. I just screamed and yelled and spat. I don't know what I was saying. I didn't even believe some of it, but I said it anyway. The best way to describe what happened was that I accused everyone by name, from Howard on down, of doing something awful to me, then expressed a great deal of dislike for the whole lot. When I came back to my senses and stopped, the look on Gary's face told me that what he'd heard was pretty bad. He slid off the edge of the counter where he'd perched himself and left the room without saying a word.

When he walked out that door, I felt that years of therapeutic progress in my relationship with Howard walked out with him. I knew Gary would tell him everything I'd said. No one should have heard what I said in the first place. It was just that Gary wouldn't leave, and I couldn't hold the rage back any longer. Devastated, I grabbed my things and ran to the parking garage. I cried all the way home.

Gary swears that he never told Howard anything, so Howard must have been picking up all the bad vibes I was sending out. I'd passed him in the hall that morning and hadn't even bothered to speak, figuring he hated me because of what I'd said the day before. He must have been sitting in his office wondering what to do because ten minutes before the show was about to start, the door of the newsroom flew open and he stepped in. I rose from my seat, but he still towered over me.

"You don't want to work with me anymore?" he began. "I'm such a bad person? Then let's just walk down the hall and tell the people in the front office that the partnership is dissolved."

There was a lot of yelling. I was only aware of trying to talk louder than he did each time it was my turn to speak. Suddenly I realized that this really was the end, that he was saying he couldn't take it anymore, or at least that he didn't want to. I thought it was probably the last time we would speak, and I didn't want to leave without letting him know what I really thought of him.

"Okay," I screamed as loudly as I could, "but before I go, I just want you to know I'm your biggest fan!"

"Well, nobody believes in you more than I do!" Howard screamed in reply.

Then we just sort of stood there thinking about the two statements still hanging in the air. Just what was it we were fighting about? Then I started crying, and for the first time admitted that I was having a tough time personally and that that was what my confusion was all about. Don't make me swear to it, but I thought I saw a few tears trickle down Howard's cheeks. Then we heard the theme song of the show, the one Howard talks over when he first says good morning. So we hugged each other, mopped up as best we could, and flipped the mike switch to On. I swore once again that I'd never fight with Howard, and this time I made the promise stick.

Learning to coexist with Gary was another story. For starters, Howard locked us in a room and told us to work out our differences because neither one of us was going anywhere. To my surprise, Gary expressed a great deal of hurt as a result of my behavior. He had mistaken my avoidance for aloofness and lack of respect. I assured him that none of what he thought was true and that he had every right to confront me whenever my actions caused him a problem. This is what led to our famous fights. Gary got the hang of just answering back pretty darn quick. I had no idea how rude and dismissive I could be. Gary was a perfect mirror, bouncing back my bad reflection. After a while these fights got to be pretty funny. We fought well. And even the loudest of our tiffs was completely forgotten the very next day.

Howard never understood this dynamic. He once walked into the middle of one of these arguments about nothing and wondered in amazement how I could reach such volume. Gary left me sitting in the office, screaming "Fuck you" as he headed for the men's room. I sat at the desk answering "No, fuck you!" Howard left a client meeting to see what was the matter. I was already laughing about the ludicrousness of the situation while still screaming "Fuck you's" at Gary to see how long he'd answer. Howard just shook his head and left the room.

I subsequently learned in therapy that I overreacted to confrontational situations because of all the anger I'd stored up over the years by never reacting to problems when they occurred. I always waited to reach a boiling point before topping off. Now I had to start dealing with things as they came up, and that meant getting in touch with my feelings instead of ignoring them. I made a point of warning everyone in the office that things could get messy.

Otherwise it appeared to be all systems go as far as the show was concerned. Infinity Broadcasting, the owners of K-Rock, were a daring breed of radio entrepreneurs who really had hired us to do what we were best at. Spared the constant battles with management, we could concentrate on show content and exploring the boundaries of good taste. Howard had even come up with the brilliant idea of syndicating the show to other markets. Proceeding with caution, Infinity chose Philadelphia, city of brotherly love, to test the theory that a morning radio show didn't have to be local to get ratings.

Gradually, my depression subsided, never again to attain the intensity of previous episodes, and the agoraphobia that had for years dictated my living arrangements began to recede. I even bought a condominium in a lovely high-rise with an even bigger staff than the one at Howard's old apartment. I was no longer afraid of running into neighbors at the elevator or dealing with doormen. The apartment was a dream come true. I'd accidentally stumbled onto the complex when I was driving around, lost, on moving to New York. I was impressed by its size and beauty and imagined that it was the kind of place I'd never be able to afford. Now I was sitting in my own apartment in that fantasy building.

One of the side effects of my upbringing had always been to deny myself the best. I didn't need good things. They weren't necessary. People like me didn't deserve luxuries. Such thoughts still cluttered my mind at every turn. I had to learn to give myself a good talking to every time I bought something new. I had to teach myself to use other people as examples. If Alison Stern treated herself a certain way, I was able to realize that that's how people who loved themselves treated themselves and imitated her behavior.

Eventually, I'd learn to luxuriate with the best of them, my seaweed wraps and foot massages becoming the brunt of Howard's on-air jokes. I even have to thank Oprah for helping me to begin the process of treating myself well. I once heard her talking about candlelit bubble baths on her show and thought that that sounded like something I'd like to do. Pretty soon this ritual became part of my nightly routine as well as more fodder for the show. That I could continue to do these things for myself in the face of so much ridicule I took as a good sign.

My spiritual search continued in the midst of all these changes. Church had again turned out to not be the answer, and after a few months I'd stopped going regularly. At the urging of the Stern clan, I went back to meditation. It seemed to be doing a lot for them, so I thought, why not? At the same time I was experiencing a block in therapy. Dr. London was trying to get me out of my house so that I could meet a guy, but I just couldn't get myself to do it. I couldn't even walk up to a stranger on the street and ask for the time. Blocked and befuddled by my own resistance, I headed to Washington, D.C., for a five-day meditation retreat.

It was quite an experience. When I'd taken the course in Ohio, I'd initially noticed dramatic effects, but sitting quietly for twenty minutes had soon become dull. Yet here I was at the Washington Convention Center being told to meditate even longer. I was as skeptical as ever, but I decided that since I was here and had paid for the course, I might as well try it. In a couple of days I was more spaced out than I'd ever been on marijuana.

I attended lectures every afternoon and evening but couldn't manage to stay awake through a single one. Besides, they were always showing videotapes of the Maharishi. I couldn't understand his heavily accented English, which made it harder to concentrate and easier to drift off. These were the only lectures I've ever attended where sleeping was okay. No one ever tried to rouse me, because just being in the room was supposed to be enough to make the process work.

Since I was only going to the talks to nap, I'd taken to sitting in the upper sections of the auditorium, where the incoherent speechifying of the Maharishi could least disturb me. Then one afternoon while I was drowsing, I became incredibly alert for a moment. The Maharishi was on the big screen, surrounded by flowers and talking as usual, but suddenly I could understand him, and when I heard it, I knew that that was what I had come to learn. Then I fell back into a deep sleep.

The weekend I got back to New York, I found myself in a singles bar talking to a man who bought me flowers and took me out to dinner. When I told Dr. London what had happened, she seemed a little miffed that I was attributing this breakthrough solely to meditation, but the fact was that I'd been talking to her for months and still hadn't been able to ask a stranger for the time. We compromised and agreed that it was a combination of the two. I began to meditate regularly and to attend meditation weekends often. Life was getting good again.

But it wouldn't really be my story if everything went smoothly from here on out. Just as it looked as if our radio careers were in for some smooth sailing, we found ourselves navigating around dangerous rocks that could sink us if we went aground. The syndication of the show into Philadelphia brought with it a new round of complaint letters, and this time those letters found themselves on the desk of a sympathetic reader at the Federal Communications Commission in Washington, D.C. The FCC is the federal body that regulates radio, assigning signals and issuing licenses.

The same kinds of complaint letters received from supposed new listeners in Philly looked just like the letters the commission had received from listeners in Washington when we'd first started at DC101, and from New York when we'd started at WNBC, and until November 14, 1986, the commission had always ruled that the sexually oriented language used on the show was protected speech. On that date, though, Infinity Broadcasting received a letter from the commission requesting comment on the same kinds of complaints they'd been handling for years. These would be the first shots fired in a legal war that continues to this day.

The FCC has proved to be a worthy and dangerous opponent. I'd fought with official bureaucracy when I was in the air force and knew better than anyone how relentless the government can be. Years after I'd left the service, still owing the government a couple of thousand dollars, I opened a letter from the Internal Revenue Service, expecting a tax refund. Instead, I found a short note indicating that the air force had finally tracked me down and gotten their money from my refund. The last time I'd fought the government I'd gone in alone; this time I was part of a team, and I thought Dr. London would be a great asset as we readied ourselves for this battle.

I can remember telling Dr. London about the first whisperings of the FCC trouble on the horizon, confident that with her help I could get through anything. Then my trusted ally dropped her own bombshell. She was leaving her practice.

19

MEN

I believed in fairy tales for a very long time. I thought that all girls eventually met their prince and lived happily ever after. I liked the stories in which the prince did all the searching, like "Cinderella," "Sleeping Beauty," and "Rapunzel." Life, however, has turned out to be like the ones in which the princess has to discover a prince by turning over a lot of slimy rocks and kissing a bunch of frogs.

Although Dr. London would no longer be a part of my life, I decided to go on with therapy. Since I was trying to confront my problems with men, I asked her to recommend a male therapist. Maybe this was all happening for the best after all, I tried to convince myself. In the weeks leading up to Dr. London's departure, I met with the new guy while continuing to see her. I didn't have the ability to evaluate a new therapist but figured any new person would seem strange. All I had to go on was Dr. London's recommendation, and I was so devastated by our impending separation that I never got around to asking why she'd recommended this particular person. I was like a bird with a broken wing, staying where I was put.

At the end of our last session it was Dr. London who broke down. She said she felt that she was abandoning me and wanted me to know that I was more than just a client to her, that she really cared. She cried when she finally admitted that saying good-bye wasn't easy for her either. She took my address and said she'd like to write or call some time, just to see how I was doing, and before the final good-bye, she rose from her chair and gave me a big hug. "I'm really going to miss you, sweetie," she sobbed.

I walked out sad, angry, and unable to tell her how much I felt I needed her. I too felt that she was abandoning me, and no matter what she'd said, someone else's wishes had been more important than my needs. I couldn't afford to share my anger with her now. I still needed to hold onto the fire that was building in my belly in order to go on. Anger was my shield when I was afraid.

It would be nice to be able to tell you that I struck therapeutic gold twice, but it was hardly possible under the circumstances. Quite frankly, the new guy never had a fighting chance. He was timid and soft and I never liked or respected him, and I never disclosed these feelings while in session.

He lost me completely the day he made the statement "Yes, women have tough lives" in response to my whining about the problems that had struck my current romantic relationship. Women have tough lives?! If he believes women's lives are tough, that's what he's going to support me in having, a tough life. I could never get that thought out of my head and afterward listened with suspicion to everything he said. I wound up getting rid of him when I slipped on the stairs in a club one night and broke my ankle. I couldn't get to his office while I was in a cast, and once it was off, I terminated treatment. I was ready once again for life on my own.

While I was still seeing the therapist, I had actually begun a relationship with a man, but I suspected that it wouldn't be permanent. I'd met Glen at a fund-raising dinner sponsored by one of the organizations of Riverside Church. He'd developed this immediate fascination with me as we spoke over cocktails and kept buzzing around me all evening, eventually wearing me down and getting my number.

He was a dark-skinned black man with a beautiful smile and an irresistible British accent. He hailed from the Bahamas and worked for his government's tourism office. He was also funny, bright, and gregarious and appeared to be available, though later I'd discover that emotionally he really wasn't. From the start of the affair I felt that it would be unwise to get too serious. It was just a feeling I had, but the shrink had challenged me, saying, "We don't know that yet." So I kept seeing Glen, red lights blazing in my head, on the outside chance that the doctor was right and I was wrong. By the time the relationship hit the rocks eighteen months later, I had actually fallen in love.

I never knew that it was possible to feel something so strong and positive for another person. When Glen opened up to me about his childhood traumas, I hated the people who had hurt him and wanted to lavish him with enough affection to make up for all the pain. In the end, I discovered that that just wasn't possible, that people have to solve their own problems. I could have loved him until I ceased to exist, but if he wasn't ready to let go of his demons, nothing I could do would ever chase them away. What I learned from that relationship was that I could fall in love and have it not work out and still live.

In fact, I was amazed at how well I had begun to handle things in general. I didn't have to run right back to therapy whenever my life developed a glitch, and I didn't stop growing either. I now knew the warning signs when I was getting into trouble and had become quite good at pulling myself aside and figuring out what it was that I needed to do. People were no longer automatically the enemy.

Over the years, I was pleased to realize, I'd developed a set of friends who also acted as good sounding boards. I was working hard to build the kind of support system some people are blessed with at birth, and I was succeeding. One of the pillars of that system was, and is, a name you'll recognize—my friend Sharon London.

Sharon had stopped practicing in order to spend more time with her husband, who had decided to give up his business so that they could travel. Every couple of months the first year after she left, I would get a postcard signed "Sharon." It took me quite a while to figure out that "Sharon" was my old therapist, since I'd never used her first name the entire time we worked together. When I finally put two and two together, I was relieved that some kook wasn't writing me at home.

After we'd been apart for a year, Sharon began phoning me to inquire about my health and to catch up on the news. One day she suggested we meet for lunch. I smiled, thinking back to that smart remark I'd made to her about having lunch the first time I'd walked out of therapy. Lunch eventually led to dinner, and it was during an evening at her house that she gave up being my therapist and became my friend.

The phone rang a couple of times while we were eating, and I noticed that Sharon would lower her voice, whispering into the receiver every time she answered. After the second call, I refused to return to the conversation we'd been having.

"Is that your husband who keeps calling?" I asked, a little miffed.

"Yes," she admitted.

"Well, what's he doing? Sitting in a car parked on the street somewhere waiting for me to leave?"

Sharon explained that he wasn't exactly on the street, but he was staying away because of my being there. She really hadn't known how to handle this situation. My relationship had been with her, and she hadn't known if it would be appropriate to have her husband around. She had also heard me say some pretty ungracious things about meeting new people during those sessions in her office.

"Look," I told her in no uncertain terms, "when I accept an invitation to someone's home, I expect that I might run into the people who live there. Please tell your husband to come home the next time he calls. I'm really not as fragile as that nut you used to see in your office twice a week."

Then I realized that she was having trouble letting go of her role as my therapist. "Sharon, you're not my therapist anymore, you're never going to be my therapist again. We're friends, and that means that not only do you get to know me, I get to know you."

When I realized I was giving her advice, I started to laugh so hard that tears came to my eyes. I was overjoyed that I was getting to help her for a change. After that she took me around the house and showed me pictures of her family, explaining who everyone was. From that moment on, we've both been completely comfortable in our new roles as treasured friends. The fact that I wouldn't be where I am today without her help only enriches our relation-ship.

Even then I thanked her for guiding me to what was really a great spot. Our troubles with the FCC notwithstanding, "The Howard Stern Show" was now enjoying such phenomenal success that it was beginning to change our lives. People like Donald Trump started paying attention. In 1987, Trump had lured Mike Tyson to Atlantic City to fight Tyrell Biggs in the convention cen-ter. Tyson, at this point, was far and away the most exciting heavy-weight to come down the pike since Muhammad Ali, and Trump graciously offered Howard two ringside seats for the match. Howard, not being a sports fan, turned them down, and when Gary told me they were available, I leaped at the chance to go. Not only ringside seats were included in the deal. Trump had also thrown in two invitations to the pre-fight party.

That Friday afternoon, my buddy Don Bernstein and I headed to Atlantic City in his Jeep, and once we got there made a beeline for that party, fully intending to stargaze. Oprah was there, wearing Steadman like a human belt, his arms around her waist the whole time. And I ran into Spencer Christian, the "Good Morning Amer-ica" weatherman. Seeing him standing there with his wife was like seeing an old friend. I'd been watching him on TV since he'd done the local weather at a station in Baltimore. Without thinking, I walked over to introduce myself. "Hi, Spencer," I began, extending my hand, "I'm Robin Quivers from 'The Howard Stern Show.'"

"Hi, Robin," Spencer responded immediately. "How's your tits?" The silence with which Spencer's greeting was met made him realize that he'd made a terrible social gaffe. His wife was aghast.

"I'm sorry," he apologized, putting his finger to his lips. "I just thought it was something Howard would say."

The bystanders weren't buying it, and the silence was becoming deafening. I could have let poor Spencer twist there in the wind for-ever, but I felt sorry for him and decided to help him down from the hook on which he'd just hung himself. Laughing good-naturedly, I said, "Spencer, Howard would never say anything like that!" then grabbed his hand and gave him a hug. I flashed his wife one of those "What can you do?" smiles and walked away, headed for the buffet.

I helped myself to a plate of hors d'oeuvres and found a seat at an empty table. Don, at this point, had run into some old friends and was chatting with them, so I sat down to survey the room on my own. I immediately noticed a line forming at one of the tables not far from where I was sitting. When the crowd parted, I saw what all the commotion was about. Muhammad Ali was in the room.

This is too good to be true, I thought to myself. I'll just sit here and breathe in the same air as Muhammad, that's enough for me. So I watched him patiently sign autographs for each person who stepped up to him.

Then Ali raised his hand, motioning in my direction to someone. He did it a second and then a third time. Finally, I turned to see who was ignoring "The Greatest," but there was no one behind me. When I turned back to Muhammad, he was pointing directly at me. I couldn't believe my eyes, so I pointed at myself and mouthed, "Me?"

He shook his head yes and again motioned to me to come over. Amazed, I rose from my seat and went to him.

"Hello, Muhammad."

"Don't I know you?" he asked.

"No," I said and laughed.

"Are you sure?"

"Muhammad," I told him, "if I'd ever met you, I'd remember it."

"Where are you from?"

"New York."

"And you're sure we never met?" he asked again.

Just then, I noticed a photographer nearby and felt perfectly natural asking Muhammad something I've never asked anyone else—"Can I have a picture taken with you?" He was happy to oblige.

We had been facing each other, and now I stepped up beside him so that the photographer could get the shot. I never planned to do anything more than stand next to my only idol, but once I was at his side, he slid his arm around my waist.

I wasn't nervous in the least, and since he was being so familiar, I put my arm around him. Then he leaned over and placed his cheek against my face. It just seemed natural for me to reach for his free hand. It was shaking from his Parkinson's syndrome, and he started to pull it away until he realized that I didn't care. Once he realized this, he relaxed and let me take his hand in mine.

All this time the photographer had been standing with camera at the ready, waiting for us to get set. She finally let the huge Polaroid drop to her waist and demanded, "Are you two finished?"

"You'll have to forgive us," I explained, smiling, "but we're falling in love."

Then Muhammad whispered in my ear, "You don't know how right you are."

We stood there smiling for the camera. Then the flash went off and I had to let him go. We uncoupled as slowly as we had embraced. First heads, then arms, then fingers once we were too far away from each other to continue touching.

People had disappeared while we were talking and embracing, but as I released him I noticed that another line of admirers had formed. I returned to my seat, leaving him to his fans. When Bernstein returned, he wanted to know what all the commotion was about, and I told him that people were having their pictures taken with Muhammad Ali.

"Really?" he asked. "Can I?"

"Sure, go over and get in line."

By the time Bernstein reached Muhammad, the champ was tired. He just stood there like a cigar-store Indian and let the photographer snap away. When Bernstein took his place next to Muhammad, I walked over and said, "Muhammad, he's with me."

Ali looked at Don for the first time and commented, "Oh, he ain't so bad," then he warmly threw an arm around him and the flash from the camera went off.

Bernstein was in awe. When he asked me if I knew Ali, I just shrugged.

"How'd you do that?" he demanded. "You talked to him and he came to life!"

Trying to be my most mysterious, I said nothing at all as we made our way toward the convention center to find our seats.

I'd already had more excitement than I could ever have imagined. The fight was simply icing on the cake. It warmed my heart to

watch Ali receiving a standing ovation from the crowd when he was
called into the ring. I could tell that he still loved the adulation.

This was my first live fight, but I instantly felt perfectly at home
among the fight fans at ringside. Fight crowds are friendly crowds.
Stangers, sensing the impending battle and the possibility of witnessing something at once great and horrifying, strike up conversations with each other, sizing up the boxers' skills and debating an
opponent's chances.

And when the bell rings, utter silence falls as everyone present
becomes gripped by fear. It's live, it's real, and it's happening right
in front of your eyes. There's a beginning, a middle, and an end all
within the space of an hour. It's two people, hopefully superbly
skilled and trained to perfection, risking everything, and four rows
from the ropes, sitting below the ring, I could actually be splashed
by the water thrown on the boxers in the one-minute break
between rounds. Not many have the guts to play this game.

I hardly knew the challenger, Tyrell Biggs, but it was hard to
root against him. He was tall and handsomely built, with a pretty
face, a young Muhammad Ali. Tyson lost in the looks department.
He was short, stocky, and had no neck, but he approached the ring
with great determination, his championship belt draped around his
shoulders like a necklace. Tens of thousands were in the stands, but
Mike didn't see any of us. I would have conceded the fight just
looking at him. I imagined what it must have been like for the little
old ladies who'd had their groceries ripped from their arms by this
brute when he was loose on the street, unsupervised. Cus D'Amato
should have been given some kind of award for making the streets
of Brooklyn just a little safer by removing Mike from the scene.

The bell rang and the fighters danced from their corners. Biggs
started out looking just like Ali, bobbing and weaving, flicking little
jabs as he circled a flat-footed opponent. Everything seemed to be
going his way until Mike landed a punch to Biggs's ribs. Biggs
gripped his side. You only had to look at his face to know that he
didn't want to ever get hit by Mike Tyson again.

The fight was basically over at that point. Biggs was understandably scared. All he could do was run, and there's not much
room for hiding in the squared circle. Tyson prolonged the agony
for seven savage rounds as he stalked and mauled his frightened

prey. A flurry of punches sent Biggs to the canvas once, and then again. Bleeding and weary, he sat, leaning against a turnbuckle for support when the referee covered his body and waved Tyson off, ending the match.

Tyson's arm was raised in victory once again, and as I looked at him, I contemplated the universe of difference between a champion like Ali and a victor like Iron Mike. Ali's a man, I thought, but Tyson's an animal. His handlers got him out of the ring to take him back to his cage. There was no way he belonged around people. All the "up close and personals" in the world couldn't make me forget the sheer blood lust in those eyes. Everything I heard about Tyson after that made perfect sense to me.

The fight had been exciting, but I'd been up since three in the morning. It was time to call this truly magical day to an end. Don and I were staying over till Saturday morning, and I could have gone to my room and crashed. But there was still one more thing I had to do. I had to find the photograph of Muhammad and me.

I wouldn't have believed what happened between us without proof, so Don and I found the Trump publicity office and riffled through the hundreds of pictures that had been taken that night to find ours. I looked at mine all the way back to my room and set it on the dashboard in front of me the next morning for the drive home. To this day it remains one of my most precious possessions, proof positive that sometimes in this life, miracles do happen.

A couple of years had passed since, as Howard often puts it on the radio, I'd thrown my mother out of my house. Birthdays, holidays, even Mother's and Father's Days came and went without a word from me. In drugstores, I used to pass the rows and rows of cards marking these happy occasions, relieved that I no longer had to browse through dozens of cards searching for the ones that told the fewest lies. I felt that I was doing a public service when I spoke openly about my family estrangement on the air. Listeners who had gone through what I did now had outside confirmation that not every family works, not every family is a happy one, and that all the bad things are not automatically forgiven once we're grown.

I was surprised that I often spoke of things that had happened in my childhood, before and after my father abused me, without the slightest guilt about not talking to my parents. But even in the worst of families, there are fun times along the way. For instance, before the abuse my father and I had always played silly games with each other. I'd hide in the laundry room when I heard him on the basement steps, only to pop out when he'd least expect it, giving him a terrible fright, then he'd do the same to me. But after he'd stripped me of my innocence, it suddenly occured to me, he'd played a practical joke on me only once.

I must have been about twelve. My father and my mother had been sitting around the house all day debating who was bigger, even though at that point they were both topping the scale at about two hundred pounds. My father figured that since my mother was a few inches shorter, she was actually heavier than he was. My mother, on the other hand, theorized that even though she tipped the scales in the same vicinity, she had to be lighter because she was female. I thought it was a stupid argument and refused to be drawn into it.

At some point they decided to try on each other's clothes to end any further speculation. My father managed to squeeze his huge form into a navy blue, sleeveless sheath. I was washing dishes in the kitchen, so I wasn't aware of what was going on.

My mother had begun to wear wigs in the early seventies because it saved money on trips to the beauty parlor and because the chemicals in the permanent relaxers were damaging her hair. Even though the plastic wig looked more like a hat than real hair, it was always straight. Now my father grabbed a spare wig from one of the Styrofoam heads in their closet and slipped on a pair of my mother's size-ten black pumps. He went over his lips with a tube of red lipstick and grabbed an empty black leather handbag. Approving of the overall effect after checking himself in the mirror one last time, he headed for the stairs.

Daddy didn't just come back into the kitchen to surprise me. Instead, he stepped out onto the porch, quietly closed the front door, then rang the bell. He had to ring twice before I finally decided to respond, annoyed that I had to do it since I was already busy. I threw the dish towel over some plates in the drainer and ran to get the door, as unbeknownst to me, my father rang the bell again.

We had been told always to check the window in the door at night before opening it. I took a quick peek, and seeing a woman, I decided it was okay to answer. As my hand reflexively turned the knob and the door released from the jamb, I began to think about the face I had just seen. It was pretty strange. But before I could change my mind, the door was already open and I was staring at the ugliest woman I had ever seen. She was so ugly, she was shocking.

"Is Mr. Quivers at home?" the ugly woman asked in a reedy, high-pitched voice. I just stood there, unable to speak.

"I'm looking for Charles Quivers," the gorgon said again.

I wanted to scream, yet couldn't make a sound as this vision from hell started to smile. I know that smile, I thought, and all of a sudden could see my father's face under that wig and behind that red lipstick. "Daddy, get in here!" I demanded, irritated. "You nearly scared me to death!"

My father was laughing hysterically and congratulating himself on pulling off such a good stunt. He was so excited about what he had done, he didn't want it to end. He wound up taking his disguise two doors farther down the street to see if he could fool his best friend, Mr. White. When I was a little kid, the rule had been that once a practical joke was played, the victim was entitled to reciprocate. I didn't really feel like playing games with my father anymore, so I never retaliated, and I guess that was the evening that the jokes ended for good.

We'd been such good friends, I thought regretfully as I sat alone in my living room in Queens. Why in the world had he willingly sacrificed that bond for the sake of a kiss and a feel? For the first time, I truly believed I deserved an apology. Without even thinking it through, I picked up the phone and dialed my parents' number. My mother's voice sang out a hello.

I hung up without saying a word. I didn't want to speak to her. I immediately redialed, and this time my father picked up. "Hello, Daddy," I said.

Before he could answer, my mother picked up the receiver in another part of the house. I froze. "Hang up the phone, Lou," my father yelled down at her. Then he returned to the phone, saying, "Robin?"

"Yes," I said. I was tense and could feel my anger building, so before he had a chance to respond, I stated my business. "I'm calling because you never gave me an apology for what you did, and I want one."

"I wrote you that letter that time," he replied.

"I never read it."

"Well, I meant everything I said in it."

"I tore it up and threw it away."

"Oh, okay. Well, I'm really sorry for what I did to you. I had no idea what affect it would have or that it would bother you for the rest of your life. I didn't know what I was doing, and it was wrong."

I was amazed that he had so much to say, that he was so aware of the enormous pain he had caused. I hadn't been prepared for so eloquent an apology. "Thank you."

"How are you doing?" he asked.

"I'm okay," I said, beginning to cry. He sounded so old.

"You know, I was sixty-seven years old my last birthday," he continued as if reading my mind.

"Really?"

"Yeah, I'm getting up there. I can't get around the way I used to. My heart gives me some trouble."

"Didn't the operation help?"

"Yeah, it's better, but I can't do much."

"Well, I have to go, Dad."

"You want to speak to your mother?"

"No, I just called because I wanted an apology."

"Well, does this mean we can call you sometime?"

"No, I don't know what it means. I just wanted to hear you say you were sorry."

"I am sorry."

"Okay, 'bye."

"Call us sometime, and take care of yourself."

"'Bye."

"Good-bye."

Two days later I came home after an evening out with friends and found a message on my answering machine from my mother. Although I'd moved into a new condo, I'd kept my old phone number. My parents didn't know where I lived, but they still had the number from the time my mother had come to visit. As soon as I heard her cheery little voice on the machine I wanted to throw it across the room. I had not given them permission to call. And the fact that she was calling after I'd told my father not to destroyed any thought of reconciliation.

I stopped short of changing my number because of the hassle of having to give everyone the new one. I was still seeing Glen at that point, so, instead, the next day I made him call my parents. He was a lot kinder than I would have been. He told my mother that I was very upset when I heard her voice on the answering machine and that if she ever used that number again without permission, I would change it and they would lose their last link to me. My mother apologized profusely.

Glen felt horrible about having to make that phone call, but it worked. My mother never dared to dial my number again.

20

HOMECOMING

Richard Simmons used to be a frequent guest on the show. When he was in town, he and I often went to dinner or to see a Broadway show. After our first outing, I remember his commenting to Howard that it was tough finding things to talk about with me. "When you meet a new person and you don't know much about them," he mused, "you figure you can ask about their family and it'll be good for about fifteen minutes of conversation. But with Robin, you bring up her family, she says they don't speak, and that's the end of it."

Coming to K-Rock was like finding a home, and the pace of our careers zoomed once we settled into mornings. Howard's goal had always been to make the show bigger and to make us bigger as a result, and right from the beginning, station management, starting with General Manager Tom Chiusano, was willing to at least listen to his ideas. Howard was already a regular on "Late Night with David Letterman." Soon we were on the air mornings in New York and Philadelphia and had instituted our tradition of going "on location."

We've taken the show to California many times. We've stood

on the red carpet at the Academy Awards. In fact, we wreaked so much havoc, yelling to get the stars' attention and then asking goofy questions once we got to them, that Army Archerd of *Variety* is now the only reporter allowed to stand outside the auditorium to conduct pre-Oscar interviews. We've been banned from backstage both at the Grammys and the Emmys.

It was at the Emmys that I really got Howard into an embarrassing situation. We were in the press room, where all the presenters and winners come to answer reporters' questions and have their pictures taken. We had a little TV monitor set up so that we could see the broadcast as well as query the people who'd just appeared on stage. I noticed that Sharon Gless of "Cagney and Lacey" had just given a rather rambling acceptance speech. We knew she'd soon be in the room and needed a question for her.

You've got to understand that before there was "Stuttering John," our intrepid, kamikaze reporter who's become known for asking outrageous questions of everyone from Imelda Marcos to Gennifer Flowers, there was Howard Stern. A group effort goes into asking the questions that can stop a press conference cold, and when Ms. Gless entered the room holding her Emmy, I whispered to Howard to ask her if she didn't think her speech was too long. He shouted out the question, his voice piercing through the din of all the other voices trying to get her to look their way. Sharon's victory smile dissolved, revealing a face full of insecurity. We both felt bad that we'd probably ruined her night, but it was worse for Howard because as Gless made her way out of the room almost in tears, all the reporters turned to sneer at him. Hey, that's entertainment. At another awards show, animosity between Howard and another reporter almost flared into a fistfight. Broadcasts like these are tough on everybody, but they make for great radio.

Since the success of the radio show bestowed celebrity status on us, on more than one occasion we found ourselves grist for the media gossip mill. Sometimes this kind of scrutiny can be downright unpleasant.

I'm usually the first one in each morning. I go through the wire and listen to a number of different news feeds as I read the morning papers. Usually, I don't realize how alone I am at that time of the day, but one particular morning I could really have used a friendly ear. Right there in "Page Six" of the *New York Post* was an item that said Howard was going to be doing a talk show for HBO and that they didn't want me. According to the paper, he was already interviewing blonds. Sitting there alone, I had no idea if what I was reading was true or not. If it was, this was a really tough way to find out. When Howard got to work, I walked into his office and asked if he'd read "Page Six."

"Is there something in it about us?" he asked, casually at first. After reading the item, he was flabbergasted.

"Robin, I swear to you it's not true."

"It's okay, Howard."

"But it's not true." I'm sure Howard was thinking about how the original NBC deal had ruined our relationship, destroying the trust between us.

"No, it's okay." I was trying to assure him that nothing like that was ever going to happen again.

"But it's not true."

"I believe you, Howard, but one day it may be true, and I want you to know that I never want to stand in the way of your career. So, if one day something like this does come up, I just don't want to read about it in the paper first."

"But, Robin, it's not true!!!"

On the air that morning, Howard called Richard Johnson, who writes "Page Six," and demanded a retraction, but Richard refused and stood by his story. Howard has never done a show for HBO, but Richard still stands by the story. The incident made me realize how hard it must be for husbands and wives in the public eye to keep it together when the entire world is looking for ways to tear them apart.

And we were definitely in the public eye. Our success in Philadelphia led to syndication in Los Angeles. We finally made it to Hollywood without leaving New York. It took us three years, but we finally toppled Philly's number-one morning man, John DeBella, from his lofty perch. With church secretary turned sex kitten Jessica Hahn in tow, we held a symbolic funeral for Philly's former radio king, which, even in a downpour, was attended by thousands. We made it to number one in Los Angeles in one year and usurped the thrones of the former kings, Mark and Brian. And right around this time, we finally made it to number one in own hometown. We were number one in New York, Los Angeles, and Philadelphia simultaneously. And they said it couldn't be done!

After each victory, I went right out and bought myself something. For the Philly win, I chose a diamond tennis bracelet. When we hit number one in New York, I selected a diamond dome ring, and when we made the triple play, I picked out a huge sapphire surrounded by diamonds and set in platinum. The rings were symbolic of our radio success and my personal success as well.

We'd come a long way, yes, but I'd been playing catch-up for a long time too. For the first time in my life, I thought I deserved to be at the top. I was living well. I had redecorated my condo, putting in a wood floor and customizing the closets. All the furniture was new. As I gazed out over the Throgs Neck Bridge from my balcony, I acknowledged my good fortune and thought it was time to give something back.

I'd been seeing a lot of those Big Brother/Big Sister public service announcements on TV and started thinking how nice it would have been if I'd had an adult like that in my life when I was a kid. I knew I'd never see Jimmy again, but I was ready to befriend another child. So why not someone who could really use the attention?

Scanning the lengthy, incredibly detailed Big Brother/Big Sister application form, I decided I was going to have to be brutally honest. I could have invented a happy, stable history for myself, but I didn't want to be assigned a child if I didn't deserve it. So, I picked up a pen and told the truth. As I wrote, I realized I had a lot more to offer as a Big Sister than someone who'd never experienced any adversity. If they rejected me, it would be a kid's loss, not mine.

My honesty earned me hours of grueling interviews in which every stage of my life was dissected by a social worker. These sessions left me so drained, I'd have to go home and take a nap. Along with all the usual letters of recommendations from friends and employers, I had to get a letter from Sharon London, since she had been my therapist. Sharon, of course, was happy to oblige and I was finally accepted into the program. Immediately, I began to fantasize about the wonderful times my small charge and I would have together.

I'd never been to a circus, although I'd always wanted to go. A seven-year-old little girl would jump at the chance, I reasoned. That was probably true, but it wouldn't apply because my caseworker was recommending me for a new program involving teenagers. Past experience had told me that teenagers could be rough and probably couldn't care less about the circus, but if that's where I was needed, that's where I'd be.

A few weeks later I was sitting at a conference table across from my new Little Sister and her mother in a mild state of shock. This could only happen to me, I thought, for so far, nothing had come to pass as I'd imagined. I'd expected a little black girl and gotten a white one. I wanted a seven-year-old. Lea was thirteen and hated the circus, to boot. The only cause for hope was her love of amusement parks and horror films. Burying my disappointment, I went ahead with the deal. Lea and I signed a contract to see each other every other weekend and be buddies for one year with an option to renew.

My new Little Sister had been in the BB/BS program before. Heidi, her former Big Sister, had gotten married and had a child before finally terminating her contract. I spoke to Heidi before Lea and I met for the first time, and she warned me that Lea's mother could present a problem. Heidi, in fact, had wound up baby-sitting and running errands for the woman. "Oh, don't worry," I said confidently, "that won't happen to me. I'm not that nice."

As naive as ever, I wasn't aware for the longest time that when I picked Lea up at the housing project where she lived, the guys who opened the door for me were drug dealers. I knew it was a bad neighborhood, I just didn't know how bad. Heidi's warning stood me in good stead when Lea's mother began dropping hints that it would be nice if we took Lea's little brother with us. I played dumb, smiled, then grabbed Lea and ran for the car.

I'd led a charmed existence where kids were concerned. Until Lea, I'd never met one I couldn't win over in a matter of hours. I took her to Coney Island, even went on a ride I knew would make me sick, but she wouldn't talk to me. She always kept our dates but never said thanks or indicated in any way that she'd had a good time. To add insult to injury, when she did start talking, it was only to tell me that she thought I was silly and laughed too much. One afternoon when I couldn't take it anymore, I dropped what I was eating and asked her a question. "Would you like me to point out everything I don't like about you?"

"No," she answered, surprised.

"Well, I'm getting a little sick of hearing what you don't like about me."

"I'm sorry, I didn't realize that's what I was doing."

The critiques ended for good, but that didn't mean the ice had been broken. Next Lea tried to impress me with tales of the shenanigans she and her friends pulled on subway passengers unlucky enough to end up in the same car with them. I countered with my own youthful escapades on Baltimore public buses. Amazed that I had similar stories of my own, Lea was the one who wound up being impressed. But not even matching her story for story could melt the iceberg. I came to believe, incorrectly as it turned out, that Lea's only interest in the program was getting out of her house for a while and that I'd have to settle for that.

After six months, I felt we'd plateaued. We had totally stopped making progress in developing a friendship, when Lea's mother suggested we start doing sleepovers. The one time Lea had seen my apartment, she'd covered her eyes and complained that it was too bright. I figured she hated my place, so I certainly wasn't going to torture her by making her stay there, but if her mother was willing, I decided I'd take her to Disney World.

My suggestion was a big hit. We spent that afternoon talking about the trip, and even visited a travel agency to make the arrangements. I couldn't believe I was talking to the same girl I had known for six months. What was it that was so different? I couldn't quite put my finger on it, but something had changed. Then it hit me. She was smiling. Two weeks later we were on a plane to Florida. If she was afraid, she refused to show it. In fact, we were on the ground before Lea confessed that she'd never flown before.

We intended to make the most of our couple of days of fun. We checked out the maps for the parks, Disney World, Epcot, and the new MGM theme park that had just opened, then determined our priorities. Saturday we did Disney in the morning right after breakfast, the only real attraction being Space Mountain, but we did go to the Hall of Presidents and on the jungle and pirate rides. After lunch we hit Epcot and did most of the exhibits and saw *Captain EO*, the Michael Jackson 3-D movie, which was in previews. Sunday afternoon we were going to have to make a plane, so we saved the movie theme park for that morning. I'd wanted Lea to confide in me, but what she began telling me as we waited in line for the rides and exhibits at the movie lot was hardly what I had expected.

At first the information trickled out, then became a stream, then that stream eventually built into a torrent. Lea claimed to have suffered years of physical and verbal abuse at the hands of her mother. As she spoke, I remembered a curious remark the mother had made in our first meeting with our caseworker. "I hit. Don't I, Lea?" she'd said with a smile. The social worker didn't pick up on it, so I didn't either. Now I was getting it from both barrels.

Lea had to get up two hours earlier than most schoolkids to get her three-year-old brother ready for day care. She was expected to do most of the chores and care for the little boy in the evening between homework assignments. She spoke of beatings that left her sore and bruised. The worst part of all was that she'd probably be in for a good tanning as a result of our little junket.

The closer we got to leaving Florida, the more agitated Lea became. By the time we landed in New York, she was absolutely frantic. I didn't know what to do. I'd taken the girl to Florida with her mother's permission and had promised to take her home when the trip was over. I had no proof of what Lea was alleging, but I'd certainly never seen her in such a state. Still, I saw no other choice but to return her to this house of horrors. When we got there, the place was dark and empty. Her mother, apparently unused to caring for Lea's brother alone, had decided to spend the weekend with a friend and hadn't yet returned. I was relieved and told Lea to go right to sleep so she wouldn't have to confront her mother till the next morning.

During the Disney World trip, Lea's feelings toward me took a radical turn. Now she began telling me she thought we were per-fectly matched and that I should have been her mother. Later, one of the BB/BS social workers would explain that the weekend in Florida had probably been the most pleasant time of her life. For the first time she found herself with an adult she could trust and rely upon, one who was taking care of her rather than demanding to be taken care of. In any event, I needed time to figure out the real nature of her home situation and to let her newly awakened identification with me diminish a bit.

Unfortunately, time had run out. The first Monday after we got back from Florida, I'd rushed home to nap so that I could stay up and watch the Academy Awards telecast that night. I'd set my alarm to go off at eight so that I could catch the Barbara Walters special that always precedes it but was having trouble waking up when the phone rang. By now, I was totally addicted to that greatest invention of the twentieth century, the answering machine. No longer did I have to be afraid of my phone, because I could screen every call.

Lea's mother didn't have a phone, so I was surprised to hear my Little Sister's voice. She was agitated and said something about my needing to come and get her. I picked up and asked her to slow down because I was still half-asleep. She told me that her mother had beaten her with a broom handle when she got home from school, that she'd taken refuge in her room and had only escaped when her mother went to the bathroom. She'd been riding the subway ever since, thinking about what to do next.

There was no mistaking the fact that I was going to have to miss the Academy Awards for the first time in years. I pulled myself together, jumped in my car, and went to meet Lea. Once she'd hopped into the seat next to me, she must have imagined that her troubles were over and that I'd be her new mom. I had a problem with that. I'd wanted to be Jimmy's mother, but that was when I was practically Lea's age. I hadn't thought about being anyone else's mother since. All I wanted to do was take a kid to the circus. This was already a lot more than I had bargained for.

Lea kept saying that she had taken her last beating and was never going back to her mother again, so to test her seriousness, I asked her, "If the difference between going home and not going home is sleeping in the street, what are you going to do?"

Without hesitation, she replied, "I'll sleep on the street."

For the next month and a half, Lea was a homeless child, shuttling back and forth between my apartment and Heidi's. Heidi lived near the housing project Lea had called home and was on a subway line that was convenient for school. I picked her up on Fridays and kept her on weekends. In the meantime, we tried to tap into that supposed public safety net out there for people in need and found it gravely wanting. We made a complaint to Social Services of alleged abuse, only to watch the investigation be botched by an inexperienced and unsupervised caseworker. The only reason Lea wasn't returned to her home was that at fourteen she was old enough to choose where she wanted to live. Her brother wasn't so lucky. He was left at home to fend for himself.

Lea's options weren't so great either. She could live with a relative, if she could find one to take her, or she could go into the foster system of private family and group homes. She'd be assigned to whatever was available.

There was going to be no happy ending to this episode: The city was being of little help. They refused to even consider Lea's case as long as Heidi and I were assisting her. We were instructed that we would have to abandon her before she could get into the social services system. Our staying in her life could possibly have landed her right back at home, but abandoning her to the city would justifiably be viewed by her as rejection. It was a genuine Catch-22.

I found myself screaming at the people who were supposed to be helping us, when I could get them on the phone, but the help we needed just wasn't there. We ended it all with a compromise. An aunt who lived in Brooklyn agreed to take her, and after a couple of nights in city shelters, Lea was willing to take her up on the offer. We were all emotionally devastated by the experience, and on top of it, I was exhausted and about to undergo major surgery.

So I wound up having to terminate my Big Sister contract before our year was up. The whole experience broke my heart. Mired in guilt, I fled to a health spa as Lea's change of custody was being made. Two days after I returned to the city, I entered a hospital for my long-anticipated surgery. I, like Lea, had to move on.

One day on the air, Howard and I were discussing a pet obsession of his, nose jobs. He'd been vowing to get one for years but never quite got around to it. This time, though, I thought he was serious, because he had made appointments with not one but three top surgeons. "If you're really doing it this time," I announced on the air, "then I'm going to have my breasts reduced."

Howard swore the nose job was a go, so I made my own appointment with a highly regarded plastic surgeon who'd been glowingly recommended by a number of women at my manicurist's. I met with Dr. Daniel Baker and immediately afterward scheduled the surgery. Howard consulted with his three recommended physicians and then decided against surgery out of concern for his voice. But this was a step I'd been wanting to take for years. Even as far back as the Shock Trauma Unit, I'd toyed with the idea. My breasts were large and pendulous, just like dear old mom's. It was more the shape of them than the size that bothered me, even though they were heavy enough to give me backaches. Dr. Baker assured me that he could both reduce them and give them a prettier shape. That was all I needed to hear.

I wasn't allowed to eat or drink after ten the night before the surgery, and I showed up at the hospital at six in the morning. I was Dr. Baker's first patient of the day, and by the time I got to my room, the gurney was already waiting to take me to the operating room. I quickly traded my street clothes for hospital togs and hopped aboard. The gravity of what I was about to do hadn't occurred to me until the orderly asked, "Have you said your morning prayers?"

My resolve to have the surgery shattered, panic overwhelmed me. The guy could see that he'd said the wrong thing and tried to make it better by hastening to add, "Don't worry, God will take care of you."

God, I told myself, must think I'm an idiot.

The anesthesiologist approached the gurney as the orderly wheeled me through the door of an anteroom. "I'm a big fan of your show," he began, but noticing my state, abruptly started shouting orders. "Let's start an IV over here and give her something that will calm her down."

Before I knew it, a small catheter had been inserted in a vein in my hand and an IV bottle hung from a pole beside my stretcher. Suddenly I was feeling okay, no, better than okay. Whatever they gave me made me think I could handle anything. No wonder people like drugs, I thought. They work.

The next thing I remember is a male nurse telling me I was in the recovery room. I was freezing, in pain, and nauseated. There was something blowing on my face. I tried to bat it away only to discover that it was attached. I was wearing an oxygen mask. How often had I nursed people through this same kind of confusion? I want to go on record as saying that the staff at Manhattan Eye, Ear and Throat was fantastic. They loaded me down with warm blankets to stop the shivering, and gave me medication for the nausea and pain.

In no time at all, I was back in my room. I had no idea how long the operation had taken, but I knew I needed to go to the bathroom as soon as I got back. The nurses refused to let me out of bed and put me on a bedpan. I felt like I was floating on the ceiling, and there was no way I could relieve myself up there. The nurse was sweet and tried all the tricks. She even turned on the faucet, hoping the sound of running water would help. Giving up after about fifteen minutes, she left me on the pan and told me to use my call light when I was finished. The moment she walked out, I slipped off the pan and down to the bottom of the bed.

I was being a bad patient, I knew, but I really had to go. As I scooted past the bed rails, I wondered what I'd do if I got dizzy but was pleasantly surprised when I made it to the bathroom in one piece. Then I caught a glimpse of myself in the mirror over the sink. It looked as if they'd put my new breasts right under my chin. Oh well, no time to worry about that now. I got back into bed and fell into a light sleep that lasted the rest of the evening, interrupted only by a liquid meal, pain shots, and the news that Howard and Alison had called, along with my friends Linda and Z from Pittsburgh, to make sure that I was okay.

A good night's sleep made a world of difference. I was up and had already taken a walk in the hall by eight the next morning. I was scheduled to stay in the hospital for two nights and was already wondering how I'd get through the next twenty-four hours of boredom. Then Dr. Baker showed up and asked if I wanted to go home. After I gave him an enthusiastic yes, he pulled a piece of tape and the entire bandage covering my breasts came off. There they were, Frankenstein's breasts with points all their own riding way up high.

I looked at my new accoutrements, then at the two little C-cup bras I'd brought with me for the trip home. There was no way I was going to be able to fit myself into those little cups. I pulled out the double-D I'd worn to the hospital, put it on, and then gingerly slipped into a warm-up suit. I was sprung. I prayed that the car wouldn't hit too many bumps on the way home, since I wasn't used to having my tits sitting so far away from my body. I felt like a suspension bridge was towering above my chest and was worried that too much turbulence would cause it to collapse.

Howard was the first person I called. Though it was his talk of nose jobs that had prompted me to make an appointment with a plastic surgeon, he'd actually been opposed to the operation from the beginning, never understanding why a woman would want her breasts reduced. When it looked as though I was going through with it, he'd implored me to rethink my decision. Now I was phoning to tell him he was right. I never should have done it.

"No, Robin," Howard said, "you did absolutely the right thing."

That Howard, I thought as he argued with me, he always knows just what to say.

Five days later I was in the doctor's office having the first stitches, the ones around my nipples, removed. "So, do you like them?" Dr. Baker asked.

"If I don't, are you going to change them?" I answered his question with a question.

"Noooooo," the doctor said, continuing to remove the little stitches.

"Then I like them," I joked.

Dr. Baker explained that once in surgery he'd determined my chest wall was large enough to support two D-cup-sized breasts, so he'd stopped at a D instead of making me a C as I had requested. The breasts were still riding rather high, but he promised me that they'd settle into place as the swelling went down. At that moment, as he explained it, I had the breasts of a seventeen-year-old.

Once the healing process was complete, I became quite fond of my new breasts. I was a perfect D and no longer spilled out the sides of bras. I could even go braless in certain outfits, and for the first time was able to wear bustiers. The pain I used to get between my shoulders when I'd walked too long became a thing of the past.

I no longer regret the surgery, but I realize that it wasn't really necessary in itself. It was really a subconscious attempt to remove a blatant reminder of my mother. Now I know I could have come to terms with my feelings about my breasts rather than have them surgically altered. As for plastic surgery, I'll still have my face put back where it belongs once it hits my chest.

Right after the operation, I met Lea in our caseworker's office to end our agreement. I wanted her to know that even though I had been unable to make her fantasies of being my daughter come true and had been forced to terminate the contract, I was still her friend and wasn't abandoning her. She hardly looked at me as I spoke, and it broke my heart to see the disappointment on her face. I told her I would always be there, even if I wasn't seeing her on a regular basis, and that she could contact me whenever she wanted to.

A few weeks later she wrote me a letter admitting that she'd been angry, but once she'd thought it over, she'd decided that I'd done more for her than anyone else ever had.

Lea is now a sophomore in college, and I'm happy to report we remain friends to this day. This past Thanksgiving, in fact, I treated her to a whirlwind weekend in Los Angeles.

Three years after Lea charged her mother with physical abuse, her brother was removed from her mother's home.

My perky new breasts certainly pointed in the right direction, straight ahead to a bright future. Undeniably, things were going great for me. Maybe for the first time I was happy, truly happy with myself and comfortable with my life. I was convinced that I had done as much evolving as can be expected of a human being. I'd given up rehearsing everything before it happened. I'd even managed to fall in love and lose and not fall apart. I still had high hopes that I might love again, but I liked things the way they were well enough not to be desperate for a man. I wasn't going to settle for anyone less than Mr. Right.

Meanwhile, the show had finally made it to TV. Channel 9 in New York, also known around the country as WOR, struck a deal with us in 1990. Howard once again attempted to take every precaution to make sure that we wouldn't be embarrassed or wind up working ourselves into bad health when the deal was set, but, as usual, we wound up doing all the work anyway. I really should say "they" wound up doing all the work because shortly after the show started, I developed a bleeding problem.

Frankly, the treatment was worse than the condition itself. I had an operation, then went on a steroid medication, all while the show was in production. Two horrible side effects of steroids can be weight gain and water retention, so I got to watch myself grow on video. The bleeding had made me anemic, and the steroids made me weaker still and caused muscle spasms, which meant that I couldn't exercise. I often felt that I was letting the others down because I could no longer pull my own weight, no pun intended. The exhaustion, the steroids, and the water retention also made me irritable. I'd get crazy over the least little thing. Everyone thought the old Robin had returned.

The morning show, the TV show, and the chronic illness all began to take their toll, and, finally, the commute from Queens was getting to me. I had no social life anymore because all the construction on the roads to the tunnels and bridges had turned a traditionally awful commute into a nightmare. Once I got home, I stayed there. Finally, at "Super Agent" Don Buchwald's urging, I moved into an apartment on the Upper East Side of Manhattan. I made the move as easy as possible by taking the model and buying all the furniture. I put my clothes in the closet, plugged in my TV, and I was settled. A few months later I couldn't believe I'd resisted moving to Manhattan for so long.

Over Labor Day of 1991, I went to Connecticut for a meditation retreat to recharge my batteries. Deepak Chopra, who was closely associated with the Maharishi at the time but who now runs his own health-related organization, was offering instruction that weekend in primordial sound technique. To the best of my understanding, primordial sounds give off vibrations that promote balance and health in the body. Having not been at my best in some time, I decided to give it a try.

After explaining the theory behind the sound, Deepak met with with each of us individually. Once inside the dimly lit room where he waited, I took a seat in the chair next to his. He asked me one question that I can't remember, then placed his hand over my heart for a moment. The heat radiating from his hand warmed my whole body. Then Deepak gave me a sound and sent me on my way. We'd learned how to use the sound in the lecture and had been instructed to immediately go to another room and practice the new technique.

While I was sitting with my eyes closed, practicing the technique, I experienced a strange sensation. The closest I can come to describing what happened is that it was as if a huge stone suddenly disengaged itself from my heart. I could actually feel the weight of it falling away. Once it was gone, I felt lighter. What was that? I asked myself, and a voice inside me answered, "I don't think I'm angry at my parents anymore."

One of the rules of a meditation weekend is to not make any important decisions while "rounding." Rounding is meditating for longer periods than normal and can alter your state of conciousness. So I put this thought aside, to be examined once I was home in the real world and no longer meditating for extended periods. I didn't even mention what I'd experienced to my meditating friends.

I got home from the retreat on Monday afternoon but didn't even think about what had happened until Wednesday. Standing in the kitchen of my apartment, I examined my feelings. Whatever had made it unthinkable to ever again be around my family had vanished. But the real test would come when I was face to face with my mother and father. The timing was perfect. The Jewish holidays were coming, so the radio show would be getting a long weekend. I had decided. For the first time in ten years, I was going home.

Once I made up my mind, I immediately booked a flight to Baltimore and reserved a room at the same hotel in Inner Harbor where I'd met Mary Beth and Dom before moving to New York. Then I made sure to call a few close friends and advisers to tell them of my plans.

I was again in the backseat of a car with Howard driving when I revealed my plan to him and Alison. They were stunned. Howard jokingly asked if I should give him my parents' number just in case I was never heard from again. Alison was simply happy for me. Most amazing to me were the number of people who said, "Make sure you take my number with you, and feel free to call at any time, no matter how late." I thought to myself, These people still don't know me. Anything that would rattle me that much would require hospitalization. There really wasn't anything my parents could do to me anymore. Quite frankly, I was more concerned for them.

When I spoke to Sharon London about my impending reunion, she almost made me cry by asking the kinds of questions a worried mother would. Her caring warmed my heart. She also wanted to help me plan the whole thing. When I told her I hadn't informed my parents that I was coming, she thought that I was setting myself up for failure. "Trust me, Sharon," I said, "I know these people. They'll be right where I left them."

I had no clue as to what my reaction would be when I saw my mother and father, but I knew it would be an honest one, completely unrehearsed and unannounced. I didn't want them alerting family and friends, because there were no guarantees. That's why I was just going to surprise them.

Before Sharon would let me off the phone, she insisted that we make a lunch date for soon after I got back to talk about what had happened, and I wholeheartedly agreed. She, after all, was one of the primary reasons I could even make this trip. She above anyone deserved a detailed account. It had always been her desire to see me strong and whole and capable of making such a journey, not for someone else, but for myself. And this truly was the first time I was going home because I wanted to.

During the twenty-minute flight, I wondered if I'd recognize anything. I was picking up a rental car at the airport, and I wasn't sure I'd be able to find my way to the city anymore. Just to be sure, I asked for directions at the rental counter. I-95 hadn't changed much, and I found myself in downtown Baltimore in a mere fifteen minutes. Finding the hotel was more of a challenge. I was awestruck by all the development that had mushroomed out around Inner Harbor. It had comprised just a couple of pavilions and one hotel when I left. Now there were hotels everywhere, one more beautiful than the next, and construction was under way on a new stadium right off the I-95 exit into the city. I felt proud that Baltimore was still thriving, just like me.

Once I checked into my hotel, I ordered room service, then meditated. After that, I planned to head for the house where I'd grown up. But once I was done, I decided my clothes were all wrong and went shopping at one of the Inner Harbor malls. Finally, I realized that I was just procrastinating, so even though I'd bought a pink silk jacket studded with rhinestones, I kept on the outfit I'd worn from New York, jumped into the car, and felt my way back to my old neighborhood, making a turn whenever I saw a sign I recognized.

In another fifteen minutes I was turning onto Grantley Avenue. As I passed my parents' house looking for a parking space, I thought it looked deserted. The blinds were closed, and the front door was shut tight. There was a new aluminum awning over the porch, a new storm door with a serious lock, and metal grates over the windows. These were all signs of the change that had happened in neighborhoods like this. This one block still looked okay, but the rest of the street was in bad repair.

Even though it appeared that nobody was home, I decided I'd climb the steps and give the bell a ring. As I approached the front steps, I saw my mother. She'd opened the front door and was standing there, looking out. I walked up the steps toward her, but there was no sign of recognition. As I was about to step up onto the porch, I couldn't believe she still didn't know who I was.

"You don't even recognize me," were the first words I spoke.

"Oh, my God. Charles, it's Robin," my mother called to my father, her eyes widening.

"Are you crazy?" I heard my father yell from inside. "Let me look." He pushed my mother aside, and his large frame filled the doorway. He looked at me, his mouth dropped open, and he started fumbling with the storm-door lock. The door burst open and they both grabbed me at once, and holding on tight, my father said, "Are you okay?"

"Yes, I'm fine," I said, hugging them back, unafraid at last. We stood there hugging and crying for a long time. I knew my father's question meant that he thought only tough times would ever bring me to his door again. But I wasn't there because I needed something from them. I was there to make sure I was okay.

They both finally stopped hugging me and stepped back to get a better look at their prodigal daughter, home after a journey that had taken years. My mother raised her hands skyward and started thanking the Lord for answering her prayers while my father invited me inside and offered me a seat in the living room. Now I could look them over.

They had gotten very old. I could barely see the face of the man who had sexually molested me among all the jowls and hollows. The frame, though still large, was no longer strong and powerful. My molester had turned into a little old man with a bad ticker, dependent on medication to keep him going. As he sat across from me, staring, leaning forward on his elbows and unable to relax, I wondered what he was seeing.

My mother was older too, but her age showed less in her face than in her body. She was hobbled by an ankle she had broken a couple of years before. It was still swollen and looked out of alignment. This was the woman who had verbally and physically abused me. She wouldn't be able to catch me now, but I bet myself that that tongue was still just as sharp.

They asked me, "Can I get you anything?" and "Where are your bags?" and finally the real question, "What are you doing here?"

"I just woke up one day," I replied, "and I wasn't angry anymore."

Again my mother closed her eyes and tilted back her head as she sang hosannas to the ceiling.

Then the conversation settled into something a bit more normal. They each began to recount their infirmities and to update me on the many deaths that had occurred in the family in my absence. "I'll be seventy before you know it," my father noted. "Never thought I'd live to see that one. Not too many people in my family made it to seventy."

"Can I call your brother and tell him you're here?" my mother asked tentatively.

"Yes, it's okay," I replied, hiding my astonishment that she'd thought to ask. She'd never asked my permission to do anything that concerned me. What a difference a ten-year absence can make.

Before the day was over, there were a lot more tears and reunions. Junior was the first to arrive with his wife, Mary, and his five-year-old son, Anthony, whom I'd never met. After the six of us spent a little time together, my mother asked if she could tell some of the neighbors I was there. Soon we were being stampeded. I was overwhelmed to discover that they had developed an information network to keep my family informed of my accomplishments. Mrs. Leak showed my parents every article she came across. Miss Thelma had invited my parents over to her house to watch me on the Channel 9 show before they'd had cable installed. My parents knew about everything I'd done professionally for the last ten years.

One woman just sat in a corner and cried the whole time she was there. Before she left she hugged me tight and pleaded with me never to leave for so long again. "Who even knew anybody cared?" I thought to myself. Still, I don't think it would have brought me back one day sooner. I had needed every moment of that time away so that this occasion could be a pleasant one.

Reflecting on my visit to Baltimore as the plane spirited me home, I felt at peace. I had reclaimed a strip of emotional territory. I could put Baltimore, Maryland, back on my map. There was no longer a place in the country I didn't feel free to visit. And, although my parents had no idea what that reunion meant, I was glad they'd enjoyed it.

I was never going to be the daughter for whose return my mother had prayed. I was the daughter who had learned to forgive but who would refuse to live as if the past had never happened. I hadn't come back to help them re-create myths of a happy family or to be the brilliant daughter over whom they could crow to their friends. I was the same little girl who'd had to fight for her life and now, in adulthood, was in full possession of it. My parents still live in the land of denial. My world is grounded in the truth.

21

EXCUSE ME!!!

That's how I met Robin.
We were on this bridge.

— Howard Stern

Howard: I don't know if this is real or not, but there's some guy on
the phone. He's got a cellular phone with him, and he says he's
on the George Washington Bridge and he's going to jump from
the bridge and kill himself.

Robin: Really?

Howard: Yeah, you know, you can't tell if it's real or not. Hello.

Caller: What do you think? What does it sound like?

Howard: Hello.

Caller: What does it sound like? What do you think is going on?

Howard: Well, I hear the bridge but I don't know if you're for real
or not.

Caller: Ohhhhhh . . .

Howard: Obviously it would be a great crank call to call me up and
say you're going to commit suicide.

Caller: Yeah, it would, wouldn't it?

Howard: What, are you a big fan of mine?

Caller: Yeah, of course.
Robin: Well, why are you leaving us?
Howard: We need our fans.

Just another typical day on "The Howard Stern Show." A jumper takes his cellular phone to the George Washington Bridge and reaches out to his only friend, Howard Stern. The King of All Media puts the caller on the air, his faithful companion Robin by his side, with failure the farthest thing from their minds.

Robin: You can't kill yourself until my book comes out.
Howard: Yeah, look at the things you have to look forward to—
    Robin's book, and I'm going to revolutionize entertainment when
    my movie comes out.

Will these two wacky radio people be able to save a listener from the icy waters of the Hudson River? Should they be on the phone with him at all? The Federal Communications Commission has already fined some of the stations that carry the show more than two million dollars for indecency. Surely they would prefer that a desperate man call someone else.

Howard: I don't understand something.
Caller: What's up?
Howard: If you're in good enough shape to have a cellular phone, I
    mean, why would you want to leave the planet? That's a reason
    to live, just alone.
Caller: Yeah.
Howard: I mean, maybe it's the bill.
Caller: Ha-ha, ha-ha, ha . . .
Robin: Yeah, maybe he made too many calls.
Caller: That's not it. It's about life in general . . . Ha-ha, ha . . .
Robin: Are you married?
Caller: Yeah.

"The Howard Stern Show" is now carried live or on a tape delay in twenty markets around the country. Later tonight videotapes of us keeping this suicidal caller on the phone, complete with a parody of a tabloid show–type reenactment, will be broadcast on the E! cable network. Right now, though, the sudden silence from the caller is deafening. Maybe the guy jumped. No, he's back on the line.

Caller: Hey, there's a chopper looking at me.
Howard: Is there a cop?
Caller: Ummmmmm.
Howard: Let me speak to the cop. Let me speak to the cop so that I can confirm that you're trying to kill yourself.
Caller: There's no cop. There's a traffic helicopter just passed by.
Howard: Is anybody, like . . . Is anybody, like, looking at you, that you're, like, ready to jump off a bridge?
Caller: The cars that are passing by.
Howard: They are? Is anybody stopping to help you?
Caller: No.
Robin: They're not stopping traffic?
Caller: Who gives a damn?

Howard Stern has been described as racist, sexist, insensitive, and tasteless, yet when a desperate man decided to make one last call, it was to us. We have always contended that the show is about entertainment; sometimes it's funny, sometimes it's sexy, it can even be informative. Today the show is downright compelling. Is this a hoax? Is the guy really contemplating suicide? If he is, can we save him?

Gary: Howard, we're the number-one show in the New York area, certainly one of our listeners driving over the bridge has a cell phone. Tell them to honk or call us or something.
Howard: If you're listening now . . . *(Honk)* Oh, there goes someone honking. *(Groans and laughter in the background)* How do you know he didn't honk his own horn?
Robin: Right. We have to have somebody call us.
Caller: Yeah, honk my own horn. Up on the bridge?
Howard: Why are you killing yourself?
Caller: 'Cause life sucks sometimes, you know? And, I've been here before. I come here often to think, and I regret the times I haven't jumped earlier.

The caller could be white, black, purple, or plaid. He could be crashing from drugs, grandstanding for his woman or his buddies, or trying to get on "The Howard Stern Show" the only way he can think of. It's possible that he might turn out not to be our favorite person. The point is, from our perspective, what he is is a human being in what appears to be major trouble.

Robin: And you've got a wife.
Howard: How is she? Is she nice?
Caller: She's alright.
Howard: Not great? *(Static)* Hello? I guess he jumped.
Caller: Hello?
Howard: Oh, I thought you jumped.
Caller: Hello?
Howard: Hello? Hello? Hello?
Robin: Oh boy, what a time to break up.
Caller: My battery's running low, and so am I, so . . .

We manage to keep this man on the phone until Helen Trimble, a faithful listener on the way to work, pulls over. She bravely wraps her arms around this stranger in a bear hug after vaulting the railings to get to him. She risks her own life because like her, he is a listener and that gives them something in common. When Helen joins him on the bridge and we know the caller is serious, Howard jumps into action.

Caller: Thank you, sweetheart.
Howard: How is she? She nice-looking?
Caller: No.
Howard: No good?
Caller: No. A fat cow.
Howard: A big fat cow.
Robin: Ahhhhh . . . He's terrible.

Howard takes a moment to explain human nature. Guys never change. A woman comes to the rescue of a guy about to commit suicide and he can still deliver the harsh evaluation that his savior is a fat cow.

By this time, traffic is blocked in both directions. In another few minutes, police from the city and the Port Authority, alerted to the story because they are listening too, will converge on the scene and take our caller into custody. His cellular phone remains behind, and another listener picks it up to fill us in on the continuing drama.

Bystander: Hey, Howard, this is a friend of yours. The police are here, they got him in handcuffs now.
Howard: That's what I was trying to do. . . . Oh, I'm a hero, call the reporters.
Bystander: That's right, I was listening and the woman and I stopped and then we got him.
Howard: Who is this?
Bystander: This is the guy who stopped. You know me. I'm a friend of Celeste's. Does this mean I can do your show? *(Groans from Quivers and Stern)*
Robin: Could you climb over that little railing?
Howard: Yeah, what about you jumping?

By ten that morning, Howard is conducting a press conference, grudgingly agreeing that he is a hero before a press contingent of about fifty reporters from newspapers, local news shows, the tabloid and entertainment television shows. He didn't get the name "King of All Media" by accident.

The next day, the *New York Times* quips in print about the incident that Miss Quivers and Mr. Stern pressed him (the man on the bridge) for details, but also interrupted him to make jokes. I like that. I figure the guy called to talk to Howard and Robin. He might have jumped had we all of a sudden become Bryant Gumbel and Katie Couric. And anyway, the bottom line is that thousands of listeners, often dubbed mutants by the press because they listen to us, banded together one morning to save a life. Yet to some FCC commissioners, Howard Stern is public enemy number one.

Yes, we talk on air about sex and other bodily functions. Howard's never been one to shy away from a lesbian story or from spanking a naked girl, and we play the phone-answering message of a self-avowed member of the Ku Klux Klan, Daniel Carver. Some say it's wrong because Carver spews tons of racist propaganda in his messages and uses the term "nigger" freely when referring to blacks. A reporter once challenged me by saying that one of her black friends was so offended by the show that she ordered the driver of the cab in which she was riding to change the station. That's what she was supposed to do. But you can't prevent Daniel Carver from expressing his views and using that word and still call this the United States of America. And what if we made him refer to blacks by some other term? Would his message really change? There are all kinds of racists in this country. Carver is the least of them because he has no money, no power, and he's honest. The racists you have to watch are the ones who are smart enough to hide it. They're the ones who do the real damage.

You know what I have to say to the black woman we offended? Black people spend way too much time worrying about what white people think of them, and not enough on what they think of them-selves. You'd think that white opinion was the black man's greatest threat, and not poverty, illegitimacy, drug abuse, and black-on-black crime.

On another trip back to Baltimore after that first family reunion, I realized that this same sad obsession with white opinion had plagued my father all his life. By then, he was beginning to have trouble with his memory and had given up driving. I hadn't been in the city all that much and became confused myself trying to find one of the malls. Another driver, confused by my moves, stopped his car in a parking lot, waiting to see what I would do next. Being from New York, I thought it was quite nice that this other driver was giving me the chance to figure things out by patiently waiting on a side road. My father's point of view was quite different.

"Those white people sure can stare, can't they?" he snarled, glaring at the man in the other car.

At that moment, I felt profound sympathy for him. All his life, he'd shrunk under the gaze of whites as a result of feeling unliked and unequal. I was seized by the desire to help him understand that he didn't have to feel this way.

"How do you know why that man is staring at you?" I asked. "Maybe he's staring at you because he thinks you're handsome. Yes, that's what he's saying. Look at that handsome man. Why, I've never seen anyone that handsome in my life."

My father began to blush and become pleasantly embarrassed. "Girl, you'd better shut up and drive," he chided me playfully, unable to keep the smile off his face.

"Yep," I continued, beginning to pull away, "he's still looking, can't take his eyes off you."

My father was audibly giggling now. I was happy to see the snarl and the negativity replaced with this bright smile, but I couldn't help but think about all the pain he had inflicted on himself for years, seeking love where he was sure none existed. I was a little sad for myself, too. This was my father. He was more than seventy now, and I was still trying to teach him how to live. It was a reminder of my childhood, and how everything even then had been backward, how these two people had become parents without ever knowing exactly what that meant.

When I hear blacks on WLIB, the local black talk-radio station, say that being black is hard, I feel most for their children because their lack of self-esteem and self-love is exactly what will be passed on. Their children will find it hard to be black too. Blacks are constantly crying that we are under siege, yet many live their lives allowing their opinion of themselves to be dictated by others and continuing to use the slave masters' practices of humiliation, degradation, and beatings to raise their children. Since the liberation of the civil rights movement of the sixties, blacks themselves have been the primary instruments of reinforcing black inferiority.

Even those who have taken advantage of the educational and employment benefits offered after the 1960s have failed to then use those gains to create a solid tax base of their own. Know why? Because just like my father, many blacks continue to harbor both the emotions of love and hate for whites. Hate because of the lack of remorse for past offenses, and a kind of love that won't be satisfied without full white acceptance. In the fantasy of equality finally bestowed by whites, black problems of high crime, illegitimacy, and unemployment will just disappear.

I see my parents as a microcosm of the problems in black families and society in general. They were immature, willful people who made rash decisions about life based on whatever felt good at the moment and then wanted to bear none of the responsibility for the consequences of their acts. For them, things just happened, no apology necessary. Later, they learned that there was an excuse for their behavior: "We didn't know that then."

When I hear angry rap artists screaming about four hundred years of oppression again and again, I think to myself, That's no longer a reason, it too has become an excuse. Black children need a lot more than excuses, and they live in far too complicated a world to be saddled with parents who can't prepare them to survive.

Even as I was throwing off the chains imposed on me by my family and community as a young girl, I thought that the other children would see what I was doing and adopt my behavior. When it appeared that I was leaving them behind, I tried to make my gestures bigger so that the trail to the exit road couldn't be missed. But no matter how many crumbs of bread I scattered along the road, no one ever took up the path. Eventually, I realized that given our beginnings, not everyone was going to be able to make it out. That's when I decided it was better not to break human beings in the first place because once they're broken, they are very hard to fix. To do it, you need their full cooperation, and by that time, they are more likely than not unable to give it.

You know, writing a book about your life is a lot like psychotherapy. It stirs up a lot of old conficts, like the ones I've described, which in turn make all kinds of memories come floating to the surface of your mind. As I wrote, my thoughts about kids and the black community, it led me back to Jimmy.

He would be about twenty-seven years old by now, I reckoned, and had passed through the most precarious years for a black man in America. Had he survived? What had he learned? Was he prepared for the obstacles he would still face? Did he have the benefit of some guidance or had he, like me, had to feel his way through alone? There was only one way to find out. I had to look for him or I'd never know any peace.

I needed to know he was okay, and for the first time I felt that I deserved to. We had spent three years of our lives together, and in that time, he had been everything to me. It was for him that I had come back to life and forced myself to lay the foundation for my future. Jimmy gave me hope when there was no hope. He deserved to know how much he had meant to me and how much I had needed him.

I started my search by calling a private detective named Mike Martin. He'd helped me before when I needed to find some old nursing school buddies. Mike told me that he'd need a name, preferably Jimmy's adopted name, to get started. Mike always makes things sound very difficult, so that when he produces results in days, his clients are really impressed. This time, though, I thought I was in for a long search. I had no idea how to find Jimmy's new name, I could hardly remember the exact dates he'd lived in our home.

Just then I remembered something I hadn't thought about in years. A few months after the adoption, Jimmy and his new family had appeared in one of a series of articles on adoption published in the *Baltimore News American*. I could hardly look at the article at the time it appeared in the paper. We didn't subscribe to the *News*, so one of the neighbors must have told us that Jimmy was in the paper. But once informed, we made sure to get a copy.

The article took up the entire front page of the Women's section of the paper and was continued inside. I remembered that it talked about how happy he was, and how well he was adjusting to his new home. Three pictures accompanied the article, showing Jimmy in various poses with his new parents. At the time, just looking at them made me cry. I didn't want to see these new people, and I couldn't tell if he missed me from these pictures. I left the article with my mother and her cackling friends as they gregariously pored over every word, just as if we'd see him in a little while.

I had never looked at it again, but I knew that my mother had cut it out and saved it with all the other old family keepsakes in the dining room buffet. I'd gone through that buffet in the summer, looking for old school photographs for the book and, surprisingly, hadn't stumbled across it by accident. I hadn't been able to find my kindergarten photo either, and had assumed that some things must have been lost. I sent my personal assistant, Sherry, off to the library to look for it, unable to even give her more than the name of the paper and a range of dates from three to six months after he'd left in the summer of 1970.

Sherry returned to my apartment each afternoon, eyes red from squinting at screens, trying to read small newsprint to no avail.

Finally, I decided to call my mother to find out if she could help narrow down the date. She wasn't much help in that department but said she'd look for the article herself. I'd made that call on a Sunday evening. That Tuesday, I found a letter bearing my mother's return address in the mail. Inside was one piece of fragile newsprint, yellowed and tattered from age. On it were two faded photographs of Jimmy and his new parents. Captions, still clearly visible under the pictures, gave his parents' full name and the name of the street on which they lived at the time the article was published.

I stared at the pictures. There was Jimmy, and he was still three years old, just as he'd always been. I hadn't seen that face in years. A few months after I'd showed his picture to Alison Stern, I'd lost the wallet where I'd always kept them. I'd had a number of wallets in the many years since Jimmy had been adopted, and each time I purchased a new one, one of my first duties was to make the transfer of those two photos to a safe compartment inside their new home. When I lost that wallet, I lost my driver's license and my social security card too, but the only thing I really cared about were those pictures of Jimmy. Unlike licenses and cards, those pictures couldn't be replaced. I hadn't actually seen his face since then.

For the first time, I looked at the faces of the other two people in the picture. His new mother and father looked like really nice people. I had never taken the time to study their faces before. My only hope had been that he'd gone to a good home, and I thought their faces looked kind. The way they looked at him showed that they were happy to have him.

I ran for the phone and dialed Mike's number. "Mike," I said excitedly, "I'm holding two pictures from that article I told you about, and his parents' name and the street are included in the caption."

Mike wrote down the information and then asked if I could fax him the pictures. I wasn't sure it would work, but I wanted him to have as much help as possible, so I tried to feed the old piece of newsprint into this new piece of home office machinery. Within seconds, the article was destroyed. I'd managed to get a glimpse of him for only a moment, and now he was gone again, destroyed by modern technology. Oh well.

Two days later, another letter arrived from my mother. She'd continued to search the buffet and had finally found the article, which had slipped behind the drawers and was trapped between the drawer slip and the backboard. My mother had had to lift the drawers out completely to get to the fragile pieces of paper. Anxious to help, she'd slipped them into an envelope and sent it to New York the next day without even calling to let me know it was on the way. It was a complete surprise.

As I read, I discovered that Jimmy had been considered an older adoption at three years of age, which had made him a perfect subject for an article. By then, most kids had already been abandoned to the scrap heap of permanent foster care, to be bounced around from family to family until they reached the age of eighteen. At least he'd been spared that.

I called Mike again to tell him that I had the whole article now if he needed it. "Oh, I've already spoken to Jimmy's father," he replied.

I'd thought Mike would just call me when he knew where Jimmy was so that I could decide how to proceed next. But he was telling me that contact had already been made. "What happened?" I asked anxiously.

"Well, " Mike continued, "his father seemed a little suspicious and wasn't real cooperative. He wanted me to send him some proof of who I was and that what I had told him was true. He asked for a letter on my letterhead explaining the situation. Then he told me that once he got the letter, either he or Jimmy would get back to me."

I was so floored by what I had just learned that I never even bothered to find out when all of this had occurred. After I calmed down, I convinced myself, for no apparent reason, that I wouldn't hear anything for the rest of the week. The next day, Sherry called me at the station just as I was about to leave. "Robin, Mike just called," she blurted into the phone as soon as I picked up. "I have Jimmy's phone number and address."

I was too excited to just walk out of the station, and I couldn't just keep the news under my hat. I ran to the back and found Fred and one of our interns, Steve Grillo, talking in an office. They had never heard of Jimmy, so I had to bring them up to speed by giving them a brief synopsis before I could even tell them my good news. Once I'd gotten it out, I felt better and then rushed home.

All the way there in the cab, I pondered what would happen

next. I found Sherry in a just slightly less excited state than I was. I had to decide either to call or write to make the initial contact. I could never have stood the wait for a written response, so writing was quickly ruled out. Once I'd settled on calling, I needed time to steady my nerves. I ate lunch, took a hot bath, and then meditated.

At two that afternoon, I could find nothing else to delay the call. I sat on the edge of my bed and punched the strange new numbers into the phone. The line connected, and my anxiety level hit the ceiling. One ring. Two rings. Three rings. On the fourth, an answering machine picked up. A basso male voice said, "We're not home right now . . . "

I hung up before the beep, ran into my home office, and made Sherry dial the number. She got the answering machine too and was about to hang up. "No, listen. Maybe that's his voice. How do you think he sounds?"

"He sounds okay," she said, puzzled.

"No. Does he sound like a good guy, bad guy?"

"No, he sounds like a good guy."

I called every two hours the rest of the afternoon and always got the machine. At seven-thirty that evening, just before bed and with "Entertainment Tonight" blaring in the background, I tried one final time. I heard the click of a receiver being removed from the phone cradle on the second ring, and the same voice I'd heard on the answering machine said, "Hello."

"Hello," I answered. "Is this James Carter?"

"Yes."

"This is Robin Quivers." I could hardly hear him. Not expecting success, I hadn't turned down the TV, and now I had to interrupt this reunion to do so. Once I got back on the phone, I realized that I didn't know where to start. "This might seem pretty strange to you," I admitted.

"No," he interjected, "it's not strange at all. I've had the name Robin stuck in my head my whole life."

I got a big lump in my throat and my eyes filled with tears. Something had stuck after all these years. Once I could speak easily again, the conversation flowed and we spoke for two hours. He'd just had a birthday and was exactly twenty-seven. His parents had planned a little celebration the Sunday before we spoke, and when he'd walked through the door of their home, his father had handed him an official-looking white envelope. At first, he told me, he'd thought he was in some kind of trouble, but his father told him it was okay and urged him to open the envelope. It was the letter Mike, my private eye, had written to reassure Jimmy's father that no one meant his son any harm.

Jimmy said that he began to jump up and down after reading it and scolded his parents for waiting to show it to him until the day of his birthday celebration. When I realized that his parents had given me to their son as a present, I was sold on them. They'd won me over before we'd even met. Because of that letter, Jimmy said, this was one of the best birthdays he'd had in years. He began to talk faster and faster. His parents had only adopted one child, so he'd never had any brothers or sisters, "So," he said sheepishly, "I hope you don't mind, but I've been telling everyone you're my sister."

He'd never heard or seen "The Howard Stern Show" even though we were broadcast in Baltimore over WJFK and the Channel 9 show had been carried by a local TV station. But later on that Sunday evening that he'd received the letter, he'd discovered he'd already seen me. A few weeks before, he had been at the home of a friend who'd shown him the tape of what they'd done for New Year's Eve. They'd popped a tape of the Howard Stern pay-per-view special into the VCR and they'd all watched our Miss New Year's Eve Pageant again. Once one of his friends recognized my name and reminded him of the tape, he ran to his friend's home and begged him to play the videotape again. Jimmy animatedly described my braids and what I was wearing, ending with, ". . . and you just laughed at all that craziness going on."

Then I asked him if he still had the scar above his eyebrow.

"Yes," he said, astonished. "They told me that I got that falling down the stairs."

"No, that wasn't from falling down the stairs. You were running in the dining room and fell, hitting your head on the iron foot of the dining room table," I told him. That's when I realized that I was the keeper of the first three years of his life. Until now he'd had to wonder about what had happened to him and where he'd been from birth to adoption. There were marks no one could explain to him, and no one could tell him what he'd been like as a baby. For the first time, I felt sure I was right to look for him, if only to fill in those blanks.

Two weeks later, on a Friday after work, I was on a plane to Baltimore on my way to meet him in person for the first time. He worked evenings as a computer programmer, so he didn't get to my hotel room until around midnight. I had no idea what he looked like, and if I was going to be shocked, I wanted to be shocked on my side of the door, so when I heard him knock, I took a quick peek through the little fish-eye peephole in the door. I discovered, to my relief, a very handsome young man on the other side.

Understandably, we both felt a little awkward at first, although he'd come loaded down with gifts. Jimmy had a nice face, but it wasn't the one that I knew. Luckily, he'd brought along photo albums that covered his entire youth. As we went through those old albums, I got to observe the three-year-old face I'd carried in my head and in my heart, as it matured into the face across from me now. When I threw him out at six in the morning, I had finally connected the dots. That afternoon, I met his parents at their home. This time, I was the one bearing gifts for everyone. His parents were as sweet as they had seemed in that newspaper article. After a while, his father let me know that I had passed his inspection by making me dinner. They regaled me with stories of Jimmy's childhood antics and teen rebellions, and then Jimmy's father quietly stole from the table unnoticed.

When he returned, he placed a frame in front of me, face down, and said, "There's something to keep the mice away." I picked up the frame and turned it over. Inside the brass-leafed edges was a family portrait of Jimmy and his mother and father. I thanked them for allowing me back into his life, and they sincerely encouraged me to stay in touch and to visit often.

Jimmy took my parents' names and address before I left him that Saturday night. He seemed anxious to meet them. I tried to explain that they were quite old now and that my father's memory wasn't all that good, but he seemed determined to visit them on his own. As fate would have it, I overslept my early-morning Sunday flight and couldn't get another until six that evening. So I wound up meeting Jimmy at my parents' home before I went back to New York.

My mother nervously sat at the head of the dining room table, making polite conversation. I did my best to steer past any unsuitable topics, and my father sat in a corner, asking the same question again and again. "Is that one of the little children who used to live here?"

"That's Jimmy, Charles. Remember Jimmy?" My mother answered my father's questions in a loud voice, as if he had a hearing problem.

"We loved all those kids," he'd answer back.

I had brought my overnight case in from the car so that I could share with my mother the picture of Jimmy and his family that I was getting to take back to New York. When it was time for me to leave, Jimmy grabbed the case and escorted me to my car. Funny, I thought, how it really wasn't strange at all to have him around. We joked and laughed and teased each other as naturally as any brother and sister. No one just looking at us interact would have guessed that we had just met.

Once comfortably settled into the seat on the plane, I realized that I had pulled off a miracle. I had made the impossible happen. I finally felt connected to someone else in this world. Jimmy and I speak often. I've even made a couple of more trips to Baltimore to spend time with him and his family, and he's been to New York to see me, once winding up on the radio show.

At first I thought I'd tell Howard to just skip all the family stuff, it would be much too confusing. But on considering it again, I figured what the hell, I've never played it safe, so why start now? Howard dove right in by announcing, "Robin calls this guy her brother, but he's really a stranger she just met."

Neither Jimmy nor I ever managed to completely explain our relationship to Howard's satisfaction, so he put an end to the confusion with the quip, "Robin, your family tree looks like a pretzel."

Family. I find I have a couple of them. My biological family, which always looked normal from the outside but wasn't really, and my family on the show, which has been accused of being twisted but is as solid as a rock inside. As a proud member of this second family, I'm the first to admit that we've had our share of crises, hissy fits, and heartbreak, but we worked through them. Each time we did, it was a breakthrough for the whole group, not just the individuals involved.

For years, Howard and I, like cogs in a well-oiled machine, had been slipping seamlessly into our roles each morning. Having discovered what a storm of emotions lies just below my surface, I'd learned to put a little emotional distance between myself and the many sensitive topics we tackled on the air each day. I always made sure that if I addressed a difficult subject, I was addressing the issue itself and not my feelings about it. This made it possible to wade into territory where others might fear to tread.

I was glad that I no longer had a problem confusing the show with reality, and that that confusion no longer plagued my relationships with my coworkers. But when I watched Howard get into heated discussions with other people on the show, I couldn't help but feel envious. It made for such good radio. Even so, I felt I couldn't risk it. A good on-air fight wasn't worth possibly dismantling years of respect and goodwill.

When I made that last promise never to pick a fight with Howard again, we never exchanged another harsh word on or off the air. In fact, communicating with Howard off the air was never the problem. It was Howard on the radio, the master button pusher, who sometimes made me crazy. Still, I didn't feel I could trust myself to yell at that guy without getting angry at the guy who was my friend once we were back in the office. That is, until the day some Los Angeles police officers were videotaped pounding on the head and legs of a prone black motorist who had been stopped for speeding. That motorist was Rodney King

King had tried to elude the police, who were attempting to pull him over, by leading them on a high-speed chase. Once stopped and out of the car, he continued to refuse to cooperate and wound up being pummeled into submission. All the media expressed outrage at the police treatment of King and backed up their views by showing a small portion of an amateur videotape of the incident.

Howard sided with the police. He felt that Rodney King had been wrong to run away from the cops in the first place, that he was driving at high speeds and admitted he'd been drinking. As far as

Howard was concerned, King had put a lot of lives at risk and deserved the treatment he had gotten, no matter what his color.

I could agree with everything Howard said about the incident, up to a point. I'm a strong believer in the American system of government. If it weren't for stupidity and prejudice, it would be the best system of government in the world. Unfortunately, we are not lacking in either, so slowly but surely we are destroying the greatest system in the world, as evidenced by cops, frustrated by an overwhelmed judicial system, who wind up administering a little justice on the side of the road. I felt that Howard's defense of this kind of police behavior was one more unneeded assault on the Constitution.

I listened to Howard exhort the police to continue this kind of curbside punishment every day after the incident occurred, and months later as the police officers involved were brought to trial. Whenever the subject came up, I took a deep breath and then tried to discuss the fine points of the laws the cops would be flaunting if they took Howard's advice. The more reasonable I tried to be, the more outrageous he became—until I finally snapped.

"That's the stupidest thing I ever heard!" I yelled at the top of my lungs.

"I'm trying to make a point," Howard screamed back.

"I don't care about your point," I replied.

"Okay, but just let me make it."

"No! I've listened to you make that stupid point over and over again and I'm tired of it."

"Are you calling me stupid, you idiot?"

In the old days, that would have been where I lost it. Even now, my mind was replaying Howard's calling me an idiot as I continued to interact with him on the air. I was listening to two separate sets of dialogue at the same time, the one with Howard and the one with myself. That was the stuff that used to make me crazy and had driven a wedge between me and the world. That was the stuff that used to run my life.

In the studio, Fred and Jackie had fallen silent. Fred visibly stiffened. He remembered incidents like this all too well. Jackie had never heard Howard and me yelling at each other before. Neither of them knew what to do. Meanwhile, Howard and I continued yelling back and forth, with me continuing to outyell him every time he tried to finish his statement. We went on like this right into commercials.

Once the mikes were off, I went to the newsroom to retrieve the faxes I knew would be declaring me a traitor, urging Howard to get rid of me and referring to me as "the bitch." There were a lot of them. Without saying a word, I walked into the studio, handed the faxes to Howard, smiled, and went back to my desk. Howard didn't speak either, but the fact that I was conducting business as usual must have signaled to him that things were different.

Then, to my surprise, Howard brilliantly turned our little tiff into a gag running throughout the show, and it was good radio. Each time we went to a live commercial he would ask if it was all right for him to do the commercial on his show. When he wanted to take a phone call, he'd ask my permission. When Rodney King came up in the news, he'd check with me to see if he was allowed to express his opinion, at which point we'd begin squabbling again.

Since no one else at K-Rock had ever heard us disagree, Tom Chiusano, the general manager, stopped me in the hall that morning. "Robin, that sounded real this morning. Were you really angry with Howard?"

"Maybe," I said with a wink, and jauntily went on my way.

Howard and I didn't have our usual meeting after the show that day because we both had other appointments, but I ran into him just as he was about to walk out the front door.

"Robin, what you did today," he said with obvious sincerity, "it was really good."

"Thanks, Howard." I beamed. "See you tomorrow."

After years of trying, I was finally free.

EPILOGUE

Maybe I'll stop at the supermarket and pick up something to eat before I get to my parents'. I don't know the neighborhood any-more, so I really have no idea where a supermarket is. I remember seeing something called Brown's Supermarket at the corner of Reis-terstown and Cold Spring Lane. Maybe that's a black-owned mar-ket. Wouldn't that be nice? Pulling into the parking lot, I realize that I haven't seen another market. I have no choice. It's Brown's or nothing. But even though I don't know the chain, a supermarket is a supermarket, right? Right.

Five to six men, grown men, sit on the railing at the door of the store. The sight is a familiar one. As I park, I wonder about the safety of the car. Women are walking across the lot, struggling with their bags on their way home. As I approach these men, some of them old enough to be my father, they ask that old, familiar ques-tion, "Do you need a ride?"

"No," I say.

As I'm entering the store, a woman carrying bags emerges.

"Need he'p with your bags?" the men chime in unison.

I walk inside this huge, cavernous, warehouse-style market. No frills here. This is the supermarket closest to my parents' home. My mind races backward. If I were a little girl now, this is where I'd walk to run those little errands for the forgotten items on my mother's grocery list. I would have to walk across that parking lot, pass those men, and enter this dingy store.

Well, I'm not a kid anymore, and this is just a day trip. I'll be back in the safe confines of white suburbia tonight. You just can't help noticing how depressing this is. Zombies with sad faces pushing carts through aisles, trying to read labels in the dark.

The vegetable section looks like there's a shortage. I pick up a few white potatoes and put them in a bag. There's some corn on the cob. They've also got some string beans, collard greens, and kale. Not a lot of fruit on display.

I decide to walk around the aisles to see what's here. This is a black neighborhood overrun with heart disease, diabetes, and high blood pressure. So what are these people buying? In the entire store I can't find one fat-free or low-fat item. There's a ton of processed foods with high sugar contents. Finally, I hit the meat section. I want to pick up some chicken.

This is a surreal experience. I have never seen a meat section like this in my entire life. There's a little chicken section. The chicken doesn't look great, but it is chicken. It's hard to find those packages of chicken parts I like to buy, and there are no brand names here. There are some packages of chicken legs. I take the best-looking one I can find.

I decide to see what else is here. A little section for beef with ground meat and some cuts of roast and steak. But the rest of this meat department is pork and cured meats. Things I haven't seen in years. Pigs' feet, pigs' knuckles, fatback. This section spans an entire wall and runs from floor to ceiling. All of the meat is brown and white. There's a lot of white too, because this stuff is full of artery-clogging fat.

Looking at this meat section, I think of the zombies in the aisles, the men outside the store, and my father sitting alone at home trying to hold on to his memory.

I can't delay this any longer. I've got to get to the house. At the checkout counter I'm behind several people all paying for their purchases with food stamps. It gives me time for one last look at this place.

I'm looking at the girl ringing up the groceries. She's young, but she looks old and bored. Her hair is a mass of severe shiny black waves that head straight for the ceiling. In her ears are those big, square, "door knocker" earrings. She's wearing two in each ear. She doesn't have a scanner. Everything must be put into the register by hand. All of the checkout people are young, bored, black girls. They're all wearing red smocks. They all have essentially the same "Marge Simpson" hairdo. They all wear big hollow gold earrings. No one smiles. No one speaks.

I wonder what they think of me, with my hands adorned with diamonds and sapphires set in platinum, long, manicured red nails, and a ready smile. They don't even notice. You cannot break that wall. These are young girls practicing to be old, tired, disillusioned women. Women whose lives are filled with suffering and heart-break.

As I exit, the male chorus greets me again. "Need help with your bags?" one man asks.

"No thank you," I say and smile back.

"Need a ride?" another man says.

"No thank you," I say again.

And as I walk away, I cry inside. Why is your manhood wasted, slumping against a rail? Why aren't you standing tall and proud, pulling your own weight? Why are all these women shopping for food with food stamps? Why are these young girls so sad?

It's a beautiful sunny day. I think I'm the only one here who is able to see it.

The neighborhood is in bad shape. The old shopping center is just a shell with only a few stores open. This used to be a thriving, lively place. When we first moved here, the Reade's drugstore was the lead store in the center. It was huge and had one of those fifties-style soda fountains. We used to stop there sometimes and order cherry Cokes. There was also a five-and-ten-cent store, a supermarket, a bank, and a Blank's fabric shop. I did my first Christmas shopping here. The McDonald's is still here, but across the street is an empty lot. The houses used to be well-kept, now they look care-worn.

At the top of Grantley Avenue, where we lived, there was a huge white house that was once called the Guest House. It was a bed and breakfast place surrounded by a white cinder-block fence, and the lawn was always a beautiful green and perfectly manicured in the summer. I always liked it that the house served as a landmark when giving directions to our house when I was growing up here.

The street I lived on shows some wear and tear too. The people who live here now are different from those of us who moved here in the beginning. When we moved to this neighborhood, it was our first crack at the American dream. A place of your own in a neighborhood with like-minded people who were proud of the title "property owner" and took care of their homes. Of course, the whites who were already there didn't see it that way. They saw colored people who were ruining their dreams and devaluing their property. They looked at us and saw what I see now. Dilapidated houses, unkempt yards, directionless, rough-looking boy gangsters walking the streets trying to figure out how to be men. Young girls pushing baby carriages. Old people afraid to go far from home.

My parents' block still holds out the hope of the original dream. This block has been relatively stable because the people who live here were, for the most part, home buyers. They were the first wave of black families in this community before speculators who smelled fear and profit swarmed in to buy up properties and turn them into cheap rentals. Rentals attracted less stable, more transient residents to the neighborhood. But instead of moving on when the area began to change on them economically, these first-wave people blindly stayed, fighting to maintain a little oasis of calm across from a metal factory and just below the railroad tracks. This is where I came of age. This is what I fought. This is what I overcame.

The neighborhood used to be very open. In the summer we often forgot to lock the doors when we were at home, and neighbors sometimes walked right in without knocking. To get inside today, there are lots of locks, and the front door, which was always wood, is now steel.

It's the first time I've spent time alone with my father in more than fifteen years. I've never spent more than a few hours here at a time. Now I've volunteered to spend the day here with him. My mother has decided she needs a day to herself and is going on a bus excursion to Atlantic City. She was going to leave my father alone, so it's not like she planned this trip because I was here. I never stay at my parents' house when I come. It's small and cramped, and I suppose that my memories of this place make it less than pleasant for me. This is another one of my bold experiments to see how far I've come in my recovery. I've decided to spend several hours in this house with my father without benefit of a convenient escape.

I ring the bell. Dad comes to the door. He's been waiting. The big steel door has been left open. He only has to throw the lock on the storm door to let me into the living room. We are not a warm family. Any show of affection is forced and uncomfortable, so my father and I eschew any physical greeting. We smile at each other and say hello. My mother is already gone.

I'm comfortable enough, though, not to stand on ceremony. I walk into the kitchen and put down the food, announcing that I'm going to make lunch. I'm full of projects today, which is obviously my defense mechanism to deal with my discomfort. I'm in the process of writing a book about my life, after all. This is research. I'm going to videotape my father while I interview him about his early years. Can't go too far. Don't want things to get too emotional. But maybe, just maybe, I want to know who this man is. How he became who he is. What forces made him.

He's certainly not who he was. Oh, the frame is still there, though. Those huge arms that I used to use for a swing. The green eyes that would flash with blood when he was angry. The huge hands that used to clench and unclench while he was trying to control his temper. The hair is thinner and gray around the edges, the skin has permanently taken on that red glow. The face is old but still handsome, but the tiger's teeth are cracked and falling out.

I decide to prepare everything for lunch before I start so that I can just pop it in the oven or microwave when the time is right. I'm wearing my two favorite rings, a gold dome ring with diamonds across the top, and a sapphire-and-diamond ring in a platinum setting. I always take them off when I'm doing messy work, so before I start to clean the chicken, I lay them on the counter. After running water on the chicken legs, I strip off the skin. When I looked in the refrigerator I noticed that my mother had left fried chicken for my father's lunch and dinner. He's had several heart attacks, has high blood pressure, and has a long scar on his chest from open-heart surgery. And she left fried chicken.

It's getting late. I'd better stop procrastinating. I finish up, put on my rings, and announce to my father that I'm ready to interview him. I set up the camera in the dining room, have him sit at the head of the table, find him in the viewfinder, and begin.

He's not much of a storyteller anymore. He used to keep people entertained for hours with his stories. Every family gathering followed a familiar pattern. My father would collect an audience, and after a few drinks, the stories would start. Stories from childhood, stories about growing up, stories about raising children and trouble with the wife. He'd regale the crowd with large gestures, a booming voice, and a raucous laugh. When he sensed he was losing his audience, he'd embellish the story a little more until he got them back. Often, the end result was huge exclamations of disbelief at his outrageous lies, but he stood by them.

Now he repeats the same things over and over again. He stops in the middle, stumped because he can't remember a simple word or name. Today he informs his listeners that his head is so muddled that one day he won't be able to get one word out of his mouth. Then he says that he'll be locked in total silence. I'll try to get whatever stories are left.

It's not easy going. He doesn't really understand my questions. He spews whatever facts he can remember, but I want his feelings. Where were you born? Who were your father and mother? What kind of parents were they? When your mother died, you were twelve years old. How did that feel? What did it mean to you? You only finished seventh grade. Why? What did you want as a young man? Who are you?

He does manage to open the door a bit. He was born in 1918 and expresses deep love for the mother who died when he was twelve. He realizes that his lack of education condemned him to a life of hard labor. He talks about hanging out in the street, getting into trouble, and joining the navy in 1937, the first time the navy took colored people.

He can't remember the name of his job, but he remembers that it was menial, working in the kitchen, serving food to officers, and cleaning officers' quarters. He says he got mad when he saw white guys going on to better jobs while he was stuck. I can imagine that what he really felt was hurt.

He was only in the navy a year. He got sick aboard ship and was sent home and eventually discharged because the navy feared that he'd never be seaworthy again. Back home, he started courting the sister of a friend. They married in 1942. It's interesting to me that he can't remember her name although he was able to rattle off the name of his first girlfriend.

Seven months after he married, he was drafted into the army. Because of the fierceness of the fighting, racial barriers were falling. My father was trained for combat. Once in Europe on the ground fighting, there was no more Jim Crow. He laughs as he tells the story of not only fighting and sleeping in the same place, blacks and whites together, but of eating out of the same tin.

And talk about bad luck. My father says that once the war was over in Germany he thought he'd get to go home, but instead he was sent to the Philippines to fight in the Asian theater. But then I guess there was some luck. Shortly after he got there, the United States dropped the bomb and the Japanese surrendered. My father was overseas for another year before he finally got to go home.

We go on until he gets to the part about meeting my mother. I know most of what happened after that. We've been talking for quite some time, and I'm getting hungry and tired from holding the camera.

One last question before I put the camera down. Now that you've lived a long time, how do you think of your life?

Without hesitation he says, "It was a pretty good life. I raised two children, took care of my family. It's better to have a family than to be nothing."

He becomes reflective and his face darkens. He looks away from the camera and then back.

"I won't say I haven't made some mistakes," he says. "A man gets to a certain age and he doesn't know where he's going. The man is the one who messes up. Sometimes a man does wrong."

He brightens.

"But if you just hold on, you'll come through," he says.

It's time for lunch, and I want to see what I have on tape. Food prepared, we head for the basement, set up TV trays, and start to watch the videotape I just shot.

My father looks puzzled. "Who is that talking about me?" he asks.

"That's you," I say.

"Well, he certainly is telling the truth," he says. "That's exactly how it happened."

"Daddy?" I ask. "Don't you know that's you speaking?"

"That's me?!" he exclaims.

"Yes," I answer.

"He's telling the truth alright," he goes on. "I have a shirt just like that too," he says.

"Daddy, that's the shirt you're wearing now," I say.

He looks down at himself and uses both hands to pull the fabric away from his body. "That's me?" he asks confusedly.

"Yes, that's you," I say.

He stares at the screen for a long time.

"He's right about that," he says with a laugh. "I know I'm saying 'he,' but I know it's me."

He's still looking at the screen intently.

"When did you do this?" he asks.

"Just now," I say.

"When we were upstairs?" he asks.

"Yes," I say.

"How?" he asks.

"Don't you remember that the whole time you were talking to me there was a camera in front of my face?" I ask.

"It takes moving pictures?!" he squeals.

"Yes!" I say.

"Mom said you were coming home to interview me," he says. "Is that what this is?"

"Yes," I say.

I'm beginning to realize how severe my father's memory problems are. It occurs to me that he held on to his memory long enough for me to return. The he just let go of it. In any case, he's riveted to his image on the screen, fascinated by what he's seeing and hearing. I decide to rewind the whole thing and dub it off on videotape for him so he can watch it whenever he wants. He sits and watches it all the way through again.

While he does that, I decide to clean up the kitchen. I had put my rings on the counter next to the sink again while I was cooking, and they're still there. I wash the dishes, put them away, and clean the table and the counters. I leave the uneaten food in the pans because I don't know how my mother would want to store it. Then I return to the basement to finish watching the tape with my father. It's about five o'clock in the afternoon, time for me to get going. I'm staying at my friend Kathi's house in Severna Park, and we have dinner plans. My mother said she'd be home at seven, so I won't be leaving my father alone for long.

The tape ends. I set up the VCR so that he can show it to my mother when she gets home. I bought the video recorder for them the day before so that my father can watch old movies. He loves westerns and action films. Since all he does anymore is watch TV, I thought he might as well be able to watch the things he likes. I have tried repeatedly to tell him how to work it, but he really can't grasp it. My mother, who had never been very mechanical, now has to do all the things that my father used to do.

I'm leaving the camera and my other equipment at the house because I'm going to interview my mother on tape the next day. I look around, decide I've done all I can, grab my purse, say good-bye to my father, and run out the door.

I've done it. I've spent a whole day with my father without incident. Not that I hadn't experienced a whole gamut of emotions by just being there. Sometimes I was fearful, nervous, sad, puzzled, loving, irritated. I felt all these emotions and held on, never losing control, never falling back into old patterns. But it is more than time to get away again.

Now that I can relax and think about the prospects of a pleasant evening, I begin to feel like myself again, but as I grip the steering wheel of the car, I realize that something is missing. There's no sound when I open and close my hands. I look at my fingers. They're bare. My rings aren't there. I forgot to put them back on after I cleaned the kitchen.

I'm just about to get on the Beltway, and debate the pros and cons of going back. Will my rings be okay? Ordinarily I wouldn't think anything of it, but these rings are very expensive. I don't want to lose them. My inner voice offers the final decision: "Turn around."

I get on the Beltway and get off at the first exit. I'm fifteen minutes from my parents' house, so by the time I get back I've been gone half an hour. I don't even park the car because I know exactly where the rings are. When I walk into the house, I find my father holding a dish towel. He had decided to finish the job I left.

When I enter the kitchen, I head straight for the counter. The rings aren't there. I turn, look at my father, and ask, "Daddy, what did you do with my rings?"

"What rings?" he responds.

"The rings I was wearing. The rings I left on the counter," I say.

"I haven't seen any rings. Are you sure you were wearing them?"

"Yes. I took them off when I fixed lunch, and I put them on the counter."

I start to run around the house looking for where he might have moved them. First I confine myself to the immediate area. Then I remember that the car is on the street, doors open, motor running. I order my father to go to the door to watch the car.

I am having no success, so after deciding that the search is going to take a while, I go outside and park the car. When I come in, I try to retrace all of our steps. I keep asking my father questions, but he can't remember anything. I'm getting agitated. He is attempting to persuade me that I hadn't worn any rings and that if I had, he hadn't moved them. I go from room to room with him following me. My voice is getting louder and more shrill. He winces and declares, "That's your mother's voice. When she sounds like that, it goes right through me."

It's beginning to happen. I'm going to lose it. He just compared me to my mother. I don't want to be anything like either of these people.

"Well, I'm trying to find those rings," I say, almost in tears.

"Robin, don't get upset," he urges me.

"Don't get upset? You have no idea where you put the fucking things!" I spit out.

This is the first time I have ever cursed in front of my father.

"You don't have to use such nasty language," he chides me.

I yell something else. I don't know what, but I see his reaction. He starts to open and close his fists. My mind is racing. This place, these people, have never been anything but trouble for me. And now this idiot is threatening me! All my buttons are pushed. There's nothing to do but launch the missile. It's already armed and loaded. Like my mother, my weapon is my mouth. Unlike my mother, it doesn't take me all day to find the target. I'm a surgeon. I know exactly where to cut.

I turn and look my father straight in the eye and scream, "Nothing ever goes right here! I should never have come back! If I hadn't come here, I'd still have those rings!"

"Robin, don't say that," he pleads. "They've got to be somewhere if you had them on."

"There's nothing wrong with my memory," I taunt him. "I know I had them on, and I know where I put them." But already my anger's subsiding, and I regret what I just said. It's my call. I can continue to let the situation escalate or let it go. I decide to walk away.

I go to the second floor, where the bedrooms are. We haven't been there all day, but I need to put some distance between myself and my father. And I'm stuck with my actions. I've yelled at a little old man with no memory. I've just given him his best day in a long time and then taken it away. He couldn't help losing the rings. He didn't do it on purpose, but that was always his excuse. He never thought, he didn't mean to, he didn't know, he couldn't help.

It's time for me to go. More than failing him, I feel that I've failed myself. I lashed out at him not for what he's done today, but for what he's done all my life. When I was a child, I was weak and needed his help. He was older and stronger and took advantage of that. Now our positions are reversed. I am taking advantage of his weakness. I realize that I didn't come here to complete the circle. I didn't come here to get my turn. I stayed away for ten years because I didn't want it.

When I come downstairs, my father asks me if I found the rings. He has completely forgiven me. There will be no further discussion. No apologies will be delivered or sought. We will pretend it never happened. After all, no blood was shed. This is how the Quivers family handles things. It's the kind of bunch where you can savagely wound without consequence. There's nothing you can do that's bad enough to lose membership. In fact, it's the opposite. The only way to escape is to become a success.

I tell my father that I can't spend the rest of the day like this, pick up my purse, and leave. All kinds of thoughts race through my head. Will my rings ever be found? Will they turn up five years from now in some strange place? I even contemplate whether or not my mother will return them to me if she finds them. Granted, my parents have never stolen anything from me, but that's how deep distrust goes.

Later that night, I call them. My father answers.

"Hi, Dad," I say. "Is Mom home yet?"

"Robin, is that you?" he asks by way of reply. "I'm supposed to tell you something, but I can't remember what it is. Let me go get your mother." He puts the phone down, and I wait.

"Hey, there," my mother eventually says. "I guess you had a time, huh? But it turned out all right."

"What are you talking about?" I demand, feeling like I've missed part of a conversation.

"Oh, he didn't tell you? I found your rings!"

"No. He said he knew he was supposed to tell me something, but he can't remember what it was."

"Oh, goodness," she laughs nervously, "he can't remember anything."

"How could you leave him alone?"

"Oh," my mother tells me, "I don't leave him often. And when I do, the neighbors look in on him."

"How do you know he won't forget that he's not capable of doing something one day and get into real trouble?" I persist. "You have to make sure he's watched all the time. He can't take care of himself anymore."

Again, I'm reminded of the irony of his needing my protection. Almost as if she can see my thoughts, my mother replies, "Yeah, he said you got terribly upset with him. I could hardly get in the door before I had to get busy looking for those rings. He said you'd had such a nice day, and then you couldn't find the rings and yelled at him something terrible."

She relates how she took the whole house apart and had even spread newspaper on the floor and sifted through the garbage by hand. Finally, she was about to give up when for some reason she decided to look in a bowl that sits on her sewing cabinet. To get to it, she had to move a box of tissues. When she lifted the box, it rattled. As she retrieved the rings, she tells me, my father said to her, "I put them in there so they'd be safe."

Now I don't even want the rings. Who needs material things when they cause such problems? For a while I think of giving them to my parents to relieve myself of the attachment.

I come to my senses during the night. I realize that although I can't undo what's already happened, I can learn from it. I don't want to be the kind of person who beats up on or takes advantage of the weak. I don't like the feeling. The rings aren't really the problem, anyway, and the effort my mother put into finding them makes me see something else. Her version of love will always be difficult for me to accept, but it's the only love she has to give. I know that there will never be room to put my relationship with my parents on automatic. It simply doesn't function on that level.

Now it strikes me that my mother adores diamonds. She's always marveled at the diamond studs in my ears. So on the way to my parents' house the next day, I stop at a jewelry store and buy my mother some diamond stud earrings of her own.

As I turn onto the street where I grew up, I realize for the first time that forgiving is an ongoing process, something I'm going to have to work on every day. I'm pleased, though, that I'm strong enough to try.